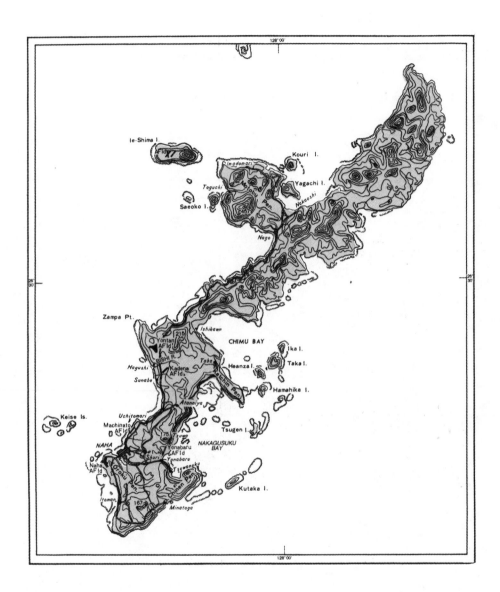

THE BATTLE
FOR OKINAWA

THE BATTLE FOR OKINAWA

COLONEL HIROMICHI YAHARA

Translated by Roger Pineau and Masatoshi Uehara

With an Introduction and Commentary
by Frank B. Gibney

John Wiley & Sons, Inc.

New York • Chichester • Brisbane • Toronto • Singapore

This text is printed on acid-free paper.

Copyright © 1995 by Pacific Basin Institute
Published by John Wiley & Sons, Inc.

A Pacific Basin Institute Book
Major funding for the English translation of Colonel Yahara's text was provided by the Japan–U.S. Friendship Commission and the Sasakawa Peace Foundation.

This publication is designed to provide accurate and authoritative information in regard to the subject matter covered. It is sold with the understanding that the publisher is not engaged in rendering professional services. If legal, accounting, medical, psychological, or any other expert assistance is required, the services of a competent professional person should be sought.

Library of Congress Cataloging-in-Publication Data

Yahara, Hiromichi, 1902–1981.
    The battle for Okinawa / Hiromichi Yahara : translated by Roger
Pineau and Masatoshi Uehara : with an introduction and commentary by
Frank B. Gibney.
      p.   cm.
    Includes index.
    ISBN 0-471-12041-3 (alk. paper)
    1. World War, 1939–1945—Campaigns—Japan—Okinawa Island.
I. Gibney, Frank B. 1924– . II. Title.
D767.99.O45Y33 1995
940.54′25—dc20   94–43765

Printed in the United States of America

10 9 8 7 6 5 4 3 2 1

In memory of
Kenneth Lamott and Roger Pineau

Contents

The Colonel's Prologue: April 1, 1945   xi
Two Views of Battle, by Frank B. Gibney   xv

PART I

PREPARATIONS FOR BATTLE
From the text by Colonel Hiromichi Yahara

1. Plans for 32nd Army:
    Yahara versus Imperial Headquarters   3

PART II

THE AMERICAN ASSAULT
Lieutenant Gibney's commentary continues

2. The Grand Strategy Unfolds   29
3. Challenge and Response   35

PART III

RETREAT UNDER FIRE
Colonel Yahara's narrative resumes

4.   Counteroffensive Halted   41
5.   World View through the Eye of a Needle   45
6.   The Headquarters Cave   49
7.   The Battle at Maeda-Nakama-Awacha   53
8.   The Bloody Action at Sugar Loaf Hill (Amekudai)   57
9.   The Arikawa Brigade Withdraws to Shuri   63
10. Choosing a Last-Stand Location   67
11. The Right Flank Nears Collapse   75
12. Retreat and Attack   79

13.	Army Headquarters	83
14.	Farewell to Shuri	87
15.	The Tsukazan Command Post	93
16.	Tsukazan to Mabuni	99
17.	Civilians at the Last Stand	105
18.	Retreat and Rear Guard Action	107
19.	Kiyan Peninsula	111
20.	Mabuni Headquarters Cave	115
21.	The Battle for Kiyan	121
22.	The Naval Base Force Is Wiped Out	125
23.	The Last Battle	129
24.	Cave Fantasies	135
25.	Final Days at Mabuni	139
26.	The End of 32nd Army	149

Part IV
Exodus
Yahara's attempted escape

27.	The Mabuni Departure	159
28.	Gushichan Cave	167
29.	Mingling with the Refugees	175
30.	Fusozaki Village	179
31.	Coolie on a New Battlefield	183
32.	Reversal of Fortune	189
	The Colonel's Postscript	195
	Epilogue: The Battle Ended—Capture and Return	199
	Prisoner of War Interrogation Reports	205
	Index	237

The Colonel's Prologue
April 1, 1945

On the morning of April 1, in the twentieth year of the Showa era, the island of Okinawa is rent by an earthshaking bombardment, vast and oddly magnificent in its effect, in preparation for the American army's landing attack.

At this time the commanders of Japan's 32nd Army are standing on the crest of Mount Shuri near the southern end of Okinawa's main island, quietly observing the movements of the American 10th Army. The commanding general of 32nd Army, Lieutenant General Mitsuru Ushijima, stands tall and composed, a fine figure of a man. The short, stout officer standing nearest to him, legs set defiantly apart, is his chief of staff, a man known for his fierce valor, Major General Isamu Cho. Ushijima's staff officers, binoculars in their hands, gaze calmly at the Kadena western shoreline, about twenty kilometers to the north. There, at that very moment, the enemy landing force is disembarking.

Since early dawn, the silhouettes of enemy troopships have darkened the coastline. Ten battleships and ten cruisers form the core of the attack force: Some two hundred lesser ships line up offshore. Stretching from Namihira to Heianzan, Kadena forms a seven- to eight-kilometer-long coast zone. There the heaviest gunfire is concentrated. Smoke and debris from the explosions and fires rise up to the sky. The enemy aircraft, looking like hundreds of oversized beans, conceal themselves in the convenient smoke screen before carrying out their bombing operations.

At 8:00 A.M. the enemy infantry disembarks from the thousand-odd landing craft, thrusting onto the shore. The sweep of the ordered military formation is impressive. It is as if the sea itself were advancing with a great roar.

Four divisions of the U.S. 10th Army, under the command of Lieutenant General Simon Buckner, now close in on the beach in succession. They take cover. They are most probably anticipating the famous "*banzai* charges" repeated time and time again throughout the Pacific island operation ever since the battle of Attu. In these assaults, masses of Japanese soldiers wearing frantic, weird expressions, brandishing swords, throwing grenades, and stabbing with bayonets, charge ceaselessly, jumping over the dead bodies of their fallen comrades while screaming "*banzai.*"

But the Japanese atop Mount Shuri show no signs of using such tactics. The group simply gazes out over the enemy's frantic deployment, some of the officers joking, a few casually lighting cigarettes. How could this be? For months now the Japanese army has been building its strongest fortifications on the heights of Mount Shuri—and its adjacent hills. Here they will lure the American forces and confound them. Hence their air of nonchalance. The battle is now progressing exactly as expected. All the Japanese command need do is to await the completion of the enemy's landing at Kadena and watch them finally head southward.

General Ushijima and his staff are full of confidence. He who wields power is unperturbed, as the saying goes. Without the least bit of doubt or worry, the Japanese are nevertheless tense with the warrior's inner excitement at the thrill of preparing to cross swords with a mighty enemy.

As senior officer in charge of operations I should be the proudest of all. As their troops land with almost no resistance from the Japanese forces, what must the enemy commander and his staff be thinking? In my attempt to imagine the minds of my opponents, I am unable to suppress an ironic chuckle.

Contrary to their expectations, the enemy meets no resistance from Japanese troops. They will complete their landing unchallenged. Advancing with such ease, they must be thinking gleefully that they have passed through a breach in the Japanese defense. They will be wrong. In that eerie atmosphere, are they not suspicious that the Japanese army has withdrawn and concealed itself in the heights surrounding Kadena, with plans to draw the Americans into a trap? What a surprise it must all be. It is amusing to watch the American army so desperately intent in its attack on an almost undefended coast, like a blind man who has lost his cane, groping on hands and knees to cross a ditch. Observe the huge amount of firepower directed at Kadena: According to American military records, a total of forty-five thousand shells were fired from the big guns (over 5 centimeters) in preparation for landing. In addition some thirty-three thousand rockets were launched with an uncountable number of bombs dropped from the air. From the viewpoint of the defenders it is exceedingly pleasurable to see this all wasted.

Spring in its fullness has already come to this southern island. The green hills and fields around Mount Shuri, where ten thousand Japanese soldiers wait concealed deep below the surface, shine brilliantly in the morning sun. It is all so splendid. The sea below is quiet and deep blue as the whitecaps breaking on the nearby reef draw a series of fractured lines that finally join together. The only sign of what lies ahead is an occasional enemy reconnaissance plane passing through the sky above Shuri—as if a reminder. Compared to the wildly menaced Kadena coastline, it is a world apart. The stillness of the Japanese 32nd Army, against the movement of the American 10th, makes a truly interesting contrast.

Yet, now, as they gaze casually at the American planes cutting across the sky, these high Japanese officers are suddenly seized by a gnawing sense of unease. Not one Japanese airplane has appeared over the battlefield. According to the original battle plans formulated in Imperial Headquarters in Tokyo, the leading actor in warding off the enemy attack on Okinawa would be the air force. Thirty-second Army was to play no more than a minor supporting role. It had been publicly stated that the best opportunity to destroy the enemy would be while he was still in his ships, before the troops had a chance to land.

Over the past week, Japanese aircraft had carried out attacks on the enemy fleet under cover of darkness, by moonlight and at dawn. Why now, with enemy landing craft swarming around the Kadena beaches, do they not overcome all obstacles, take advantage of this once-in-a-lifetime chance, and make an all-out concerted attack? Had the afternoon's "special attack" (suicide bombing) been canceled due to damage inflicted on us by enemy planes? No matter how unbelievable this thought might have been at the moment, the "special attack" planes nonetheless did not appear.

Postwar accounts of the battle have directed criticism against the Japanese army for its alleged negligence at having allowed the American forces to land. In contrast, there have been few discussions in which the Japanese air force's behavior on that day is adequately questioned. Could this be because a piece of the puzzle that would bring insight into the strategic plan is missing? Or has the truth of history become that difficult to grasp? Did the air force simply disappear without a trace—with no evidence of its activity?

This was truly an extraordinary prelude to the opening act of the battle of Okinawa. The gigantic U.S. Pacific Fleet, with its ten battleships, ten cruisers, and auxiliary craft, formed the base of operations for the attack, along with units of the powerful British navy. The infantry now landing numbered some thirty thousand men. Thousands of enemy planes were in the air, with the poor Okinawans caught in the middle of it all. So extraordinary is this opening scene of what is to be a historic and decisive battle; it encompasses land, air, and sea. It is almost unbelievable.

The American army, having pumped huge quantities of ammunition into the undefended Kadena coast, now stabs at the beach. Our air force had announced it would destroy the enemy attack force while it was still in its boats. But no planes arrive at this decisive moment.

The Japanese infantry soldiers on Okinawa come out of their caves to stand on the slopes of Mount Shuri, overlooking the battle's beginning. They exchange ironic smiles, but they are puzzled. There was a perception gap, not only between the Japanese and U.S. forces, but also between Japan's own army and air force, who were supposedly working together! This is too much to imagine. What conclusion will all this bring? What tragedies will play out in the ensuing battle? Here the fate of Okinawa is brought to light.

Since the end of the Pacific war, many histories of the battle of Okinawa have been compiled in both Japan and the United States. Detailed versions have been published by war correspondents of both sides, writers, journalists, professional soldiers, and by persons who actually experienced the battle as well. Reading such accounts, which sing the praises of old comrades in arms and the bravery of the Okinawan people, gives me great pleasure. But the descriptions of the horrible, tragic conditions of the war are heartrending. Different perspectives on military tactics have often made me open my eyes, reflect, and see events in a new light. Many accounts have also shown a lack of knowledge. Or they have been weighted down by misconceptions.

My own role in the affair was that of staff officer in charge of operations. As such I participated directly in the design and implementation of the Japanese battle plan. Yet I have to this day declined to speak directly on this matter or to talk of the defeated soldiers—in deference to them. But having once given my life to military tactics, I must express my opinions here, aside from the question of how skilled I might have been in that field.

Twenty-seven years have passed since the war's end. The island of Okinawa has long since reverted to Japan. My memory gradually fades. Yet fortunately I had the foresight to keep a record of events during the war and just after. With these as my source, I present my appeal to the facts about the battle of Okinawa. Here I must say, "This is how it really was."

Two Views of Battle

By Frank B. Gibney

Hiromichi Yahara, Colonel, Imperial Japanese Army

With his Prologue, Colonel Hiromichi Yahara began a unique account of the last great battle of World War II in the Pacific. *The Battle for Okinawa* (published in the original Japanese in 1973 as *Okinawa Kessen*) is in many ways an extraordinary document. It is one of the few accounts of battle in the Pacific war to be written not by rank-and-file soldiers or historians but by an active member of the Japanese military high command.

Yahara, as he is quick to state, was senior staff officer of Japan's last fighting army, in charge of Operations—the rough equivalent of an American army G-3. A bright light of the General Staff, whose last post had been as an instructor at Japan's War College, Yahara became both the architect and executor of the entire Japanese defense effort in what was probably the Pacific war's bloodiest military encounter, lasting from April to July 1945. It was Yahara's concept of a yard-by-yard "war of attrition" (*jikyusen*) that made Okinawa such a hellish struggle. The purely defensive strategy was a complete departure from other Japanese island defenses, which had concentrated—with a notable lack of success—in attempts to "annihilate the enemy at the water's edge." By fighting for time, not victory, and doing so despite the obligatory grandiloquent sloganry of his communiqués, Yahara recognized far more clearly than his superiors in Tokyo the inevitability of final defeat.

Yet his book, while on its face "an appeal to the facts," is not a simple military history. Behind the cool-sounding narrative beats an intense, personal story. Here was a man with a grievance. He had been taught professionally to think of military operations as a kind of exalted chess game, but he lived to see his human counters scattered and slain around him, torn and bloodied beyond all calculation. In the end his own operational narrative gives way to a desperate struggle in which survival and honor seemed to work at cross-purposes. His two generals, Ushijima and Cho, as we shall see, committed ritual suicide in the approved *samurai* tradition when the battle seemed totally lost, but only after ordering Yahara to avoid the planned final *banzai* charges and escape, if possible, to make a final report to Army and Emperor in Tokyo.

As things turned out, Yahara was captured by U.S. troops while posing as a civilian teacher and ended the war as a prisoner. This ran against all Japanese military tradition, which bothered him intensely. Throughout the Pacific war not the least of the reasons for so many military suicides was the soldiers' fear of lasting disgrace for their families if they were captured. Such fears were an ironic tribute to the "group think" that Japan's military cultists of the thirties and forties had fastened on a populace that was all too susceptible to it.

At forty-two, Yahara was, ironically, at the peak of his military career when the battle ended. The son of a small farmer in Tottori Prefecture in southwestern Japan, he took the requisite school examinations and qualified for the Military Academy, which then represented one of the few paths for social advancement open to country boys in Japan. In 1926, three years after his graduation, he entered the War College, where he led his class—in the military meritocracy, an obvious ticket to advancement. Bright, modest, and hardworking, he was an intellectualized new model of the wartime *gunjin* (military man), a word which evoked instant respect among the Japanese of that time, in contrast to its use as a virtual pejorative among later post-1945 generations. But he was more than that. From the time he was a young regimental officer, he had the unusual ability for someone in his class to stand apart from his surroundings and examine them with some detachment. This quality, combined with a strong disinclination to suffer fools gladly, often led to friction with his superiors, who wanted courage and obedience, above all, from their subordinates.

After service in the War Ministry, he spent two years as an exchange officer in the United States, including six months with the troops of the 8th Infantry and attaché service in Washington. ("Just like the Shoreham," he had said, with an ironic smile, when taken to his private living quarters after his capture.) Although in his account of the battle, he refers to the Americans simply as "the enemy," he knew us far better than his commanders did. He was fully aware of the nonsense in the militarists' propaganda—so tragically believed by Okinawan civilians—that American soldiers would habitually kill, rape, and torture any prisoners that fell into their hands. Later, after staff duty in China and a teaching post at the Military Academy, he worked as an undercover agent and, on occasion, as an intelligence officer in Southeast Asia in the years leading up to the Japanese invasion of 1941. He knew the score, although superior knowledge never seemed to get in the way of his 1940s-style patriotism. For all his later exhortations to the troops on Okinawa, no one understood better than Yahara the flaws of Japan's military position. Not only had his superiors done badly, but they continued to repeat the mistakes of an earlier era. No modern army was crueler than the Japanese, but in no high command did the capacity for self-delusion flourish so abundantly. It was Yahara's particular curse to know how badly his army was destined to fail.

Yahara's problems with Japan's rockbound military hierarchy were embodied in the person of his immediate boss, Chief of Staff Isamu Cho. Through the stormy thirties, when the militarists riveted their hold on the country, Cho played a leading role in one of the "revolutionary" young officers' groups that attempted to set up a military dictatorship in the name of the Emperor.[1] He was actually arrested with other plotters during a secret meeting at a Tokyo *geisha* restaurant but was quickly released by the army command and transferred to a post in the Kwantung Army in China. There he helped to organize the military occupation of Manchuria in 1931. This led to Japan's establishing the puppet state of Manchukuo. Later his group provoked the clash on Peking's Marco Polo Bridge in 1937 that precipitated what Japan officially called the China Incident. Actually, this was a full-scale war—the invasion and exploitation of China.

Cho was almost a prototype of the politicized officers who managed to terrorize timid civilian governments into sanctioning the army's aggressions

---

[1] His particular organization, the *Sakura-kai* or Cherry Society, resembled various other secret cabals of that time. National-socialist in nature, they were strongly antibusiness, antipolitician, and against the government bureaucracy. Strongly traditionalist, they emerged partly in reaction to the parliamentary Party governments of the "Taisho democracy" of the twenties; and they enjoyed the tacit support of many high-ranking army and, to a lesser extent, navy officers. They purported to establish a "pure" government under Imperial sanction and eliminate capitalist corruption. This they hoped to achieve by a campaign of selective violence. Such groups were behind the momentarily successful "young officers'" revolt of February 26, 1936, which was suppressed only after Emperor Hirohito, unexpectedly angered, ordered "loyal" army units to fire on the rebels.

on the Asian mainland. A ruthless nationalist, he reportedly took a leading role in engineering the mass killing of Chinese military and civilian prisoners in the Nanjing Massacre of 1938. In the field, he consistently favored attack, as opposed to Yahara's "war of attrition." His confidence in Japanese infantry superiority was unbounded. For all his fanaticism, he was superficially rather likable, gregarious, and ever ready to put politics aside for any local version of wine, women, and song. He respected Yahara's abilities; and in fact they got along rather well.

The colonel wrote his book in 1972, after long years of brooding about his last battle. Postwar living was hard for a career officer. Salary gone and pension worthless in the inflation of those days, he went back to the family home at Yonago, on the Japan Sea coast, to try to eke out a living for his wife and six children. He worked a small farm and found a supplementary income as a kind of salesman for a textile company, later setting up a small store. But he remained obsessed with the issues that Okinawa had raised in his mind. He managed to gather every scrap of literature he could find about the battle from both Japanese and American souces.

Part of his motive was defensive. His capture was regarded among surviving members of his army peer group as a disgrace. Defeat had not changed that mindset. Militarily, his reputation had suffered from the accusations of Major Naomichi Jin, the only other survivor of the 32nd Army staff. Jin, 32nd's air officer, had been ordered to report to Tokyo during the battle in an attempt to secure more air support, and he had succeeded in getting off the island. After the war, he loudly blamed Yahara for adopting a purely defensive strategy and giving up airfields that might have been the base for Japanese bombers and fighters. For Yahara, arguments like this amounted to nothing more than wishful thinking.

In a wider sense, however, the failure of the promised air support for Okinawa underlined the incompetence, indeed, the mendacity of Japan's top military leaders in sacrificing tens of thousands—military and civilian alike—to a hopeless cause. The colonel felt a continuing sense of national betrayal. And it grew with the years. When a reporter from the *Yomiuri Shimbun* came in 1970 to interview Yahara about the war, he found the story so fascinating that he urged Yahara to write a book.

Even almost three decades after the Pacific war ended, Yahara's perspective remained a very special one. Among the brave, but on the whole simple-minded, military officers of that day, Yahara was a rare bird indeed.

"A heretic," his Japanese biographer, Takeshi Inagaki, called him.[2] Keen-minded intelligence officers have their careers constantly at risk in almost any army. On the whole it is the line officer, "good with the troops," who is generally promoted first. This was nowhere more true than in Japan. The Imperial Army, the last big infantry army of modern times, was dominated by a kind of "blood and guts" offensive spirit. Since the Sino-Japanese War of 1895 it had never been beaten. Brutal in its discipline—corporals kicked privates, sergeants slapped corporals, and for that matter, majors slapped lieutenants—its philosophy, if it could be called that, held that Japanese "spirit," backed by a willingness to die for the Emperor, could overcome any material advantage possessed by an enemy. (The dearly bought victories of the Russo-Japanese War followed successes in China. And at the outset of the Pacific war, General Yamashita's early triumphs of pell-mell attack against the British and the Americans had reinforced the generals' confidence.) Except for the use of air power, modern tactics were, in the minds of its leadership, generally suspect. The Japanese army's pioneers in armored warfare, for example, received little support in their plans for tank divisions. For most Japanese commanders, a good bayonet attack was deemed the adequate response to most military problems.

Yahara thought differently. His was a world of high strategy; he had, after all, spent almost half of his military career at the General Staff and the War College. In his mind, action was useless unless based on cool, rational assessments of a situation. His exemplars were Western theoreticians like Carl Clausewitz or, reaching back to classical Asian tradition, Chinese intellectual "strategists" like Zhuge Liang of Three Kingdoms fame. *Bushido* (the Way of the Warrior) had no place in Yahara's military estimates. He had no illusions about the effectiveness of Japanese "spirit" against bombs and naval gunfire, unless it was carefully entrenched.

His superiors found him useful, which is why Yahara was chosen for difficult intelligence assignments. Ushijima and Cho valued him because he was the best brain their military culture could produce. But his pitilessly rational view of military situations was uncomfortable, stripping away as it did the bulk of the *samurai* bravery myths by which they lived—and were to die. In turn, Yahara felt isolated from his peers by his very perceptiveness.

---

[2]I am indebted to Inagaki's book *Okinawa: Higu no Sakusen/Itan no Sambo Yahara Hiromichi* (Shinchosha, 1984) for this comment, as well as for further information about Yahara's life after his return to Japan.

His frustration at the folly of Japan's military leadership deepened with the years. He wrote the book in the spirit of a man betrayed.

Frank B. Gibney, Lieutenant (jg) United States Naval Reserve

There is another perspective from which this book has been edited and in part written. That is my own. And since my life at several points intersected with Colonel Yahara's, it would be well to mention it now.

On Easter Monday, 1945—L plus one in the language of invasion—I left the navy attack transport on which we had sailed from Pearl Harbor, jumped down into an LCVP (for Landing Craft, Vehicles, and Personnel) bobbing in the offshore swells, and headed for the beach. It was my first landing. Unaware of 32nd Army's decision against a beachhead attack, all of us in the boat were excited, tense, and scared. We were also puzzled. Our small group of Intelligence specialists—army, navy, and marine officers—was attached to G-2, Headquarters 10th Army. Along with our fellow passengers, mostly construction engineers and air traffic controllers, we had been ticketed to disembark on L plus six or seven, after the infantrymen, artillerists, and other more obviously useful combatants had landed to clear the beaches. Through some planning mistake, our ship had been ordered to land us far ahead of time, then clear the landing area to make one less target for the *kamikaze* suicide planes that had been spotted heading our way.

Thus it fell out that my colleague and Honolulu roommate, Lieutenant (jg) Kenneth C. Lamott, and I—Yale College, Class of 1944 and 1945, respectively—spent the late afternoon digging our flea-ridden foxhole on the Hagushi beach, just west of Kadena, listening respectfully to the naval gunfire against real or imagined Japanese positions and wondering whether we would be hit in a *banzai*-charge counterattack. We were also keenly interested in what we were expected to do. For the past year our work had been prisoner-of-war interrogation. Based at the Pearl Harbor POW Interrogation Center of CINCPAC (for Commander in Chief Pacific), we could claim by extension to belong to Admiral Chester Nimitz's staff (although we ranked about as low as possible on that well-populated totem pole). Our particular unit was the Joint Intelligence Center for Pacific Ocean Areas, called JICPOA for short. JICPOA was responsible for collecting and disseminating intelligence information in the vast Central Pacific theater of operations, which stretched from California to the coasts of Japan and China, with notable emphasis on the islands between.

Lamott and I were both recent graduates of the U.S. Navy Language School at Boulder, Colorado, an intensive yearlong course in the Japanese language, designed to be of military use. The very existence of such a school, along with similar army institutions, underlined the almost total lack of Japanese speakers (not to mention readers) in the United States at the start of World War II. (The considerable reservoir of linguistic talent available among mainland Japanese-Americans was denied us, since the bigotry of that time, masking as wartime security, had already imprisoned them in the infamous "relocation centers.") Students at the Boulder school included some Americans with Japanese backgrounds; for example, Lamott, the son of a missionary, had grown up in Tokyo. The majority of us, though, were recent college students who had been selected on the basis of real or fancied language-learning capability. (My own college major was classical Greek.) As things turned out, most graduates spent the war translating captured Japanese documents, deciphering code transmissions, or serving with Marine Corps combat units. A few of us had been selected, rather casually, to serve as interrogators.

Prisoners captured on Pacific islands were questioned in the field for immediate tactical information, such as "What was the size of the Nakagawa unit? Where is the attached artillery battery? How much ammunition is left?" Afterward they were sent to us for interrogation—both tactical and strategic in nature—on matters ranging from tank unit tactics to rear-area industrial sites. Because most Japanese language officers had little experience in questioning prisoners, we were often sent out on landing operations to interrogate POWs on the spot and, on occasion, escort them back to Pearl Harbor. Lamott had landed with the marines in their attack on Tinian Island, in the Marianas, where he was wounded in an unsuccessful effort to talk some Japanese soldiers out of their cave hideaways. I had participated in the marine invasion of Peleliu in the Palau Archipelago east of the Philippines and that past December had escorted a shipload of Japanese army and Korean military construction workers back to Pearl.

General Buckner's 10th Army was placed under the authority of Nimitz's Pacific command for the Okinawa operation; hence we had been sent from Pearl Harbor to set up an army-level Interrogation Center as soon as possible after the landings. After screening by front-line units for immediate tactical information, prisoners of war would be sent to us for detailed interrogation. In addition, POWs of particular importance should go to Army immediately.

Until then our major problem had been how to get prisoners. Less than a thousand had passed through our stockade at Pearl Harbor's Iroquois Point, many of them captured while unconscious or seriously wounded. So powerful was the militarists' indoctrination that the average Japanese soldier or sailor regularly chose to die rather than be captured. Soldiers and sailors were officially told that to be taken prisoner was a total disgrace for themselves and their families. Official propaganda warned Japan's people, civilians as well as military, that prisoners would be tortured and killed by Allied troops. This was not hard for them to believe in view of the widely known atrocities already perpetrated on captured Americans and Australians by the Imperial Army.

It was not always so. No official action was ever taken against the sixteen-hundred-odd Japanese officers and men released from captivity after the Russo-Japanese War, although they faced some popular displeasure. But by the time of the China Incident in the thirties, the revived cult of *Bushido* enjoined military men at all costs from surrendering. The folk history of that time held out as a glorious example one Major Kuga. Captured by Chinese soldiers while severely wounded in the 1931 Shanghai fighting, he was repatriated to Japan only to commit suicide, after long brooding, at the tomb of his old superior officer.

At the Pearl Harbor camp, when we asked POWs to give basic information that could be forwarded to Japan under rules of the Geneva Convention, the reply would almost invariably come: *"Naichi e namae wo shirasetakunai"* (I don't want my name sent to the homeland.) The words would rush out as their eyes filled with fear. Almost all the prisoners felt that disclosure of their captivity would bring down reprisals on their families. Their worry was manifest in their maddening use of false names. Most of the aliases were chosen hastily, in panic, and originality was not their strong suit. Kazuo Hasegawa, for example, was a famous *Kabuki* actor whose name was as familiar to Japanese of that day as Frank Sinatra's was to Americans. During any given POW registration we would turn up at least a dozen Kazuo Hasegawas. Many would later forget their new names, thus making identification difficult.[3]

The good side of this, from our point of view, was that Japanese pris-

---

[3]One such incident still stands out in my memory. Going through some forms filled out by POWs from the Marianas campaign, I found that one prisoner had scrawled the name "Amelia Earhart" in barely intelligible English script on the back of his registration. Here was tantalizing evidence that the missing American aviatrix had gone down in the Japanese-held islands when she disappeared on her prewar flight over the Pacific. We repeatedly called out the POW's name at roll call, but could not trace him.

oners, with only a few exceptions, showed few signs of security consciousness. It was not like interrogating SS-men. Assuming that a good soldier would not be taken prisoner, Imperial Headquarters had not bothered to instruct them what not to reveal under questioning. The good treatment given a prisoner was in itself surprising. It was completely different from the death and torture that his superiors promised would await captives of the Americans. He had been deceived. Add to this a sense of disillusionment in Japan's military invincibility and awe at American strength, and you had a numbing sense of loss; the more intelligent the prisoner was, the more intense.

Thus most prisoners, officers included, were quite willing to tell us all, or almost all they knew. (One man, we were told by the POW sergeants, had even threatened suicide because he had not been interrogated. Was he that worthless? It made for an interesting study in group relationships.) For those of us with no prior knowledge of Japan, our work at the POW camp and in the field was extremely useful. Very early in the game we were able to put aside the wartime American stereotypes of Japanese as nearsighted, buck-toothed fanatics with no minds of their own—an illusion that often proved dangerous to those fighting against them—and see them as individuals who were good, bad, indifferent, boastful, modest, honest, deceitful, intelligent, not so bright—once the carapace of their army's group thinking had been lifted. We tried to teach them something about the realities of the American "enemy." Many ended up writing leaflets for us advocating surrender and the promise of a future "democratic" Japan. In turn we learned a lot about the nation we were fighting, as well as the curiously formidable military machine that served it.

Thus equipped, Lamott and I trekked through the low hills and sweet potato fields until we finally came to the tents then being set up for XXIV Corps headquarters. We found the G-2 and offered our services, since our own army G-2 had not yet landed. We were fortunate, since no one at XXIV Corps had ever heard of us, to find an army colonel whom we had previously met in Honolulu. ("Good boys—know 'em socially," he witnessed.) No Japanese prisoners were yet forthcoming. For those first few days, in fact, there was very little actual combat. After the first U.S. forces to land had raced to secure the airfields, 6th Marine Division units probed their way north and XXIV Corps's divisions began working their way southward toward Colonel Yahara's entrenchments. As it happened, we found ready employment with XXIV Corps Artillery trying to discover just where those entrenchments were.

Throughout the landing bombardments, Japanese artillery had returned scarcely any fire. Gunners obviously waited in their emplacements, but they were anxious not to give away their positions prematurely. So neither Corps Artillery nor the massed armada of fighting ships offshore had much to shoot at. Thousands of Okinawan civilians, however, many rendered homeless by the heavy shelling, were being gathered into improvised Military Government compounds, while thousands more remained in their homes in the sparsely populated northern two-thirds of the island. Sadly, even more civilians, heeding the orders of their governor and 32nd Army headquarters, had fled to the south, to take shelter with the Japanese troops. (Some twenty thousand Okinawans had been drafted into Home Defense units, the *boeitai,* to serve as army auxiliaries.)

Each night we would return to Corps headquarters laden with notebooks and sector maps to piece out possible emplacements from the construction workers' testimony. ("How big was the hole you dug there? Did the Japanese engineers pour concrete there?") After Artillery had made its educated guesses on gun locations, word would be flashed to the ships offshore. More naval gunfire would result, but to what effect we could not be sure. Meanwhile the defenders on Mount Shuri waited.

During that first week I had a chance to meet a great many Okinawans under rather stressful conditions. Their fields chewed up by the bombardment, their revered tombs that dotted the landscape—oddly graceful rounded stone structures shaped, as tradition had it, to resemble a woman's womb—destined to be wrecked for pillboxes or gun positions, their families scattered, high school boys and girls drafted to serve the Japanese army, they bore it all with the stoicism of an island people abused for centuries by pirates and typhoons. The Japanese treated them as second-class citizens. Racially distinct, although speaking a strongly dialect version of Japanese, they had preserved a cultural identity for centuries. Until their final absorption by Japan, they had their own kings and had indeed enjoyed the prosperity of maritime middlemen between China and Japan. Slower-moving and more relaxed than their Japanese cousins, they were now mostly small farmers and fishermen. Theirs was the poorest of Japanese prefectures. And their suffering transcended even that of Hiroshima, Nagasaki, or firebombed Tokyo. They were—and remain—nice, courteous people, remarkably patient under terrible hardship. Caught between two armies, they were the victims of both. But the worst of their experience was their ruthless sacrifice by their Japanese leaders.

Having now introduced the scene of action and a partial cast of characters, it is time to set the battle of Okinawa in context. In the following chapter, the first from Yahara's book, we can see the forecast of the oncoming battle, as the senior staff officer and Imperial Headquarters envisioned it. Their views were strikingly different.

Part I

Preparations
for Battle

From the text by Colonel Hiromichi Yahara

1

Plans for 32nd Army
Yahara versus Imperial Headquarters

Japan's 32nd Army defending Okinawa came into being on March 22, 1944, about one year before the American troops landed. Its assigned task at that time was to defend the Ryukyu Islands. From the north, the major islands included in this area were Amami Oshima, Tokunoshima, Okinawa, Miyakojima, Ishigakijima, and Iriomotejima, as well as the Daito Islands far out in the Pacific to the east.

At that time ground forces for the new army were almost nonexistent—no more than a few garrisons armed with out-of-date coast artillery on Amami Oshima, Okinawa, and Ishigakijima. Three sizable units from the 21st Independent Mixed Regiment (Tokunoshima) led by Colonel Inoue arrived much later, as did Major General Suzuki's 44th Independent Mixed Brigade (Okinawa) and Major General Miyazaki's 45th Independent Mixed Brigade (Miyakojima and Ishigakijima areas). These troops were not scheduled to arrive until July. The Daito Islands detachment, which arrived in late April, was the first to set up its defenses. Part of this unit, along with its commander, Lieutenant Colonel Tanaka, was lost in an American submarine attack.

Thirty-second Army was specifically charged with the rapid construction of numerous airfields throughout the entire Ryukyu Islands, as well as the defense of airfields and major harbors from small-scale surprise attacks by enemy submarines.

On March 9, just before 32nd Army was activated, I was transferred to its staff from my post as an instructor at the Military Academy. I was given an office in the senior officers' section of the General Staff Office at Ichigaya, where I was to begin preparations to establish the army. At the Staff Operations Section, I was given an explanation of the character and mission of 32nd Army, as I have described. A protest escaped my lips: Was there really anything that could be accomplished with such a weak force?

The operations section chief, Colonel Hattori, and his junior staff assistants replied:

> The defenses in the Marianas, our front line in the Central Pacific, are now impregnable. We call this the "Tojo Line." Thus, large numbers of ground forces are not required in the Ryukyu Islands. Even if the Marianas line were broken through—of course, such a thing could never happen—once a large number of airfields had been constructed in the Ryukyu Islands, the air power based there would be able to provide adequate defense. Even if seaborne supply lines to oil and other raw material sources in the South Pacific were disrupted, the chain of airfields would make it possible to utilize gliders.

Colonel Hattori was one year my senior at the Military Academy. We had once worked together on the Operations Section staff before the Greater East Asia War, and we were good friends. So he encouraged me, saying in a low voice, "Although you have an easy job now, you'll probably get busy later."

The room next to mine in the bleak officers' area was set aside as a liaison office for 31st Army, which three months later was completely wiped out defending the Marianas line. At that point the rear echelon officers there had not received orders for the front. They complained that they was too rushed to get anything done. Yet General Headquarters had declared fortification of the Marianas complete. I had my doubts about whether that was actually true.

If the Marianas line collapsed and in its place our Ryukyu Islands became the main line of defense, this could mean the end for Japan. With that in prospect, ensuring defense of the Ryukyu Islands by air power alone left much to be desired. It is true that in March 1944 our air forces were worth pinning considerable hopes on. If these hopes faded, the Pacific war would end in total defeat.

There is no naval supremacy without air supremacy, and without naval supremacy there is no way to defend the Pacific islands. This axiom is not just a theory, but an ironbound rule that the Japanese military had flouted to its sorrow time and time again in its past island strategies. Our high command at Imperial Headquarters were firm believers in the doctrine of air supremacy and did everything possible to build up air capability. While this of course meant an emphasis on aircraft production, headquarters in Tokyo also worked hard to train air corps personnel. Many promising officers of field rank had in fact transferred to the air arm. They tended to be promoted a year ahead of those in other branches of the services. Defense of the Ryukyus, accordingly, was faithfully based on the principle of top priority for air power. But as the days passed and the gap between American and Japanese air power widened, differences of opinion arose between air and ground forces about the actual condition of the air arm.

In late March I went ahead to Okinawa to begin organizing 32nd Army headquarters. I chose the Okinawa Hotel as temporary quarters. It was a good Western-style hotel, rather elegant for Okinawa at that time. I had previously visited airfields in Okinawa when traveling to and from Southeast Asia and the South Pacific, but this was the first time I had set foot in the interior.

My first glimpse of the town of Naha was one of glare and dust whirling up in the spring breeze. The clothing and homes of the islanders had a strange air about them, suggesting an exotic atmosphere. After taking a bath I looked out from the window of my room. The breeze was cool, and the sight of the town as evening approached reminded me of an early summer back home. I could hear the music of a snakeskin *samisen* coming from beyond the green trees. Memories of Thailand and Burma, where I had once wandered on special assignment, began to flow through my mind. I was also reminded of small towns in the southern United States. Having just arrived from a war-wracked Tokyo on an urgent mission, I was struck by the relaxed atmosphere on Okinawa. The people of the island seemed so unhurried and carefree. I was overcome at the thought of the fate that awaited this peaceful island and its inhabitants.

> The very guardians of the island bask
> In pleasant serenity;
> But from the interior they keep
> One eye on the sea.
>
> The sails, some furled, some spread wide,
> Each held its own picturesque charm
> In the brief calm
> Before the typhoon.

These two awkward verses lamenting the times reveal my mindset at that point—close to nihilism, one might say.

On March 29, Lieutenant General Watanabe, the original 32nd Army commander, flew into Okinawa accompanied by Major General Kitagawa, the chief of staff. After careful deliberation, a decision was made to situate the headquarters at an experimental silkworm factory located halfway between the towns of Naha and Shuri. The house of the manager of the Okinawa branch of the Kangyo Bank was offered to the army commander. Major General Kitagawa and other staff members were quartered nearby. For those of us from the mainland expecting to find guerrilla war conditions in Okinawa, the mayor of Naha's official residence, with its panoramic view surrounded by tropical foliage and cooled with abundant breezes, was indeed a pleasant surprise.

As it happened, General Watanabe and most of the officers, including the chief of staff, were to be transferred out of Okinawa in August of that same year. Thus they would have no direct effect on the battle for Okinawa. I need to mention them, however, for sake of order in the story. General Watanabe had participated in the battle of Burma as commanding general of the 56th Division. Later he served as the director of the Army Technical School, before appointment as an army commander. I was in Burma as a staff officer, but around the time the 56th Division landed in Rangoon as a reserve unit I was sent back to Japan because I was suffering from amoebic dysentery and dengue fever. After recovering from my illness, I was appointed as an instructor at the Military Academy. Thus, I missed a chance to work closely with General Watanabe, except for a brief encounter during a "Burma Party" held in Tokyo. As a commander, he was quite different from Lieutenant General Ushijima, who later took over 32nd Army command. Watanabe, a man of medium-sized build and a sharp look, was not one to intimidate others, but a man of swift action and pure heart. I became very fond of him and learned much during my brief service under him in Okinawa.

In those days, our transports were quite often sunk by enemy submarines, and the bodies of dead soldiers were washed upon the shores of various islands. General Watanabe ordered the entire army to treat the corpses with dignity and pay strict attention to gathering and examining articles found with the dead, so that we could identify their names and the companies they belonged to. I was touched by his order, even though it was an action expected of him. To this day I remember his expression, filled with deep feeling as he gave these orders to his army. There were times, though, when I could not bear the overzealous fire drills, in which he would lead the officers in bucket relays.

   Major General Kitagawa, the chief of staff, was my senior by six years at the Military Academy, although we graduated from the War College the same year. We were the best of friends and I admired him for his integrity. Kitagawa was a graduate of the artillery program but later transferred to the flight division. He was in charge of the Military Flight Officers School when he was called to Okinawa. There could have been no better choice for army chief of staff than he, since his chief duty was to dot the Ryukyus with as many airfields as possible, in the shortest space of time.

With almost no ground forces to deploy, 32nd Army was idle as a fighting force. There was little to do but devote ourselves to the construction of airfields. The Marianas line was still standing strong. New Guinea was under fierce attack by American forces, but the fires of war had not yet spread to the Philippines. I considered all the possible scenarios by which the war in the Pacific might reach the Ryukyus, and arrived at the following forecast.

   There were two principal axes of operation along which the American forces could move. ("Principal axis of operation" is an operational term meaning the direction in which the main body of a large fighting force advances.) Advancing along one axis, the American forces could capture the Marianas and proceed on a direct course to the Ryukyus. Even if the Marianas were taken, a direct attack on the Ryukyus would require crossing two thousand kilometers of open sea. U.S. forces in the Marianas would need time to prepare for such a difficult undertaking. An attack from that direction would probably not come before the autumn of that year.

   The other probable axis of operation would follow the chain of islands from New Guinea through the Philippines and Taiwan to the Ryukyu Archipelago. This attack would also proceed in leapfrog fashion and require the capture of all but a few islands along the way. Judging from the enemy's rate of progress through the Pacific islands so far, their island hopping would take them to the Ryukyus at about "cherry blossom time" the following year. I judged this latter axis of operation to be the more probable. At every available juncture I openly declared that the fate of our army would be decided when the cherry trees blossomed in 1945. This pronouncement served on the one hand to allay some people's anxieties, since combat in the islands was not immediate. At the same time, it heightened our sense of inevitable disaster, emphasizing that fact that we were less than a year away from meeting our fate. Though consequently in an ambiguous state of mind, we devoted our full energies to our army's primary duty of building bases for the air forces. Scheduled to be completed late in July, some eighteen airfields were then under construction on Okinawa and the other islands of the Ryukyus.

Preparations for air warfare centered on building a large number of airfields and coordinating these as a functioning network. Air power based there was intended to break up the enemy's attack and reduce losses to our ground troops. The air bases would also serve to ensure effective air defense, speed up command operations, and facilitate the movement and assembly of war materiel.

The sweeping precedence given to air defense, however, was to prove very costly. Airfields were built wherever suitable land could be found on each of the islands. Large airfields were created on the tiny island of Iejima off Okinawa's northwest coast, and numerous airfields were constructed all over the Okinawan main island. No consideration was given to how much ground force would be needed to defend these airfields. Following the reckless thinking then dominant in the military, it was thought enough simply to build them.

In previous battles in the Pacific, large numbers of landing strips had been similarly constructed, but in many cases these had been occupied by American forces before our defenders could use them. It was as if our ground forces had sweated and strained to construct airfields as a gift for the enemy. Later, trying to prevent the enemy from using them, those same ground forces sacrificed countless lives in futile attempts to retake the occupied airstrips.

We therefore felt some discontent about building countless air bases but faithfully performed our duty. Unfortunately, only a few of the units assigned to this work actually specialized in airfield construction; most of them were organized for airfield operation. Most construction had to be performed manually, using primitive picks and shovels. This necessitated mass mobilization of the islands' civilian populations. The approximate number of those drafted for this work was two thousand on Tokunoshima; twenty-five thousand on Okinawa; five thousand on Miyakojima; and three thousand on Ishigakijima. The sheer number of citizens and labor service students working at each of the construction sites presented quite a spectacle. Also impressive was the local citizens' spirited determination to defend their islands. Due to these "human wave" tactics and the zeal shown by both military and civilians, work proceeded slowly but steadily to completion according to plan.

Although our sole duty at that time was to construct air bases, 32nd Army took pride in the fact that it was under the direct command of Imperial

Headquarters. It seems somewhat childish, but we vaingloriously regarded ourselves as standard-bearers. Our conceit was short-lived. In early May, orders from Imperial Headquarters placed 32nd Army under the command of General Shimomura's Western Army, whose duty was the defense of Kyushu. Although intended merely to simplify the chain of command, this came as a blow to our staff officers. Morale sagged. We suspected that Imperial Headquarters, confident that the Marianas line was securely defended, no longer attached much importance to the Ryukyus.

The Marianas line, also known as the Tojo line, had been considered impregnable, but a ferocious battle erupted there in mid-June 1944. The focal point of this fateful showdown was the island of Saipan, headquarters of 31st Army under the command of Lieutenant General Obata. The fortunes of 32nd Army were to be closely tied to that of 31st.

At the outset I dispatched a telegram in the name of our commanding general, wishing the defenders a vigorous fight and the best fortunes of war. Because I had a brother-in-law in 31st, my hands trembled as I drafted the text. After that we received no word from either 31st Army or Imperial Headquarters. As the days passed, we had no idea whether or not the battle was going in our favor.

Suddenly, on the morning of June 20, the naval operations base at Naha sent word that the Combined Fleet (*Rengo Kantai*) would put into Okinawa's Nakagusuku Bay. They asked for our cooperation in security and all other matters. Naval base officers then called on our headquarters. Discussion was limited to army assistance to the fleet, however. No mention was made of the fleet's operations. Not knowing the current war situation, we were in high spirits, thinking that at last there would be a showdown between the main battle fleets of Japan and the United States. Orders were handed down to Colonel Shibata, commander of the Nakagusuku Bay Fortress, to give full cooperation to the navy.

One after another, coastal lookout stations phoned in encouraging reports of fleet sightings: battleship off Katsuren; ten warships now entering the harbor; large ship, probably aircraft carrier, seen near Tsukenjima. So they ran.

Having spent long miserable months of idleness, I was too excited to wait patiently in the staff office. Binoculars in hand, I took a car to a hill west of Yonabaru and looked down over Nakagusuku Bay. Twenty-odd warships, from battleships to smaller craft, were moored in the bay, floating motionless in the dark waters under low-hanging clouds. Not a single soul could be seen on their decks. There were no aircraft in sight. There was not a trace of the buoyant gallantry of men going to battle; the fleet appeared speechless and forlorn. On the road to Yonabaru I had passed Rear Admiral Shinba of the naval operations base, going in the opposite direction. I was bothered by the grim expression on his face, but my head was still full of grand thoughts of the fleet sallying forth to a decisive battle.

I found out in Tokyo a week later that the battle for the Marianas line was already over. The fleet I had seen had been soundly trounced by the enemy and had pulled back in defeat. That night, the fleet had silently departed Nakagusuku Bay, its destination unknown to me.

The battle in the Marianas had gone badly beyond anyone's expectations. Imperial Headquarters' faith in the Marianas line had been shattered, yet war preparations in the Ryukyus were still close to nil. We had completed deployment of only one battalion on Daitojima and the 21st Independent Mixed Brigade on Tokunoshima. If the enemy were to follow up his victory in the Marianas with a swift advance across the ocean, the Ryukyus would be in jeopardy. A storm was brewing in the East China Sea. I felt a sense of personal satisfaction, a sudden stirring of the will after a long paralysis.

A conference of the chiefs of staff of the Defense Forces had been convened in Tokyo. I flew up on June 27 in the company of Western Army Chief of Staff Yoshinaka. It was there, at Imperial Headquarters, that I heard the shocking details of the crushing defeat in the Marianas. Now the General Staff Office, far from fretting over this defeat, was desperately seeking ways to cope with the changed situation.

Both the General Staff and the Defense Headquarters had their offices in Ichigaya. While the chiefs of staff were in conference, Defense Headquarters held high-level command exercises for the air defense of the mainland. These exercises had been planned before the fall of the Marianas. I quickly lost interest when I found that Okinawa was being given no more than a minor supplementary role in the defense of the mainland. Of course the two staffs had different objectives. While the General Staff was in charge of the entire military war effort, Defense Headquarters had only the specific task of preparing for an American assault on the home islands. Yet I was amazed that these two staffs, occupying adjoining offices in Ichigaya, could have such different perspectives. During the exercises there was a discussion of the importance of Daitojima in view of the fall of the Marianas line. The general opinion of both Defense Headquarters and the General Staff was that the

Americans would follow their victory in the Marianas by seizing Daitojima, using it as a foothold to swoop down on the Ryukyus; the defense of Daitojima, it was argued, should be strengthened.

When asked, I stated my own opinion of the situation. I began with a strategic analysis. To me, Daitojima, only three hundred kilometers east of Okinawa, was a small island, "an isolated rock" with almost no strategic value. Rather than waste energies against Daitojima, an aggressive enemy would probably prefer to strike at Okinawa directly.

I then presented my tactical ideas for the defense of the islands. If we were to strengthen our defense of the Ryukyus, we should drop this fixation with Daitojima and concentrate on building up troop strength on the keystone, the main island of Okinawa. In Pacific island battles so far, we had deployed insufficient numbers of ground troops at the last minute to one island after another; one after another they fell to the enemy. I felt it was crucial that we select those islands where we could expect the enemy to attack, place decisive troop strength there, and make adequate combat preparations while we still had the chance.

This proposal I placed before Defense Headquarters Chief of Staff Lieutenant General Kobayashi, Western Army Chief of Staff Lieutenant General Yoshinaka, and the other chiefs of staff. Apparently thinking my views too extreme, Yoshinaka ridiculed them. "If we took your ideas one step further," he said, "we'd discard Okinawa and concentrate our strength on the more important island of Kyushu."

Our strategy in the Pacific war followed our supreme commanders' unswerving policy of relying on the air force to win battles. My dissenting views stemmed from my doubts about that policy. I was saying that with our air and sea fighting strength having fallen far below that of the enemy, we should place greater emphasis on our fighting strength on the ground.

In the end, the General Staff recognized the danger of a land invasion. Their offices were thrown into a commotion as they set about to mass a large fighting force in the Ryukyus. The tense atmosphere, so different from that of Defense Headquarters, was as refreshing to me as a springtime breeze. After a long and agonizing stretch of inactivity, 32nd Army was at least moving into the spotlight. What could be more agreeable?

In Tokyo I ran into General Isamu Cho, who, as chief of staff, would later play a leading role in the tragic battle of Okinawa. The first thing he said, in his usual high-spirited fashion, was, "I'm going to teach your army and the army in Taiwan, tactics that will assure victory!" This he punctuated with a burst of hearty laughter. Standing silently beside the general, looking tough, was Lieutenant Colonel Kimura, who would later serve as one of our staff officers. I learned that Major Tadahiko Hayashi, formerly a student of mine at the Military Staff College, had already left for Okinawa to serve as a staff officer.

The sense of urgency at Imperial Headquarters reached new heights at the end of June, when it was learned that the transport *Toyama Maru* had been sunk by an enemy submarine off the coast of Tokunoshima. On board the ship had been the 44th Independent Mixed Brigade, one of our army's most prized units. This attack was taken to be a harbinger of the coming assault on the Ryukyus.

Plans to build up troop strength in the southwestern islands were quickly drawn up and forcefully implemented. First, it was decided to airlift Colonel Mita's 15th Independent Mixed Regiment from Tokyo to Okinawa immediately. This was the first time the Japanese army had ever attempted to airlift such a large fighting force. Naval warships, among them the battleships *Yamato* and *Musashi,* were also mobilized. General Hara's 9th Division and Lieutenant General Kushibuchi's 28th Division were rushed to Okinawa and Miyakojima, respectively. Plans were also made for further reinforcements. I went to pay my respects to Colonel Nishiura, chief of the Military Affairs Section of the War Office. Nishiura gave me his enthusiastic encouragement, telling me he would give highest priority to sending military supplies to our army in the islands.

The conference of the chiefs of staff drew to a close. Before returning to our posts, we received instruction in winning tactics from General Atomiya, vice-chief of staff of the Imperial Headquarters Army Department. The general was a straightforward man, full of ardor and humor. His bald head fairly steaming with enthusiasm, he outlined for us the following tactics:

> First, we cannot hope to match the enemy's strength on the ground, at sea, or in the air. Therefore, we should attack the enemy from "underground."
>
> Second, in order to prevent the enemy from using his superior ground, sea, and air strength to the full, we should make use of the cover of night to pull up behind the enemy or penetrate enemy lines. Enemy troops would be thrown into a state of confusion, unable to distinguish friend or foe.
>
> Third, the greatest threat above ground is enemy tanks. We have only a few antitank guns, and these would be quickly destroyed by the enemy's bombardment. If a poor man fights with the same tactics as a rich man, he is sure to lose. Therefore, the Japanese army has formulated new "patented" antitank tactics. These involve hand-carried makeshift explosive devices containing ten

kilograms of yellow powder.[1] Our experiments have shown ten kilograms of powder to be enough to blow up enemy tanks of any size. Delivery of these explosives would be in the nature of a suicide attack, of course. Soldiers assigned to this duty should be promoted three ranks.

General Atomiya seemed very pleased with himself, and wanted to know if we didn't agree that it was a splendid battle plan. I had previously served under the general in the War Office's personnel department. I was now 32nd Army's senior staff officer, about to stand at the focal point of a great battle. The general therefore seemed anxious to know how I received his views. "Well then, Yahara," he asked, "am I correct? I haven't gone senile yet, have I?" He stared at me long and hard and repeatedly pressed me for an answer.

I smiled and replied that his battle plan was highly insightful and realistic. The "winning tactics" Major General Cho had earlier boasted of probably followed the same line of reasoning. During the battle of Okinawa, I was to adhere consistently to these tactical ideas. My only reservations concerned the fact that the overall battle plan did not go beyond ground tactics. I was anxious to hear a broader strategic analysis with guidelines for coordination of air, land, and sea forces.

In any case, the few days spent at Imperial Headquarters in the turbulent aftermath of the fall of the Marianas line had totally swept away my earlier feelings of emptiness and futility. Charged with a sense of heroic purpose, I rode over to Azabu airfield in a car sent around from Imperial Headquarters and boarded the airplane that would return me to my post.

My flight stopped overnight at Akinogahara, then continued on the next day, passing over the coastal waters of Tosa in eastern Shikoku, eastern Kyushu, and Tokunoshima, where the *Toyama Maru* had met its fate. I was greeted by a beautiful sunset as I landed in Naha late in the afternoon of July 2.

I was preceded by General Cho, who had already gone into action on several fronts. General Watanabe was deeply troubled by the sinking of the *Toyama Maru* and the fall of the Marianas line. Staff Officer Major Miyake and his aide, Captain Sakaguchi, had been dispatched to Tokunoshima to do what they could.

Colonel Shibata, commander of the 1st Infantry, and more than four thousand troops, had perished on the *Toyama Maru*. The only survivors were

---

[1]These so-called "satchel charges" were used to considerable effect in the battle of Okinawa.

the 2nd Infantry's Colonel Udo and two hundred troops. Colonel Shibata had commanded the fortifications at Nakagusuku Bay; I remembered him as an amiable man who had been of great assistance to me since my first days in Okinawa. Coming soon after the death of the Daitojima Battalion Commander Lieutenant Colonel Yokota, this deplorable event reminded me of the cruel turns of fate awaiting men who chose a career in the military.

It may seem odd that we were so deeply grieved over this particular incident, considering that as many as seventy thousand soldiers had met the same fate on ships sunk in the Pacific. As commander of the naval escort, Rear Admiral Shinba felt a deep sense of personal responsibility and called on our headquarters to express his regrets. The navy staff officer accompanying him remarked bitterly that the *"shinsengumi"*[2] had struck again. He told us that there were three groups of enemy submarines in the waters nearby. One group in particular did a great deal of damage whenever it came close to the southwestern islands.

Lieutenant General Hara's 9th Division headquarters and Colonel Mita's 15th Independent Mixed Regiment arrived by air during the three days from July 10 to July 12. There were reports of newly landed officers and soldiers drawing their swords and shouting "Where's the enemy?" The sense of urgency pervading Imperial Headquarters had apparently made itself felt to these men. Many arrived thinking the enemy had already landed.

The 15th Regiment was placed under the command of Major General Suzuki of the 44th Independent Mixed Brigade. That brigade was assigned the defense of the Nakagami district north of an east-west parallel running through the town of Futema near the island's center. (See map on page 21.) South of that line was the defense sector of the 9th Division. Additional large units were to be steadily dispatched to the islands, but the unit names and arrival dates were not specified. Recognizing the urgency of the situation, we posted successively arriving units to temporary defense positions that would gradually be shifted in the months ahead. An enemy invasion might come at any time; we had to be prepared. Until our full fighting strength was assembled on the island, we were obliged to reassign constantly and move the various units as new reinforcements arrived. If Imperial Headquarters had been able to give us an overall plan with specific unit names and arrival dates,

---

[2]The *shinsengumi* were improvised special police units organized by the Tokugawa Shogunate in the 1860s to suppress the revolutionary activities of anti-shogunate elements in Edo and Kyoto. They became well known for their ruthlessness and swift action. Ambushes were their specialty.

we would have been able to follow a consistent policy, disposing units in an efficient manner instead of constantly moving them left and right. Imperial Headquarters itself, however, had to take gradual measures to make troops available, so such specification was probably impossible.

In the account of the battle that I made public after the war, I pointed out that the 44th Independent Mixed Brigade had its defense position changed seven times during the ten months before the actual battle of Okinawa.[3] Officers and soldiers normally work to build up their defense positions with zeal. It is bad policy to change the operational plans of large fighting units in such a reckless manner.

I had cited such cases to illustrate my dissatisfaction with the gradual troop reinforcement procedures of July. The full troop strength planned by Imperial Headquarters had been largely completed by early September. Composed chiefly of four divisions, five mixed brigades, and one artillery regiment, troop strength in the islands then totalled 180,000. The number of troops and their disposition in the islands had been decided by Imperial Headquarters. The question of total troop strength aside, it would normally be the responsibility of our army to plan and implement their disposition. Considering the urgency of the situation and the necessity of transporting troops across dangerous waters, Imperial Headquarters no doubt felt compelled to decide these matters arbitrarily.

The recommendations of Major General Cho, who departed for Okinawa while I was in Tokyo, seem to have been taken in consideration. Cho, who soon became my chief of staff, told me he had demanded that five divisions be stationed on the main island of Okinawa. He laughed uproariously as he told me how he had browbeaten the General Staff Office, saying, "If Okinawa should fall because you didn't take my recommendation, the section heads of the General Staff Office will have to commit *seppuku.*"[4]

The Marianas line having fallen, it was certain that the enemy would soon advance toward one of three places: the Philippines, Taiwan, or Okinawa. Under the circumstances, Imperial Headquarters made the right decision to give our army the largest troop strength. Unfortunately, their ar-

---

[3]The 44th Independent Mixed Brigade had lost the 1st and 2nd Infantry Regiments in the *Toyama Maru* sinking. The 1st was not reactivated. The 2nd was reformed with troops raised on Kyushu and Okinawa late in the summer. The 15th Independent Mixed Regiment was added to the 44th Independent Mixed Brigade in July.

[4]*Seppuku* is another reading—and the preferred one—for the characters of *hara-kiri,* or ritual disembowelment, as practiced in the *samurai* tradition.

bitrary disposition of troops throughout the islands only scattered our combat strength. Altogether too many troops were stationed at Miyakojima, and I thought it ludicrous that, in spite of my statements in Tokyo, one entire regiment from the 28th Division had been posted to Daitojima. It may be unfair to belabor the point. As of the summer of 1944, both the navy and air force had considerable strength, and Imperial Headquarters was holding firmly to its operational policy of fighting battles primarily with air power.

As this great flood of troops was flowing into the southwestern islands, our 32nd Army was detached from the Western Army and placed under the command of 10th Theater Army (Army of Taiwan) on July 15, 1944. It was thought appropriate to shed peacetime dispositions and place our army with 10th Army, which both in name and in fact was an operational fighting force. If, however, command relationships between different Pacific islands were not established with great care, serious problems could arise. Once troops are dispersed among the islands, limited transport capacity and the dangers of the open seas make it difficult to move and concentrate troop strength. Furthermore, it is only natural that each commander expect that the island under his command will be the next target of the enemy, whatever the overall strategic situation. The problem was particularly apparent in the relationship between 32nd Army command headquarters in Okinawa and 10th Area Army in Taiwan. The resultant clash of opinions—only basic human nature—was to intensify with the passage of time and the growing urgency of the situation.

Together with these troop reinforcements and changes in the line of command, our army now underwent a reshuffling at the top. Major General Cho was appointed chief of staff, while Major General Kitagawa was transferred to 10th Area Army as vice-chief of staff. General Cho's career record and personality were well known to everyone in the military. Tough and decisive, Cho could be aggressive and forceful. He was paternalistic on a grand scale to his subordinates, extending his care and protection even to those prone to be insubordinate. He was also known occasionally to defy his superiors. I sometimes heard stories of drinking parties at which Cho had reportedly thrown punches at brigade and regiment commanders.

I first knew of General Cho during my days at the Army Staff College. I was the youngest student at the school, and Cho outranked me by six or seven terms. I remember very well the dashing figure of the young captain in those days. He was then only two years ahead of both myself and my former chief of staff, Major General Kitagawa. Practicing my horsemanship one afternoon, I had led a horse from the stable and was about to mount. I saw a young captain mount his steed and, lashing his whip, take off for the riding grounds at nearly full gallop. Normally a rider starts out at a walk and gradually works up to a trot and then a canter. My horsemanship was very poor then, and I was astounded at the unconventional approach of that dauntless officer. I asked a classmate who he was and learned that he was Captain Cho.

In 1936 I was working in the War Office's personnel department. At the time, young officers were active in politics, and I attended a meeting called by Lieutenant Colonel Kingoro Hashimoto.[5] Cho was also present. They were both very active in the "young officers" military clique.

Because I worked in the personnel department, I knew a great deal about Major Cho and his political activities, but I had not yet had the occasion actually to speak with the man. My chance came when the Japanese army advanced into Indochina in 1941. Officially, I was listed as the military attaché to the Japanese Embassy in Thailand; unofficially, I was at work collecting strategic data for later operations in Thailand, Malaysia, and Burma. My duties required frequent travel between Bangkok and Saigon.

One night Cho and I were both staying in the Majestic Hotel in Saigon. Seeking some diversion from our cares, we went to the cinema next door. The feature that night was a European film, *Waves of the Danube*. Later, just before the general committed suicide during the battle of Okinawa, he said, "Yahara, I remember the scenery and music from that film we saw in Saigon." After the film, we had walked to a favorite haunt of the general's, a Japanese-run *sukiyaki* restaurant on the banks of the river, and drank till we were thoroughly besotted. I had always held an image of the general as a fine, spirited fellow. Our revels that night confirmed it.

There is no dearth of colorful anecdotes about Cho. Once, during the Zhanggufang Incident—a veritable war between divisional-strength Soviet and Japanese troops on the border between Manchuria and Mongolia—he had astonished Soviet officers by lying down to take a nap on the borderline. As a brigade commander, he would instruct his officers by singing to them in the old-fashioned *naniwabushi* style. Invited to a party with French officials in Saigon, he showed up in a *Kamishimo* gown and astonished everyone by

---

[5]Hashimoto was a leading advocate of aggressive warfare in China during the 1930s and played a prominent role in Japanese army incursions there. In 1937, he engineered the artillery and air bombing of the U.S. Navy gunboat USS *Panay* in Yangtze waters.

reciting a classical *joruri* narrative. I was to serve under this remarkable man, fighting by his side in the battle of Okinawa.

The first commanding general of 32nd Army, Lieutenant General Watanabe, had worked diligently to cope with the changes in the war situation, but finally succumbed to fatigue, aggravated by his chronic gastroenteritis, and had to be confined to bed. The chief of staff and other officers close to the general kept his illness a secret and prayed for his speedy recovery, but his condition steadily deteriorated and eventually became known to our superiors in Tokyo. In August we received orders to report on the general's condition. Our staff carefully deliberated about this matter. Finally taking into consideration the general's grave condition, and the fact that he was a widower with young children, we had no choice but to submit a full medical report from the army surgeon. Immediate transfer orders followed.[6]

Despondent, General Watanabe departed from Naha airfield. His replacement, Lieutenant General Mitsuru Ushijima, arrived in Naha on August 11. He displayed great dignity and composure as he assumed his fateful command on the island. Tall and heavyset, General Ushijima was an imposing figure with ruddy cheeks and a benign countenance. I had occasionally seen the general when he was a high-ranking adjutant at the War Office, but I did not know him well. He had served as the superintendent of the Military Academy before coming to Okinawa. After I began working under his command, I was to discover that he was the complete opposite of his predecessor, General Watanabe.

Ushijima, as a rule, entrusted all operational details to his subordinates but always took full responsibility for the outcome. In this respect, he was faithful to long-standing Japanese military tradition, going back to the great Takamori Saigo, a fellow native of Kagoshima.[7]

Shortly after he assumed command, I drafted several very important orders, submitting them for the general's approval with some trepidation. Without reading my draft, he rolled up the paper and with a straight face

---

[6]The rumor persists that Watanabe had grown very negative about further prosecution of the war, feeling it hopeless. This, rather than his illness, may have actually prompted his transfer.

[7]Takamori Saigo (1827–1877) was one of the leaders of the Meiji Restoration of 1868, Japan's extraordinary political and cultural revolution, which modernized the country and led to Japan's becoming a great power. A military man who set great store by the *samurai* spirit, Saigo ultimately led a revolt against his peers in the new Meiji government. Although reluctant to break with Tokyo, he was urged on by Satsuma *samurai* who felt that excessive central government control conflicted with long-standing clan traditions. He committed suicide in 1877 after his revolt failed.

asked me where he should sign. I was appalled. This seemed a dangerous practice to me, and I realized that I would have to devise ways to ensure that my commander read the orders he signed.

While our top ranks were being reshuffled, newly appointed staff officer Hayashi died on a mission to Imperial Headquarters, when his plane crashed on Mount Hakone. During his short term of duty, Hayashi had been active in many areas. Majors Hazeyama and Yakumaru were assigned to replace him. In addition to myself, 32nd Army now had six staff officers: Kimura, Kugimiya, Hazeyama, Yakumaru, Yasaka, and Miyake. With a staff befitting a first-rate army, the atmosphere at our command headquarters grew lively and invigorating.

Reacting to the fall of the Marianas, Imperial Headquarters quickly formulated new plans for a decisive showdown with the enemy. These plans were given the name "Operation Victory." Plans were numbered one through four, according to the four probable directions in which the enemy might advance: (1) the Philippines, (2) Taiwan and the Ryukyus, (3) the Japanese mainland, and (4) Hokkaido. When the direction of the enemy's offensive became evident, the greater part of army and navy air power, it was said, together with the Combined Fleet, would annihilate enemy landing forces while they were still seaborne. Enemy troops managing to reach land would be neutralized by ground units. Of the four plans, Imperial Headquarters took the greatest interest in Operation Victory Plan No. 1 (the Philippines) and Operation Victory Plan No. 2 (Taiwan and the Ryukyus), since it judged that attacks in these quarters were most probable.

The army and navy operational officers in charge of the defense of Taiwan and the Ryukyus met in Taipei in mid-August to reach mutual understanding on the guiding concept for Operation Victory Plan No. 2. I went to Taipei with General Ushijima and was a key participant in the conference. The main points were as follows:

1. The air forces deployed in Kyushu, the Ryukyus, and Taiwan were to annihilate enemy landing forces in the water.
2. The Combined Fleet, then on alert in Brunei Bay, would rush to take part in the battle, arriving within a week.
3. The China Expeditionary Army command would assemble the crack 1st Division in the Shanghai area; the 10th Theater Army com-

mander would station the 1st Mobile Brigade in Keelung. Both units would be on alert, ready for battle.

4. Any enemy troops to escape the attacks of our navy and air force would be mopped up by ground units, as soon as they reached land.

Troop strength given to 32nd Army for Operation Victory Plan No. 2 amounted to four divisions, 9th, 24th, 28th, and 62nd, and two independent mixed brigades, the 44th and 45th, along with several heavy artillery regiments, antiaircraft units, shipping engineers, antitank and machine-gun battalions, and numerous units of specialized troops. Of these, three divisions and one mixed brigade were to be located on the main island of Okinawa, along with the greater part of the artillery, organized into a special artillery group.

In addition to these formations we had numerous powerful navy units, chiefly shore battery, antiaircraft artillery, and rapid-fire gun units on various islands. By agreement between the army and the navy, these units would be directed by the army commanders of the respective islands.

Thirty-second Army set the following guidelines for defense of the islands:

1. The decisive action was to be fought on the main island of Okinawa.
2. Units on Miyakojima would mainly wage a protracted defense but take the offensive under advantageous conditions.
3. Defense garrisons on all other islands would concentrate on a protracted defense, keeping air bases secure for as long as possible.

Troop disposition would conform to local terrain; troop strength would be concentrated; and an extensive system of subterranean fortifications constructed.

A plan of operations for the main island of Okinawa was decided upon by 32nd Army. (See map on page 21.) I drafted the entire plan, which ran as follows.

With some units left on Iejima to wage a protracted defense, our main fighting strength was to be placed on the southern half of Okinawa. Units would move in the direction of any enemy landings, launch an offensive, and destroy the enemy near the coast. The American forces would probably make their landing at one of three fronts: Itoman, South airfield, or Kadena. We labeled these operations Numbers 1, 2, and 3, and swiftly brought all three fronts up to full

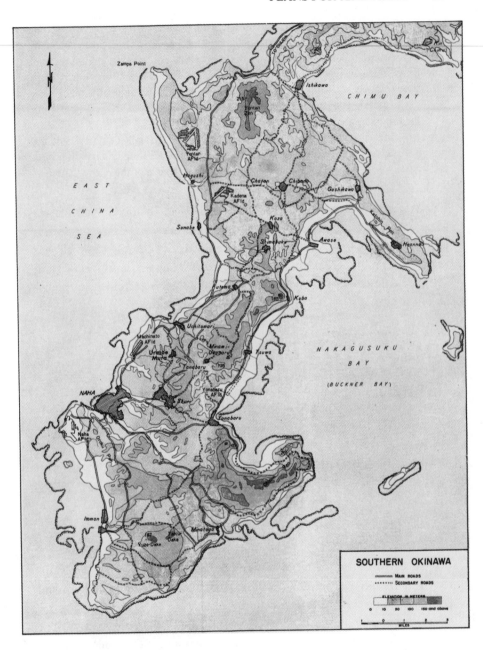

SOUTHERN OKINAWA

MAIN ROADS
SECONDARY ROADS

ELEVATION IN METERS
0   10   50   100   150 and above

MILES

operational readiness. We then turned to preparations at Minatogawa on the south shore, Nakagusuku Bay, and Kinmu Bay.

Operations 1 through 3 followed the same pattern, differing mainly in the deployment of the attacking divisions. In each plan one division was to hold the enemy landing force at the beachhead, while a force of two divisions would move to the front and prepare to take the offensive, heavily supported by artillery. Alternately, one division would attack, while another was kept in reserve. Early in the second night after the enemy landing, army and division artillery were to direct their full firepower at the beachhead, annihilating the main body of the invasion force. Later that night, infantry units would attack and mop up the enemy at the beachhead.

In each of these operations, the 1st, 2nd, and 3rd Sea Raiding units on the central coast and the 26th, 27th, 28th, and 29th Sea Raiding units on the south coast would assault the American transports on the eve of the enemy landing.

Thirty-second Army's Operation Victory plans were finalized in mid-August when our last reinforcements, the 62nd Division, arrived. I drafted the strategy and tactical troop disposition for this plan of operations, which was accepted without reservation by both my commander and my chief of staff. The plan reflected my judgment of the general situation. Herewith, my analysis of the plan and what I hoped to accomplish with it.

1. Timing of the American Invasion

As I stated earlier, I had anticipated an enemy assault on Okinawa at around cherry blossom time the following year; in other words, April 1945. In July and early August, however, I could not discount the possibility that the momentum of the victory in the Marianas might carry the enemy to an early attack on Okinawa. Thus, I had to prepare a plan of operations to cope with an enemy attack at any time.

2. The American Landing Place

If the enemy invaded the southwestern islands, his main force would be directed at Okinawa. The other islands, including Miyakojima and Amami Oshima, had no real strategic function.

If the enemy invaded Okinawa, where would he choose to land? The island is actually much larger than it looks, measuring 120 kilometers north to south and between 8 and 20 kilometers east to west. The southern half of the island is mostly flat and densely populated. The main cities, harbors, and airfields on the island are in this southern half. The northern half of the island is mountainous and sparsely populated. Except for the town of Nago and

Iejima, the north has little military value. Therefore, enemy landings would probably be limited to the southern half of Okinawa.

Assuming that the enemy would make a landing in southern Okinawa, where exactly would that be? There are two main bays on the east coast, at Kinmu and Nakagusuku. But behind Kinmu Bay lies some very hilly terrain, and it would be difficult to advance on key strategic points. The enemy would very likely be wary of entering Nakagusuku Bay from the start. Thus enemy troops would probably land on the west coast at Kadena, from which they could swiftly occupy the north and central airfields, or at Oroku, close to the southern airfields. They could also land on the coast north or south of Naha, and thus be able to utilize Naha harbor.

When judging the probable movements of the enemy, however, one must not limit the possibilities. The only way to be certain of where the enemy will land is to detect his intentions beforehand or observe his actual landing maneuvers. One must be prepared for an enemy landing wherever a landing is theoretically feasible. While our plan of operations, therefore, anticipated landings at three places on the west coast, we also planned to prepare for possible landings at Nakagusuku Bay and Minatogawa on the south coast.

3. Enemy Troop Strength and Landing Methods

In order to gain their objectives, invaders must have at least three times the troop strength of the defenders. This fact has been amply demonstrated throughout the history of warfare in Japan and other nations. The American military had adhered to this rule in all previous actions in the Pacific. American forces invading Okinawa would thus have to have between six and ten divisions, three times our army's troop strength.[8]

The enemy would probably pick one spot to make a landing. It is rare for an invasion force to make two or more landings at a time. The enemy would secure a narrow strip of land on the coast a few kilometers in length, extending one or two kilometers inland. The superior forces of the enemy's navy and air force would fend off counterattacks by the Japanese army, while troops on the ground unloaded munitions and made preparations to advance inland. The advance would normally be staged several days after the landing.

---

[8]In the event, 10th Army comprised XXIV Corps (96th, 7th, and 77th Divisions) and III Marine Amphibious Corps (1st and 6th Marine Divisions). The 27th Army Division was also committed, while the 2nd Marine Division remained in reserve.

One also cannot discount the possibility that the enemy might stage landings at two or more different locations, or advance immediately after landing. But in any of these cases as well, the Japanese army was committed to the kind of plan that would attack and destroy the enemy immediately after landing, in a narrow strip of land on the coast.

4. Reliability of "Operation Victory"

The plans adopted for the decisive battle of Okinawa were based on the policy of Imperial Headquarters to use the navy and air force to crush advancing enemy forces at sea. To their way of thinking, ground defense units were needed only to mop up enemy remnants after they landed. It would be fortunate if this actually turned out to be the case; 32nd Army obviously hoped that it would. After the fall of the Marianas line, however, 32nd Army's senior officers no longer had much faith in the fighting strength of the navy and air force. We questioned whether we would stand a fighting chance against an invasion force if it landed without sustaining great damage. The ground fighting strength ratio between their forces and ours, given their heavy logistical support, could be as much as 10 to 1. With the addition of the American Pacific Fleet and its air power, the overall fighting strength was 20 or 30 to 1. Did we have a chance of successfully defending Okinawa against such a powerful enemy?

For the following reasons, I felt hopeful that we could thwart the American forces' landing scheme.

1. The effects of bombardment by the American navy and air force could be nullified by keeping our forces in underground tunnels that would withstand enemy bombs and gunfire. Against steel, the product of American industry, we would pit our earthen fortifications, the product of the sweat of our troops and the Okinawan people.
2. The Americans might put as many as ten divisions into the field, but no more than a few could land initially. There would doubtless be confusion in the ranks, as the troops would be exposed on a narrow strip of land without fortifications.
3. Holed up safely in our fortified areas we could, as our chief of staff put it, "laugh in the face" of the enemy's bombardment. We would be able to maintain firepower and organization and keep order in the ranks.
4. Because our army was on the defensive, we could concentrate large-

caliber artillery guns in the field. We had 400 guns of $7\frac{1}{2}$-centimeter bore or above; of these, 120 guns were 15 centimeters or above. The firepower of these powerful guns directed at the enemy's narrow beachhead from the tunnel emplacements would have a devastating effect.

In modern warfare, tanks and artillery wield greater offensive power than infantry. Unfortunately, our 32nd Army had only one regiment of light tanks; we did, however, have considerable artillery strength. With an eye on this, I devised tactics for effective bombardment of the beachhead. On the basis of these tactical concepts, I made recommendations to the central command for further artillery reinforcements. Stressing the necessity of unified command operation facilities, I made a strong case to headquarters and succeeded in having the 5th Artillery Group placed under direct army control.

5. In the Pacific islands so far, American landing forces had first secured a beachhead and then progressed step-by-step toward an advance a few days later. We could not discount the possibility that the enemy might stage an advance immediately after landing, with numerous tank units breaking through infantry resistance and striking at artillery positions. If this happened, our army would be at a disadvantage. If, however, we increased the longitudinal depth of infantry tunnel positions and made substantial preparation for antitank warfare, the infantry lines could hold out for the two days our army would need to prepare for a counteroffensive.

6. Given the enemy's sea and air supremacy, it would be difficult to move large fighting units through the narrow corridor of land connecting Nakagami in the southern half of the island with Shimajiri in the north. For the following reasons, I believed that this problem could be solved:

   a. The distance to be crossed was no more than twenty-five kilometers.

   b. Units could be moved under cover of night. Units unable to complete the move at night could adopt the procedures devised in Manchuria for troop maneuvers under enemy-controlled skies. The 9th and 24th Divisions had been thoroughly drilled in these maneuvers in Manchuria.

   c. Because the invasion would proceed from water to land, enemy aircraft would be based on aircraft carriers and would probably make no more than a few night air sorties.

d. We could prepare four north-south roads for troop movements, place repair materials at those key segments most likely to be bombarded by the enemy, and construct alternate roads.

e. Underground positions would be constructed beforehand for units to take up after maneuvers.

f. The 9th and 24th Divisions and artillery units would undergo drills to master these maneuvers.

g. Munitions would be stockpiled separately in the north and in the south.

Part II

The
American Assault

Lieutenant Gibney's commentary continues

2

The Grand
Strategy Unfolds

Events would prove the accuracy of Colonel Yahara's forecasts about the time and place of the Okinawa invasion, although the scale of the American attack was beyond even his cool and pessimistic reckoning. This was due largely to two factors: the success of American air power, principally the carrier sweeps of the Pacific; and the continued attrition of Japanese shipping by the U.S. submarine force, the unsung heroes of the Pacific war. Thus the strategic estimates for the encirclement and invasion of Japan were being outdated by the very speed of the Allied advance.

As events unfolded in 1944 and 1945, Yahara's forebodings about the loss of the Marianas and the disintegration of Japanese air power were confirmed, far beyond the worst-case scenarios of the Japanese staff planners. In 1943, when the Joint Chiefs of Staff in Washington had approved the design for the ongoing war against Japan, the plan was to invade South China, Taiwan, and ultimately, the main islands of Japan, but only after a continuing series of strikes and landings at island outposts across the Pacific. This at least is how the war was viewed from Nimitz's headquarters at Makalapa heights, overlooking Pearl Harbor.

General MacArthur saw things differently from his vantage point. He envisioned a steady push northward through New Guinea and Borneo to the attack on the Philippines. This offensive would proceed regularly, first with the reduction of Mindanao, then Leyte, and finally the Japanese strongholds on Luzon.

Events intervened, however, to speed up both timetables and, in a sense, combine them. While the steady push northward continued in the Southwest Pacific area, the Central Pacific theater became the scene of a series of successful long-range strikes at Japanese sea power and air power. The result was the destruction or isolation of most of the beleaguered island garrisons in the Pacific. Japanese losses in the battle of Midway had already taken away the best of Japan's well-trained, carrier-based navy pilots and some of its aircraft carriers. The battle of the Philippine Sea, which destroyed the superbattleship *Musashi,* among others, took a fearful toll of Japanese air power. Air strikes by the American task forces leading up to the attack on the Marianas virtually completed the job. In those engagements of June 1944, the so-called "Marianas turkey shoot," U.S. Navy pilots took care of most of Japan's remaining carrier strength. Thenceforward, Japan's air war would be carried on by hastily trained aviators with only a few surviving carriers. The end result was the desperate strategy of the *kamikaze* suicide planes which, as it happened, took a heavy toll of U.S. Navy ships in the Okinawa campaign.

By July 1944, U.S. forces had secured the Japanese stronghold of Saipan, along with the adjoining islands of Tinian and Guam, the former American possession. The attack on Leyte in October of that year bypassed Mindanao and opened the way to a move north for the final assault on Luzon. The September attack on Peleliu, which proved to be a very bloody battle indeed, was overtaken by events before it began. (The island was supposed to serve as a base for aircraft in the attack on the Philippines, but with airfields on Leyte, no further bases were needed.) Iwo Jima was attacked and captured with similar heavy losses on both sides late in November 1944. It served as a base for the B-29s then raiding the Japanese mainland. By October, the Joint Chiefs canceled plans to attack Taiwan. They chose Okinawa instead. The Ryukyus were closer to the Japanese main islands and presented a far more tempting and immediate target.

The B-29 raids continued in 1944 with ever-growing intensity, culminating in the ghastly firebombing attacks of 1945. Less heralded, but in the end far more effective in undermining Japanese military strength, was the extraordinary success of the U.S. submarines. In 1944 fully 2 ½ million tons of Japanese shipping was sunk by U.S. submarines—more than the total achieved in the early years of the war. By the middle of 1945 when the Okinawa invasion began, it was hazardous for Japanese troop ships to attempt travel much outside the main islands. Indeed, U.S. submarines had their periscopes locked on the entrance to Tokyo Bay.

At JICPOA's Interrogation Center at Pearl Harbor, it was easy to project from staff requests for interrogations which way the winds were blowing.

In mid-1944 I had spent a great deal of time interrogating Taiwanese seamen who had been picked up by the navy, with a view to an invasion there. By the time I returned from the Palau operation with some 250 Japanese POWs and 300 Korean conscript laborers in tow, Taiwan was a dead issue. It was clear that we were after Okinawa and then the main islands. Most of our interrogation at that time centered on strategic targets in Japan. But when we received orders to board navy transports in early 1945, heading west and north with only a stop at Leyte on the way, it was quite clear where our target lay.

By late summer, as we have seen, the fall of the Marianas and lost carrier battles west of the islands had convinced Imperial Headquarters that Okinawa must be reinforced. The 62nd Division, a battle-wise unit from China, was ticketed for the island as well as the 24th, which had served in Manchuria. The bulk of the troops from the new 44th Independent Mixed Brigade was lost on June 29, 1944, when a U.S. submarine torpedoed their transport. Almost five thousand men were killed in that disaster.

Worse was yet to come. On October 10, 1944, a week after Nimitz's staff had finally decided to bypass Taiwan and go for the Ryukyus, waves of carrier-based aircraft from Task Force 58 gave Okinawa its first brutal taste of war. The capital city of Naha was almost destroyed. Since the U.S. air strike's principal target was the harbor there, great quantities of munitions went up in flaming explosions. The rest of the island was not spared. Two airfields were heavily damaged and more than eighty Japanese aircraft destroyed on the ground. The civilian toll was worse. More than one thousand Okinawan men, women, and children lost their lives, far worse than the military casualties—and a sad foretaste of the tragedy to come.

There was some fortuitous irony in the timing of the raid. The night before, at a banquet in Naha, Lieutenant General Cho had boastfully told his audience that the Okinawa battle would result in certain victory for Japan. He did nothing to dispel the impression that Imperial Headquarters' grand strategy lay in luring American air and sea power into a deathtrap, only to be finished off by waves of aircraft from the mainland and the Combined Fleet, while 32nd Army eliminated those American troops unfortunate enough to reach the beachhead. Perhaps he believed it. The next morning the very restaurant where he had made his claims was a smoking ruin.

These blows from the Americans were now compounded by a major strategic error on the part of Imperial Headquarters in Tokyo. Worried about the progress of U.S. forces in the Philippines, Tokyo ordered the entire 9th Division shipped out of Okinawa to the Philippines, via Taiwan. The twenty-five thousand men who left in December represented the cream of the Okinawan defense force. They were the very people whom Cho and Yahara had counted on to fight off the Americans from heavily fortified defenses along the west coast beaches.

Thus, several months before the American landing on April 1, 1945, Yahara had been forced into a change in plans. There would now be no attempt to repulse the Americans at the beachhead because there were too few troops.

On the contrary, while a few units were left to act as guerrilla irritants in the northern two-thirds of the island, the main force of 32nd Army was to be concentrated in the southern third, behind several heavily fortified lines north of army headquarters at Shuri Castle. The battle was to be, as Yahara frequently wrote, a *jikyusen,* a war of attrition. For this, his preparations were impressive. Almost all of the Japanese artillery strength in the Ryukyus—there were two divisions on Miyakojima and Ishigakijima, we must remember—were concentrated on Okinawa and placed under General Wada's 5th Artillery Group. Their guns would bolster an elaborate system of interlocking defenses. Dugouts and pillboxes dotted the honeycombed caves of the area and provided a kind of interlocking defense.

The airfields at Yomitan and Kadena would be abandoned to the Americans. If others at 32nd Army headquarters still hoped for a massive surge of avenging aircraft and paratroopers from the mainland, Yahara had few illusions on that score. As he saw it, the war in Okinawa would be fought on the ground. It would consist of a bitter yard-by-yard defense of the island. Ultimate defeat was inevitable, given the weight of American sea, air, and land power, but Yahara's aim was to delay the reduction of the island fortress for as long as possible. Thirty-second Army's persistence would in turn gain time for the Japanese armed forces to build up their resources against what all felt would be a coming invasion of the main islands.

At the close of Easter week, on April 6 and 7, Imperial Headquarters launched its long-promised two-pronged attack on the American fleet off Okinawa. Almost seven hundred aircraft took off from bases in Kyushu and Taiwan in an effort to destroy the U.S. Fifth Fleet. Most were shot down. The damage they did was considerable—some eight destroyers and smaller ships were sunk and ten damaged—but it was nothing like the sixty warships that Japan's Imperial Headquarters announced had been sunk. Some of the airplanes were *kamikaze,* piloted by officers of the *Tokkotai,* the Special Attack Force of suicide fighters, who pledged to crash their airplanes into enemy ships in acts of self-immolation. There would be more of these *kamikaze* later, though not in such great force. The suicide attacks were responsible for the highest rate of U.S. naval casualties in World War II.

Also on April 6 and 7 the superbattleship *Yamato,* the world's largest,[1] made its fateful sortie south from Kyushu in a desperate effort to reach the American fleet offshore, where *Yamato*'s 18-inch guns could be expected to wreak heavy damage. It was a suicide mission. All acknowledged this, from Vice Admiral Seiichi Ito to the lowest ensign in the wardroom. The *Yamato* had been given only enough fuel for a one-way trip. The huge, sleek, oddly graceful ship raced south through the Bungo Straits toward the Ryukyus at flank speed. In addition to having the world's heaviest naval guns, the *Yamato* also was the world's fastest battleship. But for its last run, Imperial Headquarters could provide it no air cover whatsoever.

The *Yamato* was attacked by swarms of American carrier aircraft from Task Force 58 on April 6. She finally sank on the morning of the seventh, after having taken nine torpedoes and several bomb hits. The cruiser *Yahagi* and most of the destroyers in the accompanying screen were lost as well. Almost the entire crew perished, with only two hundred survivors. As ensign Mitsuru Yoshida reported, in what later became a bestselling book in Japan: "The desolate decks were reduced to shambles, with nothing but cracked and twisted steel plates remaining . . . the big guns were inoperable because of the gathering list and only a few rapid-fire guns were intact. . . . As though awaiting this moment, the enemy came plunging through the clouds to deliver the *coup de grâce* . . . it was impossible to evade. . . . I could hear the captain vainly shouting, 'Hold on men, hold on men. . . .' "

It was an ironic commentary on the war's changing fortunes. Three years later the *Yamato* had met the same fate dealt out to the British battleship HMS *Prince of Wales* and the battle cruiser HMS *Repulse* when they were sunk by Japanese carrier aircraft off the Malay coast in early 1942.

On the land, however, the fighting told a different story. Five days after the successful landing, the two lead divisions of U.S. XXIV Corps, soon followed by the 1st Marine Division, ran into the heavily fortified Japanese line. For the next two weeks the war settled down to the most bitter, ruthless kind of hand-to-hand fighting, as GIs and marines desperately tried to claw

---

[1]The *Yamato,* like its sister ship the *Musashi,* displaced seventy thousand tons and mounted a main battery of nine 18.1-inch guns. Built in defiance of the prewar Washington Naval Treaty regulations, they were, as Japanese chief petty officers were wont to say, "the biggest 16-inch guns in the navy."

their way up heavily defended rocky escarpments. The advancing troops were exposed not merely to constant mortar, machine gun, and rifle fire, but they took a pounding from General Wada's artillery. It was the worst fighting of the Pacific war, its sustained intensity surpassing even the brutal combat of Tarawa, Peleliu, and Iwo Jima.

3

Challenge and Response

The southern third of Okinawa proved to be ideal terrain for Colonel Ya-hara's war of attrition: wooded, hilly, and easily honeycombed with caves and dugouts. North of the headquarters on Mount Shuri several jagged lines of ridges and rocky escarpments stretched on east-west lines across the narrowed waist of the island. Japan's 32nd Army had spent the greater part of a year turning them into formidable nests of interlocking pillboxes and firing positions. Connected by a network of caves and passageways inside the hills, their positioning enabled defenders to shift their strength constantly in response to attack. The infantrymen of 32nd Army rarely built their entrenchments on hill crests. Instead, in time-honored Japanese military tradition, they dug in on the reverse slopes. When U.S. troops advanced to the top of a hill, thinking they had it almost secured, they would be met by a withering fire from just below the crest line.

A little more than a week after the easy landings, General John Hodge's XXIV Corps ran into serious trouble. The Kakazu Ridge was merely the first of Ushijima's heavily entrenched strongpoints, but it brought the U.S. Army's 96th Division up against the sort of desperate hand-to-hand fighting that would characterize the Okinawa land battle. Carefully concealed anti-tank guns and mortars seemed anchored into the terrain. Their intense fire partly nullified the considerable firepower of the tanks advancing with the American infantry. While marine and army units swept north to capture Iejima, the offshore airfield island, and occupy most of Kunigami in the north of the main island, things were getting stickier in the south. The American command would later rule out a flanking amphibious landing on the south coast because of logistical difficulties, but operation timetables were being

35

altered to bring the two marine divisions of III Amphibious Corps to join XXIV Corps in what promised to be a grueling and costly attempt to breach 32nd Army's Shuri line.

It was at this point, just when Yahara's war of attrition was working well, that the chief of staff had his first outburst of *samurai* offensive fever. It was time, Cho argued, to strike back. Unduly encouraged, perhaps, by Imperial Headquarters' glowing but hugely inflated accounts of air force successes against U.S. fleet units offshore, Cho persuaded Ushijima to launch a counterattack. It was to be a night assault, in the best Japanese army tradition. Crack battalions of both the 62nd and 24th Divisions were to jump off on April 12, infiltrate the American positions, and attack them from the rear. Infiltration tactics were preferred so that large concentrations of advancing troops would not furnish obvious targets to U.S. Navy units waiting offshore for just such a possibility. Once Japanese units had penetrated the American lines on a broad scale, 10th Army's advantages of air power and offshore firepower would be largely negated, for American and Japanese units would be hopelessly entangled. The infiltrating troops had only to sever supply lines and generally cause confusion in 10th Army's rear areas. Then Ushijima's front-line troops could come out of their entrenchments and attack.

In vain Yahara argued that this kind of offensive effort would only waste men. Against a determined and superior enemy it was bound to fail. But Cho swept his superior and the divisional generals along with him. Here, they agreed, the vaunted Japanese offensive spirit would obviously overcome those foreigners with all their machines. All Yahara succeeded in doing was to cut down the number of battalions committed.

In the event, the attack failed. Although some of the infiltrators temporarily gained their objectives—one battalion actually penetrating a mile behind the American lines—they were all mopped up after hard fighting. The net loss amounted to almost four battalions, which 32nd Army could ill afford. Some amphibious landings had also been planned for April 12; Shipping Engineer units were to attack the U.S. west coast beachhead from the rear. They were discovered, however, and destroyed.

Earlier, a week before the April 1 landing, U.S. units had successfully occupied the Kerama Islands just west of Okinawa. Japanese planners had hoped to use these islands to launch a swarm of suicide boats in attacks on the American transports. With the failure of the April 12 landings, all such efforts came to an end.

Back in their entrenchments, however, the infantrymen of 32nd Army remained as formidable as ever. From the huge cave headquarters beneath Mount Shuri, where they were secure from any amount of aerial or naval bombardment, Yahara and his staff assistants continued to deploy their defenders. For the Americans, each strongpoint received its local nickname: Conical Ridge, Flattop Hill, Chocolate Drop, Tombstone Ridge, and so on. Each involved sustained, bloody, seesawing advances and retreats, to the point where progress could be measured only in yards. Militarily speaking, Yahara was satisfied. In no other Pacific island operation had the Japanese side held out so long and with such relative success against superior force. But holding operations were not what a fire-eater like Isamu Cho had joined the army for.

In a second heatedly argued conference, Cho once more talked the commanding general into ordering a general counterattack. This time the 24th Division, less heavily engaged than the badly bruised 62nd, would take the lead. Before dawn on May 4, after the heaviest Japanese artillery bombardment of the campaign, the 24th Division and the 44th Independent Mixed Brigade moved up to the attack, in what Cho hoped would lead to a decisive battle. But no breakthrough was achieved. Under attack, the American units rallied, and the Japanese gained almost no ground. Indeed, out of their entrenchments, they were veritable sitting ducks for 10th Army's big guns.

Cho was disheartened and chastened. Ushijima, for his part, now regretted yielding to his chief of staff's persuasion. The attack had gained nothing and had cost him five thousand men. Although Cho had once again been impressed at the prospect of a simultaneous assault by the air force, that, too, had failed. It was at this point that the commanding general sent for his senior staff officer.

Here we resume Yahara's own narrative.

Part III

Retreat under Fire

Colonel Yahara's narrative resumes

4

Counteroffensive Halted

At six o'clock in the evening of May 5 I was sitting quietly at my desk when Lieutenant General Ushijima, our commanding officer, sent for me. I walked woodenly as far as the adjoining office of the chief of staff and stopped, with a silent salute. When Ushijima spotted me, he shouted, "Come on in, Colonel Yahara, senior staff officer!" Entering his office I was tense, dreading what he might say. Would he order a final charge? Would this be the end?

As usual the commander in chief was sitting cross-legged on the worn *tatami* floor. I stood at attention. He looked at me pensively and then spoke softly:

Colonel Yahara, as you predicted, this offensive has been a total failure. Your judgment was correct. You must have been frustrated from the start of this battle because I did not use your talents and skill wisely. Now I am determined to stop this offensive. Meaningless suicide is not what I want. When I left Tokyo, both War Minister Umezu and Army Chief of Staff Anami urged me not to be hasty in ordering a last suicidal charge. Now our main force is largely spent, but some of our fighting strength is left, and we are getting strong support from the islanders. With these we will fight to the southernmost hill, to the last square inch of land, and to the last man. I am ready to fight, but from now on I leave everything up to you. My instructions to you are to do whatever you feel is necessary.

What an outrageous thing for Ushijima to say! Now that our forces were exhausted, he finally recognized what I had been advocating from the start of the Okinawa battle. It was now too late to accomplish anything. I was not only frustrated, I was furious. Still, I appreciated his sincerity and

41

the fact that he could admit the truth. I could feel his remorse about our situation.

Up to now General Ushijima had left major decisions to the chief of staff, the recently promoted Lieutenant General Cho, and his subordinates. The outcome was inevitable, and I must acknowledge certain unpleasant facts. He was not alone to blame. I had not performed to the best of my ability. Since I truly believed in my own strategic plan, I should have stuck to that belief and staked my life on it. I thought I had done my best, but I regretted that so many things were left undone.

I was aware that General Cho, sitting next door, could overhear every word of our conversation. I could only imagine his feelings. When he ordered the May 4 offensive, he had said that we would all die together.

General Cho had staked his life on this offensive, and it was a complete failure. I felt sorry for him, but the results had been predictable. Until this offensive Cho had been responsible for our military decisions, but now General Ushijima was leaving everything up to me. Naturally, this was discouraging to Cho, but he understood the situation. He even said jokingly to me, "Hey, Yahara, when will it be okay for me to commit *hara-kiri?* Is this a good time?" He not only had assumed responsibility for the failed offensive, but now had lost all hope for success in any further operations.

Some accounts of the battle for Okinawa have made much of General Ushijima's overruling me at the start of the offensive, but they overlook the fact that when the offensive failed, he left all decision making to me. It is ridiculous to have told only half the truth; I feel it is now my duty to set the record straight.

With the defeat of our offensive, there was no miracle medicine to heal the critical wounds of the May 4 debacle, but to afford at least temporary relief, I immediately put into effect my original plan of action, as follows:

1. Trusting to the courage of each unit, our forces would continue to punish the enemy where possible, while conserving strength to improve our chances in a continuing war of attrition.
2. The 24th Division would at once cancel its offensive, return to its original entrenchments, and force the enemy to shed his blood.
3. The 44th Independent Mixed Brigade would return to Sugar Loaf Hill (Amekudai) immediately and prepare to assist the 62nd Division in its operations. The 6th Special Regiment would serve under the command of the 44th Brigade, wherever located.

4. The 62nd Division would continue its present assignment.
5. The Army Artillery Group would cooperate closely with the front-line divisions. Ammunition supplies would be conserved in accordance with our strategic war of attrition.
6. The Naval Base Forces would continue their present duty.

Our intelligence officer Yakumaru, who had proposed counterlandings on both coasts of Okinawa, was thoroughly somber and depressed; his counterattacking units had been lost. Major Tadao Miyake, our logistics officer, quite a cynical fellow, said to him: "So all your China experience was for naught."

Young, aggressive staff officers are not to blame, however, for such military failures. Their training has taught them to rely instinctively on the sheer offensive. Young blood cannot just wait silently for a suicidal death charge.

To myself I summarized the results of the May 4 counteroffensive in this way:

1. The fighting strength of the 24th Division was down to one-third of its original strength.
2. The Artillery Group's ammunition supply was almost exhausted. Sunano, a senior officer of the group, proposed limiting each gun to ten rounds per day so that supplies might last to the end of May.
3. Two shipping Engineer Regiments and many naval suicide squadrons had been totally annihilated.
4. During the two-day counteroffensive our forces suffered the loss of five thousand seasoned soldiers, killed and wounded.
5. Without the counteroffensive, the 24th Division, the Mixed Brigade, and the 62nd Division, in cooperation with the Artillery Group, could have been well prepared for defense. We were well aware of the coming decisive battle for mainland Japan. (At the time we never dreamed of a surrender by August 15.) It was now too late to consider, but if we had not gone on the counteroffensive and instead remained in our well-prepared fortifications, reinforced by our powerful artillery, we could have prolonged the Okinawa battle for another month and saved thousands of lives. Failure of the counteroffensive forced the Mixed Brigade to draw back to Sugar Loaf Hill (Amekudai), where they were doomed to defeat. The 24th Division

was similarly handicapped, while our artillery activity was restricted to sporadic firing.

6. The counteroffensive had at first eased the pressure along the 62nd Division's front, but its failure placed them in even greater danger.

7. Arai, the prefectural police chief, visited our headquarters and confirmed that everyone on the island—military and civilian—had suffered a loss of morale as a result of our failed counteroffensive. The one possible benefit of this disaster was that it might make the enemy more cautious about our future course of action.

5

World View through the Eye of a Needle

Busy as I was with the daily battle situation, I tried very hard to keep up with the news of other war developments, the homeland, and the general world situation. On Okinawa we were very conscious of our heavy responsibility in the glaring light of world attention. I continued to hope that the fate of our army would improve with each new outside development. At the start of the war Domei News Service had provided accurate world news reports, but as time passed they did not cover world news at all. Toward the end we had to rely on the army radio for outside news. I encouraged our intelligence officers to pull together better coverage of world news, but they were too busy with day-to-day operations to gather useful outside reports.

In early April 1945, seemingly authoritative information came from one of the secret Special Service Organization units in Harbin saying that if our air attacks on the U.S. Navy could continue for another ten days, the enemy would be forced to break off operations on Okinawa. This lifted our spirits and led us to believe that we might again succeed in regaining enemy-occupied territory. Then came the glorious news (for us) on April 12 that President Roosevelt was dead. The staff officers were ecstatic. Many seemed convinced that we would now surely win the war!

Meanwhile, in the homeland, the Koiso cabinet was replaced by the Suzuki cabinet. There was no explanation of this change, and soldiers did not pay much attention to it. I felt myself that the ease with which the enemy had landed on Okinawa, as well as the urgent insistence from Imperial Headquarters that we counterattack, had caused some political disorder. I also guessed that the collapse of Nazi Germany and developments in Europe were inducing the new cabinet to end the war.

If we were to sue for peace, I wanted it to happen before many more thousands of soldiers and civilians had to make the supreme sacrifice. After the war I read a newspaper article by former Prime Minister Suzuki in which he suggested that if Japanese soldiers in Okinawa could have pushed the enemy into the sea, it would have been a propitious moment for Japan to ask for peace. I was infuriated. He knew nothing about the battle situation on Okinawa. His sources of information were not aware of the situation there. He must have actually believed that an all-out air offensive was the solution.

The fact is that we never had a chance for victory on Okinawa. Months before the enemy invasion, General Sugiyama informed Colonel Takushiro Hattori, the operations chief at General Headquarters, that he could not bear responsibility for the defense of Okinawa. Just three months before the Okinawa battle started, the high command moved our powerful 9th Division to Taiwan and other forces to the Philippines.

At that time, nonetheless, we reported our intention to fight on the beaches of Okinawa when the enemy landed at Kadena. Imperial Headquarters' response was to say: "We will have the decisive battle on Japan proper. Okinawa is merely a front-line action." Yet when battle was joined on Okinawa, the Emperor solemnly declared that its outcome would determine the nation's future. If he truly believed that, why did he not send the forces needed for the defense of Okinawa? And why had he referred to us as merely a front-line action?

I would not have resented a firm decision simply to wage the final battle on mainland Japan. Once the Okinawa battle began, however, such a goal was contradicted by forcing our "front-line unit" to fight *the* decisive battle and then expecting us to win. It was naive for anyone to believe that Okinawa was an excuse for ending the war. Since October 1944 not a single person from Imperial Headquarters had come to Okinawa or even given us a word of encouragement. Never once did any individual speak to me concerning the defense of the Ryukyu Islands, even though I was the senior staff operations officer. Instead they merely sent me documents and messages. Nothing more.

From the very start of the Okinawa battle we were out of real touch with Imperial Headquarters. Our fighting men made cynical and sarcastic remarks such as, "Headquarters people will never come to Okinawa because Tsuji Town [Naha's red-light district] was burned down in the air raids last October," or "They are afraid of enemy submarines and airplanes." What a contrast to the leaders of enemy countries, such as President Roosevelt and Prime Minister Churchill, who appeared in combat areas to speak words of encouragement to their fighting men.

On April 26 Prime Minister Suzuki made a special radio speech to encourage the troops and civilians on Okinawa, but I missed the broadcast. In mid-May came news of Germany's capitulation. We now realized that we were doomed. It was nonsense to continue the war in this corner of the Pacific after our only real ally had collapsed.

A man may ruin himself as a matter of pride, to save face. He should not, however, jeopardize his nation for such a reason. A nation should never be sacrificed for the sake of its leaders. Japan's leaders got us involved in the China Incident out of a sense of self-preservation. They started that war to preserve their own power, status, and honor. Who would not despair at knowing that soldiers were dying in the interests of such leaders?

6

The Headquarters Cave

When our May 4 counteroffensive was terminated, all troops returned to their original positions. General Ushijima, his staff, and the troops were thoroughly discouraged, yet overall there was a strange sense of relief. Then one day a liaison officer brought me an order from Generals Ushijima and Cho saying that staff officer Major Jin, an aviator, was going to Tokyo. Puzzled by this surprising decision, I asked what it meant, and was told, "We are sending him to Imperial Headquarters to request approval for our air forces to attack the enemy fleet in strength, force their withdrawal, and thus end the Okinawa operations."

At first glance this might have seemed like a brilliant move to spare us military losses, yet every effort was already being made to destroy enemy shipping from the air. The fliers were already claiming that *they* were the main strength in this operation, with 32nd Army being merely a bunch of stagehands. Our *Tokkotai* special suicide (*kamikaze*) units had been striking almost daily, but enemy air strength remained far superior to ours.

As a matter of fact, air power was never a prime factor in the battle for Okinawa. The enemy had established a firm position ashore by landing six army and marine divisions. We knew that our forces were attacking them bravely, but we needed much more than bravery. Furthermore, it was ridiculous to think that the enemy would withdraw from this operation.

Japan was frantically preparing for a final decisive battle on the home islands, leaving Okinawa to face a totally hopeless situation. From the beginning I had insisted that our proper strategy was to hold the enemy as long as possible, drain off his troops and supplies, and thus contribute our utmost to the final decisive battle for Japan proper.

Since it was foolish even to dream of victory here in Okinawa, I disagreed with the idea of sending Major Jin to Tokyo. From the strategic point of view I was against it. As a tactical matter, I certainly agreed that our suicide planes should destroy as much enemy shipping as possible, but this was no more than a hope. The order for Jin's mission was already signed and sealed. There was no way for me to stop it.

The problem was how to get Jin out of Okinawa. The two possible avenues were the sea and sky, but the powerful enemy forces were serious obstacles, and we would need a miracle to overcome them. The plan was for Jin to go south to Mabuni and take a seaplane to Tokyo.

Jin and I had completely different military points of view. He naturally favored the use of air power. I was opposed to placing heavy emphasis on it. If he somehow managed to reach Imperial Headquarters, how would he present my views of the Okinawa operation? I was deeply concerned that he might misconstrue or even ignore them. If that happened, my position would be lost forever. I thought about this as I asked him to carry a notebook to my father in Tokyo.

Shortly before Major Jin's departure, we were diverted by a minor force. Lieutenant Moriwaki of the Mixed Brigade approached Jin, saluted him, and startled him by saying: "Sir, will you please teach me how to fly an airplane? Any plane, even an enemy one will do. I want to fly myself home."

I understood Moriwaki's feelings. An instructor at the infantry school, he had been assigned to Okinawa for only temporary duty, to accompany Major Kyoso, an antitank specialist. Unfortunately for Moriwaki, he was caught by the enemy invasion and was going to be in combat whether he wanted to or not. When he heard that Jin was leaving, he made his desperate plea. In a way I was responsible for his being here. I had asked headquarters for an antitank expert to help us work out tactics against enemy tanks. The two officers, once they arrived, seemed fated to share our destiny. Some time later we learned that Moriwaki was ordered out of Okinawa; I hope he made it.

About the time that Major Jin left our underground headquarters for Tokyo, I ordered all women occupants (nurses as well as comfort girls) to leave the cave and go south.[1] After the failure of our May 4 offensive, conditions in the caves had become miserable. Sanitation facilities had broken down. Food was in short supply. Morale was deteriorating. It seemed certain

---

[1]"Comfort girls" were women forced into prostitution by the Japanese army.

that everyone in the headquarters cave would die in battle. I wanted to get the women out of this depressing situation and send them to rear areas, where they could care for wounded soldiers. When I ordered their retreat to the south, they objected violently. "You order us out," they cried, "because you think of us only as women. We are no longer just women. We are soldiers, and we wish to die with you."

Despite their loyal objections, they had to go. We gave them a few small mementos. General Cho contributed his precious teapot. The oppression of the cave was eased somewhat as we saw them safely on their way south and wished them luck. Carrying heavy bags on their backs, they disappeared into the Hantagawa valley on May 10. Enemy artillery fire diminished as the sun began to set.

7

The Battle at Maeda-Nakama-Awacha

Seen from the enemy lines, the heights of Maeda and Nakama soar into rugged hills, forming an escarpment seventy to eighty meters high. Fortifications on these hills posed a serious threat to an advancing enemy. Our defense was not fully protected because the connecting underground network between the hills had not yet been finished. If either wing of these entrenchments was lost, the other would be isolated. That is what ultimately happened.

We had fallen back from Uebaru hill in the south on the evening of April 23. Since then, survivors of the 12th and 14th Battalions and the independent infantry battalion had been led by Lieutenant Colonel Kaya to Maeda hill. These battalions, along with 32nd Regiment led by the Shimura Battalion, took shelter in the command caves of the 33rd Brigade and continued to fight tenaciously against the Americans attacking the hills. Colonel Kaya, famous for his ingenuity, followed the example of Masashige Kusunoki, the great fourteenth-century warrior, and harassed the enemy by dropping human excrement on them.

Elsewhere, at Nakama and Awacha, Lieutenant Colonel Yamamoto commanded the independent infantry units—the 23rd Battalion, the 14th Independent Machine-Gun Battalion, the 22nd Regiment, the Tagawa Battalion, and Lieutenant Nakamura's antiaircraft defense troops. They established a nest of strong positions, fought brilliantly, and inflicted heavy losses on the enemy.

Kaya and Yamamoto, who commanded the two battalions, were the "twin chargers" of the 62nd Division. They had previously fought in China and were decorated with the highest honors. Until May 10 these courageous leaders had fought in complete isolation for three weeks under total siege by the enemy. They finally rejoined our main force by breaking through powerful enemy lines. Unfortunately, the Shimura Battalion remained pinned down in caves until the battle was over and thus could not join Colonel Kaya's force.

With the hills of Maeda and Nakama in their hands, it appeared likely that the enemy forces would concentrate against our Shuri headquarters. As expected, Shuri was soon being torn apart by heavy bombardment. In the annals of warfare it is rare for a headquarters command post to be located within a few kilometers of the enemy lines for a sustained period. That our commanding general and his division leaders remained close to the front line provided encouragement for our soldiers and maintained their spirit to fight to the bitter end. On the other hand, this situation made it inevitable that the high command would be too directly influenced by the day-to-day successes and failures along the front line.

At midnight on May 10, after Major Jin had left and the women had all headed south, I was studying our war maps with their red and blue markings. I heard the continuing roar of enemy artillery only as the steady hum of cicadas. Now that the hills of Maeda and Nakama were lost, I realized that our remaining strongpoints were hopelessly inadequate.

While staring at the chalk-marked maps, my concentration was suddenly disturbed by my realizing how close we were to the front. It occurred to me that our main defense line was on the verge of collapse because of the very location of our headquarters. I realized that if we withdrew a distance of two kilometers to Tsukazan we could have a more balanced and positive view of the battle situation.

Once that became clear, my perspective changed drastically. The hills of Shuri were higher and much wider than those at Maeda and Nakama. The Shuri hills could provide a superb defensive stronghold. By connecting Shuri to Yonabaru on the right flank, and Amekudai and the Kokuba River on the left, we would have a tremendously deep defense line.

Why had we not thought of this simple but brilliant plan earlier? We had been too preoccupied by the location of the present headquarters. Not only was it an insecure and dangerous situation for our headquarters to remain so close to the front line, but our soldiers must have felt that they were fighting a losing battle. And if our leaders, too, inevitably felt insecure, then the entire army was in danger of collapse.

For a proper view of the whole picture, the mind must be clear of preconceptions and personal danger. We were not yet in a major catastrophe.

By thinking of Shuri as not simply our headquarters but as the keystone of a unified fortification along the front lines, we would still have a chance to prolong the battle considerably. As army leaders we had a responsibility to stand above transient sentiments. We should not distort our ability to think wisely, nor limit our potential in any way.

Deep inside me a new confidence welled. In my own mind, I knew that withdrawal was necessary. Happy with my changed perspective, I prepared to disclose this new strategic view to General Cho and his staff the next morning.

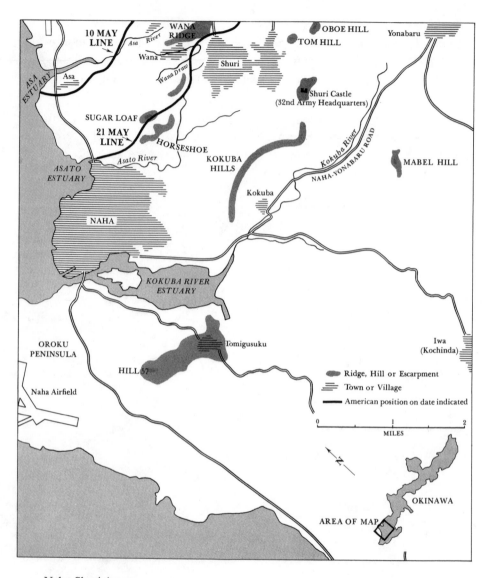

Naha-Shuri Areas

8

The Bloody Action at Sugar Loaf Hill (Amekudai)

After the failure of the May 4 counteroffensive, our 44th Independent Mixed Brigade left Bengadake hill on the night of May 6 and returned to its original position on Sugar Loaf Hill.[1] Meanwhile, on the left flank of the 62nd Division, the Arikawa Brigade was overwhelmed by American marines. The 62nd managed to escape from the town of Takushi and proceeded to Uchim and Jichaku where they made a precarious stand. American marines broke through these fortifications by way of the Asa (Aja) River and were preparing to assault Amekudai. At the same time, the 44th Independent Mixed Brigade, fresh from Bengadake, rushed to Amekudai for what would be one of the bloodiest battles of Okinawa.

I never knew if it was by chance or design that our brigade had been ordered to proceed from Amekudai for a counteroffensive at Bengadake on the night of May 3. I had been opposed to this action, and now our troops were not prepared to face the enemy. In defending ordinary field positions it takes only a couple of days to study the terrain, assemble required ammunition, and prepare proper fortifications. It takes more than a week, however, even for fresh troops to establish strong underground defenses. Because of heavy enemy daytime bombardment it was impossible to get out of our caves for even a quick glance at the terrain. Even at night, when we thought we were free to come out, the enemy bombardment continued. Day and night we were forced to stay underground, idle, waiting for the shelling to subside. When our men did leave the caves it was always difficult for platoons and squads to find their intended positions. It was a challenge to occupy a position because it usually took an entire night just to locate the assigned area.

---

[1]Amekudai consisted of a chain of hills, of which Sugar Loaf Hill (Hill 52) was only one.

On May 9 the enemy occupied Uchina and then crossed the river the next day. As soon as Colonel Mita's 15th Independent Mixed Regiment reached assigned positions they were immediately engaged in heavy combat. Our front-line troops, with no knowledge of their location, were totally unprepared for the ensuing chaos. It was folly for our troops to fight in such circumstances.

General Suzuki's independent 28th Battalion initiated battle on the far left flank of the Asa-Amekudai line. The Asa River is about sixty meters wide, and it is possible to wade across at ebb tide. On its southern bank, a strong underground fortification faced the enemy on the main road. Along the coastline the enemy's amphibious tanks faced a formidable chain of escarpments. I had firmly believed that our fortifications were impregnable against the strongest enemy forces and that we could hold out there for a long time. To our dismay the enemy broke through our lines easily, and blasted and sealed those underground fortifications. (See map on page 56.)

It was a shocking disappointment to find that the independent battalion was so inadequately trained and equipped. After it was overwhelmed by the enemy, Captain Kitamura's antitank troops used artillery to defend their positions at the Ameku Primary School. In two days of bloody fighting, they too were annihilated.

Amekudai is on a cultivated plateau, easily open to enemy naval assault and the maneuver of enemy tanks, making it extremely difficult to construct and organize defensive positions. Therefore, our main brigade troops were forced to abandon the hill at Amekudai and retreat to the positions at Makabe, Asato, Hill 52 (Sugar Loaf Hill), the Sogenji Temple, Takahashi, and Tomari hill. Our high command and brigade commanders feared that the enemy would overrun Amekudai and penetrate Naha City.

The anxiety at headquarters was reflected directly in the actions of the brigade commanders, who were located in nearby cave positions. Brigade Commander Suzuki, planted beside his erratically functioning telephone, continued to encourage Colonel Mita at Masagawa. He spoke in a low voice, compassionately, as if calming a frightened child. Major Kyoso, finally out of patience, rushed back to regimental headquarters through a storm of artillery fire, with Colonel Mita following close behind. The enemy was as determined to take Naha City as we were to defend it.

At Makabe, the right flank of our brigade was defended by Major Nishimura's battalion, and the central heights by Captain Ozaki's battalion. Captain Inoue defended Tomari and Takahashi, to the left of the brigade's right flank. Also joined in the battle were the 2nd and 7th Battalions of our brigade.

Because our troops were unyielding and fought so intrepidly, the battle at Amekudai lasted much longer than expected. Even after Amekudai was captured by the enemy, it was so unbelievable to our troops that they continued to fight. Not only did our troops fight brilliantly, but we were helped by terrain favorable to our defense. The fortifications at Amekudai were ideal. Our stronghold on the escarpment was located within deep depressions which led to a network of caves and tunnels. These kept our troops relatively safe from artillery attack. From the top of the heights we had a bird's-eye view of the enemy. We had observation posts at Shuri with the army Artillery Group and at Shikina with our brigade artillery. Lieutenant Commander Nii's naval gun units assisted our forward positions at Amekudai. During the May 4 counteroffensive, however, we had used up most of our artillery ammunition, so our destructive power was short-lived.

With adequate ammunition we could have had a victory at Amekudai. We had planned to have two more elite battalions available to march along the Asa River on a west-east line to smash the enemy. Because we missed this opportunity to apply pressure at the front line of our brigade, we planned to use our naval troops for a large-scale, last-ditch infiltration. Unengaged, they had been waiting two months in the Oroku (Naha) airfield vicinity for a chance to fight. They were eager for battle, and this was an ideal time to use their strength.

The Naval Base Forces totaled about eight thousand troops, but only three thousand were regulars; the rest were Okinawan civilian conscripts. No more than half of the regulars were well-trained sailors, so we organized them into one hundred infiltration units of three to five men each. They were assigned to the 62nd Division and scheduled to attack the enemy from the rear on two consecutive nights. Rear Admiral Minoru Ota, the Naval Base Force commander, was so enthusiastic about this plan that he left Oroku Peninsula for army headquarters in Shuri to observe his men's infiltration into enemy territory. The staff officers were excited about this all-out attack on the rear lines of the enemy. The naval units advanced deep into enemy territory, but we never learned the result of their attack because none of them survived.

By May 18 most of the four thousand picked troops of our Mixed Brigade were still tenaciously holding strongpoints, while American marines began moving through Tomari and Takahashi and into the city of Naha. Lieutenant Hiraga's 6th Special Regiment engaged the advancing enemy in hand-to-hand combat. We had lost the battle at Sugar Loaf Hill, but we were determined to continue the fight at Shuri, Shikina, and the Kokuba River. A seasoned battalion of the 1st Special Brigade was assigned to the hill north of Matsugawa to establish a solid defense zone on the right flank of our brigade. We also assigned the naval battalion to Major General Suzuki and stationed them on the hill line of Shikina, Kokuba, and Kohagura (Kufanga). If they could hold this line, the key Tsukazan fortifications would remain safe even if Shuri came under siege. If the right flank of the 24th Division could hold, the Shuri line would still remain a solid defense fortification.

In the midst of this fierce battle, our 10th Area Army on Taiwan broadcast an enemy news report: "The 6th Marine Division fought a bitter battle at Sugar Loaf Hill and had 250 casualties in one company. Only eight soldiers survived." Overjoyed, we relayed this information to Colonel Mita, one of the 44th Mixed Brigade's regimental commanders, who was engaged in a brutal fight against the enemy. He replied at once, "You are right to push us and encourage us to fight well, but I find this kind of news even more encouraging."

Mita's regiment fought remarkably well. In the April battles his men had done better than the forward battalions of the 62nd Division, who were well prepared, in strong positions, and supplied with plenty of ammunition. Mita, on the other hand, had been thrown into action unexpectedly and with limited ammunition. Still, his troops did very well.

We received many reports of valorous fighting, such as: "Our soldiers jumped out of their caves as soon as the enemy tanks passed, crawled forward, and engaged in hand-to-hand combat with enemy soldiers."

Lieutenant Commander Nii, in charge of the naval gun troops, observed the situation on the Oroku hilltops and highly praised the heroic fighting of our men at Hill 52, north of Asato. "The garrisons at Hill 52," he reported, "remained quietly in their caves while we took the fire of enemy barrages. When enemy guns stopped firing, our men dashed from their caves and engaged the enemy in hand-to-hand fighting." The battle lasted more than a week, during which Hill 52 changed hands repeatedly. The site of that mighty struggle for Hill 52 at Amekudai was given a new name by the Americans. They dubbed it Sugar Loaf Hill.

A stirring American account of the bitter struggle for Sugar Loaf Hill is given in the *History of the Sixth Marine Division* published by the Infantry Journal Press in 1948. In summary, it describes the May 12 fighting by the 6th Marine Division as

the most bitter, costly, and decisive action on Okinawa. Few Americans realized the tremendous importance the Japanese attached to this "ragged, chopped-up area." After several days of facing fierce and well-coordinated resistance there, the 6th Division realized that General Ushijima regarded the place as key to his main defense system.

In the May 12 fighting, the 22nd Regiment was brought sharply to a stand-still before Sugar Loaf Hill. It was one element of a triangular system of defenses forming the western anchor of the enemy's line, blocking the corridor into Shuri from the west. Southeast of Sugar Loaf lies a hill named Half Moon, and to the south was Horseshoe. The three formed an arrowhead, with Sugar Loaf as its point, aimed at the advancing 6th Division. Holding these three hills, the Japanese felt they had little to fear from any flanking movement from the west, and had organized the terrain strongly in a static defense.

The beautiful, peaceful countryside of the Amekudai plateau, where in times past I had enjoyed riding with General Ushijima, was now steeped in the blood of thousands of soldiers—Japanese and American. Enemy tanks fired at our headquarters, and direct hits echoed ominously throughout the limestone caves. Machine-gun fire day and night was punctuated by the rumble of artillery. As our forward troops withdrew we began to hear friendly fire from Mawashi village to the rear and left of our headquarters. It was gratifying to hear the sound of our own guns, indicating that our troops were fighting bravely, and not just hiding in caves.

The Inoue Battalion was almost totally annihilated, including its leader. As the left flank of the 15th Independent Mixed Regiment began to collapse, it was replaced by expanding the front of the 6th Special Regiment. Individual unit reports kept streaming in: "I can see American troops in the shrine garden." "Thirty enemy tanks are advancing toward the center of Naha." "Our troops are still holding out at the Teacher Training School." Hearing these reports, I knew that the war was finally entering my own garden.

One evening, indomitable Kyoso of our staff went into Naha and met Lieutenant Colonel Hiraga of the 6th Special Regiment. Upon his return to headquarters, he reported a curious incident. "On the way back I saw a platoon from Hiraga's regiment preparing for a night attack. They each carried a pistol in the right hand, a canteen in the left, and wore a bag around their waist containing toilet articles. They really looked strange." Everyone in headquarters laughed at the idea of soldiers garbed as if going on a picnic. But this was no laughing matter. On their mission they might face battle and death at any moment. Naturally they carried personal possessions. My heart went out to them.

The accomplishments of the 6th Special Regiment were a good example of Colonel Hiraga's bravery and the marvelous spirit of the soldiers he commanded. Despite their lack of training and equipment, they fought brilliantly. On our left flank were the 15th Independent Mixed Regiment, backed up by the 6th Special Regiment and the special Naval Base Forces. The enemy virtually annihilated these units, but the men all fought on to the death.

At headquarters we took encouragement from reports that the enemy was getting "desperate," but the opposite was true. The battle was at fever pitch, but we were losing. Like the last flare of a dying candle, we sent a message asking Imperial Headquarters for more air support: "We have wrought havoc on three enemy divisions, which are disintegrating. Three other enemy divisions are under heavy attack. We have lost many elite troops, but still believe in the immortality of the Empire. We are surrounded by the enemy, but our fighting spirit remains strong. Please continue air operations to destroy all enemy naval forces in the Okinawa area."

Japanese planes had been carrying out special (suicide) attacks against enemy ships since the operation began. There was no reason to think that our urgent message could effect a miracle. This last appeal was little more than an effort to raise our own morale.

Imperial Headquarters had meanwhile changed its view that the land battle of Okinawa was merely an adjunct to aerial strikes. They were now realizing the importance of conserving our remaining soldiers. We were admonished to stick to our fortifications and wage a war of attrition to the end. Our special attack squadrons were striking at enemy ships every evening, and the sounds of their attacks encouraged us. From a tactical viewpoint, however, the air attacks did not contribute materially to our land battle.

On the night of May 24 a special suicide attack squadron plunged down on the enemy-held airfields at Kadena and Yomitan. Captain Okuyama led a force of 120 fearless airmen in this attack. We would have been better off if they had landed at Naha and joined us directly in the land battle.

Nevertheless, on that evening I saw tremendous flares light the sky in the direction of Kadena and Yomitan, and imagined that our special attack squadrons had struck a mighty blow on our behalf. Such nightly attacks did not inflict notable damage on the enemy, but they gave us assurance that we were not alone in our desperate battle, and I was deeply moved.[2]

---

[2]In the event, all but one of the troop-carrying aircraft were shot down. When one bomber crash-landed, a squad of men leaped out, firing and hurling grenades as they ran; they managed to damage numbers of American airplanes before they were killed.

9

The Arikawa Brigade Withdraws to Shuri

On May 10 the 64th Brigade of the 62nd Division, commanded by Major General Arikawa, absorbed a number of other troops and withdrew from the Maeda-Nakama-Awacha line to take positions on the Kyozoka-Takushi line. Major Sugimoto's transportation unit and Hongo's regiment of the 24th Division occupied the rugged terrain between Maeda and Onna. General Nakajima's 63rd Brigade retreated into Shuri. Hongo's regiment was originally in charge of the right flank of the 62nd Division, but as they were not familiar with the terrain, Sugimoto's transport unit remained to assist them. The enemy failed to detect the transport unit, because it was securely based in numerous underground locations.

While marching toward Shuri the American troops were careful to avoid the rugged central terrain and instead converged on the town from the left and right. Arikawa's brigade thus had to face fierce frontal attacks. When the enemy appeared on the Amekudai plateau, the left flank of the brigade was exposed. The brigade command post and the 15th Independent Infantry Battalion at Takushi village came under assault by the enemy's dreaded "horse-mounting" attacks,[1] as did the 21st and 23rd Battalions in Kyozuka. It was obvious that Kyozuka and Takushi would eventually be taken by the enemy, but we had to hold the entrance to Shuri. Accordingly we ordered the Ozaki Battalion of the Mixed Brigade, then defending Yonabaru, to

---

[1] In Japanese, *hōi umanori kōgeki* (encircling horse-riding attack) was the name given to the American tactic for assaulting occupied caves. While concentrating fire at a cave entrance to keep the Japanese defenders inside, the Americans would take a position above the entrance, as if mounting a horse. From this vantage point they would shoot cave occupants trying to escape.

switch positions with the Yamaguchi Battalion of the Naval Base Force, and put them under command of the 62nd Division. We then directed them to take up defensive positions on the Onna-Sueyoshi line. Thus we prepared for the collapse of the Arikawa Brigade.

Although the situation was critical, the 62nd Division trained the Ozaki Battalion for only two days before putting them on the defense line. The 62nd Division was notorious for throwing new troops into difficult situations and must have been aware of its reputation. It is pointless to put untrained troops onto a battlefield because their fighting effectiveness is only half that of trained soldiers. They are subject to intolerable combat losses—40 to 50 percent. The 62nd Division, despite its battle experience on mainland China, was the only outfit consistently to ignore the statistics of using untrained troops in combat.

On May 12, the command post of the Arikawa Brigade came under heavy enemy siege and "horse-mounting" assault. Even Arikawa himself was said to be hurling grenades at the enemy. It became a question of Arikawa making a last stand there or trying to break through the siege and retreat to Shuri. General Arikawa, a simple man from the hills of Kagoshima Prefecture, was known to be a heavy drinker. He and General Ushijima, also from Kagoshima, were good friends who spoke to each other without reserve. Ushijima once jokingly said to his friend, "A few years back you were only a farmer, but now you are a general and really look like a warrior." Arikawa replied, "Your excellency, you are beginning to resemble a commanding general, but you still have a way to go."

There was a rumor that our chief of staff, General Cho, once argued with Arikawa at a banquet, accused him of being impotent, and knocked him to the floor. It was known that Cho and other 62nd officers did not care much for Arikawa because he often boasted of coming from Ushijima's hometown. Furthermore, while Arikawa's brigade was struggling in the Machinato and Iso battles, the combat results were not good. This distressed the leadership at army and division headquarters and did not help Arikawa's already difficult situation.

On the evening of May 13, I had a phone call from Colonel Ueno, 62nd Division chief of staff. In a troubled voice he said, "Colonel Yahara, as you well know, General Arikawa is now under fierce enemy 'horse-mounting' assault. Our division commander has sent him a personal letter saying that he should hold the strongpoints to the last man. In such dire circumstances, however, a commander is normally ordered to withdraw. I cannot turn my back and leave him to die. Many of his men are still alive. I want to rescue them and give Arikawa another chance in the future. Our division commander has already ordered them to fight to the finish. There is nothing more I can do. Can you find some way out for them?"

Tactically speaking, I knew it was useless to waste an entire battalion at Takushi. I said, "The 62nd Division commander, General Takeo Fujioka, is the one to give such orders, and I am sure he does not want his men to die at Takushi. Please order General Arikawa to withdraw at once." I had checked my opinion with Generals Ushijima and Cho, and both agreed with me. When I reported that decision to Colonel Ueno, he was elated. Late that night General Arikawa and his men successfully broke through the surrounding enemy and returned safely to Shuri.

10

Choosing a
Last-Stand Location

Thus far I have described the battle front situation for the left flank of the Mixed Brigade and the central position of the 62nd Division. What was the position of the 24th Division on the army's right flank? Overall, the situation appeared stable, but in reality, after May 20, it was comparable to a patient in the final stage of tuberculosis. He may look normal, but his chest cavities are hollow.

For a while, Hill 146, east of Shuri airfield, had been a focal point of the battle, but it was soon captured by the enemy. They also seized Hills 140 and 150 and called them Chocolate Drop Hill.

The heroes of the 24th Division—the Ito Battalion of the 32nd Infantry Brigade—were sent to recapture these hills, and they suffered heavy losses. The sole survivors were Major Ito and twenty men. The key piece of our domino game was Chocolate Drop Hill. After it fell, the chain of strongholds in front of Shuri toppled one by one. We still had one solid piece of ground in front of Chocolate Drop Hill. It was held by Lieutenant Colonel Murakami's 27th Tank Regiment, with its Type-90 field pieces. From their secure defense position they had successfully repulsed a number of enemy tanks attempting to break through our lines by way of Shuri airfield, then under construction. Those Type-90 field pieces were one of our greatest threats to the enemy, who I knew respected their destructive power.

On our war map, the front lines of the 24th Division still held firmly onto the key line along the coast of Nakagusuku Bay, Untamamui, the northeast hills of Bengadake, and Ishimine. Their positions, however, were still incomplete and not well prepared. Day after day their troops were so exhausted that a small enemy force could have crushed them with a single coordinated charge. The enemy finally made an unexpected surprise attack, and enemy tanks were able to break through.

Earlier, we had sent a victory telegram to Imperial Headquarters. Realistically, however, we knew that our fate was sealed. We were so busy with staff work that there was no time to think about the demise of our army. I was absorbed in making troop assignments, just as, before the Okinawa battle began, I had been directing training maneuvers.

Imperial Headquarters acknowledged that we were facing defeat at Shuri. I had another idea, however, which was to withdraw to the Kiyan[1] Peninsula, set new fortifications, and try for a final battle there. Some of my critics on the staff said I had insisted on a passive war of attrition from the very beginning. Therefore, if I were to suggest that we abandon Shuri and retreat to the south, tough-minded General Cho would be certain to oppose me.

After many weeks of battle, I finally realized that my practice of adhering strictly to principle and theory was wrong. Simply being correct was not enough; it was necessary to orchestrate my plans patiently from behind the scenes. Even if I was right, I could not move people without some political maneuvering. Accordingly, I pretended that the southward move was staff officer Nagano's idea, and I had him introduce my plan to the chief of staff.

Fortunately for me, Nagano shared my view of not taking our final stand at Shuri. It was conniving on my part, but I asked Nagano to develop a plan for withdrawal of our headquarters. I carefully avoided putting any pressure on General Cho to accept this idea. I merely submitted three possible locations where a last stand might be made, as follows:

1. To withdraw to the Kiyan Peninsula, with key positions at Hanagusuku, Yaezudake, Yozadake, and Maezato.
   a. Yaezu and Yoza hills were natural fortifications with eight-kilometer-wide escarpments facing north. Our remaining forces could defend this area without dispersing.
   b. The enemy could not climb these escarpments, which were thirty to forty meters in height, so we would not have to position troops there.

---

[1]Composed of three characters (KI happy, YA roof, MU brave), the name is rendered variously: Kiyamu, Kyan, Kiyan. The U.S. Geographic Survey gives Kiyan.

    c. We could withdraw to this area with a minimum of difficulty because the roads could carry trucks and mobile artillery.

    d. Army forces could be accommodated quickly and easily because the 24th Division had already built underground fortifications. There were many natural caves in the area.

    e. This was the old area of the 24th Division, which would be the nucleus of our army strength from now on. Officers and men of the 24th were familiar with the area terrain and strongpoints. Plenty of ammunition and provisions were available.

    f. One drawback of this area was that enemy tanks could maneuver easily and at will. We had lost almost all antitank artillery, and we had no satchel charge replacements to distribute to the infantry.

2. To withdraw to the Chinen Peninsula.

    a. With water on three sides, there were many natural caves. The defense area was compact. We had never lost a strongpoint there. It was favorable for antitank warfare.

    b. In the present battle situation, the terrain and roads made it difficult to withdraw to this area.

    c. It had been formerly occupied by the Mixed Brigade. There were not enough fortified caves. Ammunition and provisions were lacking.

    d. The defense area was too small for our remaining troops.

    e. The top of the flat plateau was vulnerable to enemy bombardment from all directions.

3. To remain at Shuri.

    a. There would be no need to move troops and ammunition.

    b. The small defense area was vulnerable to attack.

    c. Underground fortifications could not accommodate our remaining troops.

    d. There were not enough positions for artillery units.

    e. Should both flanks withdraw for a circular defense zone, the enemy would surely break through our frontal positions. We had war-gamed this maneuver, and it was almost impossible to station all units at both flanks in the southern area.

    f. During a withdrawal to Kiyan and Chinen, we could take advantage of a war of attrition.

g. For a short time, we could obstruct the enemy's use of ports at Naha and Yonabaru, and the airfields at Yonabaru, Shuri, Oroku, and Machinato. At present, these ports and airfields were not worth the effort for the enemy to occupy them.

If we were to withdraw to Kiyan or Chinen, would enemy attacks stop? Loss of Shuri would mean, in effect, loss of the whole island. Would the enemy therefore be willing to make more sacrifices by moving south to attack? It was reported that Admiral Nimitz had no intention of assaulting our main strength after gaining the airfields at Kadena and Yomitan. In that case we would survive in isolation, as had our troops at Bougainville, Rabaul, and Luzon. Surviving thus, would we not be guilty of abandoning our honorable mission to fight to the end? Would we not be accused of being concerned only with self-preservation?

It would not be difficult, however, for the Americans to strike a final blow at our retreating, dispirited army. It was unlikely that the enemy would stop at the Shuri line and not advance to the south. It was crucial for the enemy to occupy the southern part of Okinawa in order to use the island as a base for launching attacks on mainland Japan. If, from the beginning, we were concerned only with survival, we would have occupied the northern part of Okinawa instead.

I concluded that we could not waste precious time further debating my first two options. On the morning of May 22 I set up my war operations plan as described and had Nagano submit it to the chief of staff. I did not want my name associated with it.

General Cho was reluctant to decide on the retreat plan. Perhaps he was still thinking about remaining at Shuri. Finally he summoned me and said, speaking very slowly, "It is important that we decide how to end this battle. What is your opinion?" My time had come. As planned, I explained the pros and cons of each option, and then gave my clincher: "I have long considered the option of remaining at Shuri, so it is difficult to relinquish it. Nevertheless, I feel that retreat, especially to Kiyan, is the most desirable." I felt that Kiyan Peninsula was our only choice, but I did not want to appear too enthusiastic about it.

I was well aware of Cho's frame of mind. After the failure of the May 4 counteroffensive he kept saying, "Yahara, is your war of attrition still on?"

He had heard General Ushijima tell me, "From now on, operational planning is entirely in your hands."

It was clear that my response should not appear to be a snap decision, so I continued with thoughts for General Cho to consider. "Since last year when the 9th Division was moved to Taiwan, we have mapped our war plans for southern Okinawa. Some division commanders feel that it would not be right to offer their opinions. In making this crucial decision, which may determine the fate of our entire army, may I suggest that you ask each division commander for his opinion?" Cho promptly agreed with this suggestion. I, of course, knew the opinions of each division commander.

That evening, May 22, the chief of staff and his deputy from each division came, through heavy rain and enemy bombardment, to the headquarters cave. In addition to myself and the other headquarters staff officers, the participants were:

62nd Division—Ueno and Kitajima
24th Division—Kidani and Sugimori
Mixed Brigade—Kyoso
Artillery Group—Sunano
Naval Base Force—Nakao

We all gathered in the staff officers' quarters next to General Ushijima's office. Knowing that most of the assembly would be reluctant to speak out frankly in front of General Cho, I acted as chairman of the meeting.

All the faces were familiar, but after two months of incredible struggle everyone looked worn out. Staring a dark fate in the face, they treated each other with kind dignity and kept up an air of calm. On the table were canned pineapples, canned clams, and *sake*. I described the overall battle situation, pointed out that we must decide about our future, and asked for their frank opinions regarding the three options.

Chief of Staff Ueno, less passionate than usual, spoke rapidly in his hoarse voice. "After all we have endured, we cannot retreat. Our 62nd Division dutifully followed your directives and prepared Shuri's formidable fortifications. Even if we abandon them and try to withdraw to the rear, our transportation is inadequate. There is no way to transport a thousand wounded soldiers and stores of ammunition. Our division determined from the beginning to fight to the death at Shuri. We cannot leave behind thousands of dead and wounded who dedicated their lives to our motherland. We want to die here."

Soft-spoken Colonel Kidani of the 24th Division endorsed the Kiyan retreat plan, as did Lieutenant Colonel Sunano. Major Kyoso endorsed the Chinen option. Nakao, of the Naval Base Force, expressed no opinion. In the end, each command insisted on sticking to its own territory. I avoided endless debate by saying, "I do not know General Ushijima's decision, but it may be the Kiyan Peninsula." I described the pros and cons of each option, adding that transportation of the wounded and ammunition would be provided by Nakamura's transport regiment. Depending on available facilities, the front forces could complete their withdrawal in five days. I assured them that the 24th Division could provide enough ammunition for itself and the Mixed Brigade.

When the business was concluded, we took time for a social meeting at which more wine softened all hearts, before returning to our posts. Because I was feeling tipsy, I did not go to see General Cho but went directly to my room. There I told Yakumaru and Nagano about the meeting and then boasted, "When I was in the military academy, instructors praised my skill in tactics and strategy. My judgments and decisions were outstanding." I glanced at nearby General Ushijima, who was absorbed in reading but was also listening. I continued, "Our last stand must be at Kiyan." Ushijima's concentration yielded to a slow smile. He did not say a word, but I knew he endorsed my opinion. I was thrilled.

I reported the result of the meeting when General Cho returned to his office. "The 62nd Division wishes to die here. This is understandable, but it is impossible for all troops to assemble at Shuri. If we are to contribute to the homeland battle, we must continue to fight. Thus, to remain at Shuri is unthinkable, and Kiyan is the most realistic option. It suits the goal of army operations." The chief of staff must have already considered this matter, and he promptly accepted my advice.

Wednesday morning, May 23, Cho handed me a letter from Lieutenant General Takeo Fujioka, the 62nd Division commander. "A senior staff officer of army headquarters recklessly invited all division chiefs of staff to a serious discussion of military operations. In the event, he forced a decision contrary to my wishes. This is unforgivable. I wish to know if yesterday's meeting was held with the approval of the commanding general and his chief of staff." Cho and I exchanged smiles. Either Fujioka misunderstood, or else he was too naive to be a general. Of course our commanding general had approved the meeting. Furthermore, we did not have to invite the other staff officers, but we did, and we also had given them a chance to speak their minds.

I did not get to see General Fujioka in person because he arrived in Okinawa just before the battle began. He had always impressed me as being a reasonable and responsible leader, but the start of his letter made him appear very obstinate. His closing remark, however, changed my mind. It read, "You should not summon my valuable chief of staff to your head-quarters through a hail of enemy gunfire. Please do not do it again." Discovering that he really cared for his subordinates, I respected him.

11

The Right Flank
Nears Collapse

The main strength of Colonel Kanayama's 89th Regiment occupied key fortifications of the army's right flank at Untamamui hill. To the southeast, the Yamaguchi Battalion of the Naval Base Force occupied the town of Yonabaru. The remaining troops of the 23rd Shipping Engineer Regiment held Amagoimui hill, south of Yonabaru. Colonel Higuchi's Heavy Artillery Regiment was at Ohzato Castle, perfectly sited for any enemy attack on Untamamui hill. These fortifications all supported each other in defending the far right flank of the army troops. While we were maintaining the battle line at Amekudai plateau, however, the right flank of our battle front had started to crack.

Enemy warships in Nakagusuku Bay directed such heavy gunfire at Untamamui hill that the 89th Regiment had to withdraw to the reverse slope. On Tuesday evening, May 22, while we had been debating the withdrawal, enemy troops crawled through a blind spot on the eastern slope of Untamamui hill and entered Yonabaru. They scattered Yamaguchi's battalion and by dawn on Saturday had captured the saddle-shaped hill west of Yonabaru.

I learned of this situation on Saturday morning when I dropped by the 24th Division command post. The enemy troops at Yonabaru numbered no more than fifty or so. I had evaluated our defenses in this area and was not concerned, but this was just the beginning of enemy infiltration here. I cautioned that they had to make every effort to drive back the Americans. When I met the 24th Division commander, Lieutenant General Tatsumi Amamiya, he said, "Don't worry, Yahara, we will turn back the enemy tonight, and tomorrow I'll serve you a Truman bonus."[1] I said, "I'm looking forward to that bonus."

---

[1] In Japanese, *Torūman kyūyo* probably derives from the interest (and delight, see page 45)

The next morning I was up earlier than usual and hurried to the command post. The officers all looked depressed. They explained events: "We failed in last night's attack. Yamaguchi's battalion was farther back, but they managed to hold out at the western ridge of the saddle-shaped hill. At Yonabaru the enemy numbered more than two hundred, and we could barely defend Amagoimui hill. The 89th Regiment is barely able to hold Untamamui and cannot send any support to Yonabaru." The tide had turned against us more violently than ever. There would be no Truman bonus.

The 101-meter hill at Untamamui was the control tower for our rear area. If we lost the Untamamui-Yonabaru-Amagoimui hill line, the enemy would rush into the Tsukazan area. We had to hold that line long enough for our troops to withdraw to Kiyan Peninsula.

I immediately phoned my friend Colonel Higuchi, the commander of the Heavy Artillery Regiment, and requested that he make every effort to hold Amagoimui hill. I also asked Lieutenant Colonel Sunano at the Artillery Group command post to concentrate his entire firepower on Yonabaru. Higuchi readily agreed, but his regiment could not move a step out of Ohzato Castle because his guns had been destroyed by warship bombardment. Very few men of the 23rd Shipping Engineer Regiment remained at the key positions on Amagoimui hill.

All of our trained reserve forces were lost in the fierce battles for Amekudai and Naha. All the key pieces for our game plan were spent in the emergency. We still had considerable force, but they were not battle-ready. Our various support and maintenance forces and the conscripted civilians had lost most of their arms and equipment. Since they could not perform their regular duties, all we could do was put them directly onto the battlefield. (Postwar history books recorded that the Americans had underestimated Japanese military strength and were surprised at Japan's "versatile" tactics for troop replacement.)

Yamaguchi's naval battalion had allowed the enemy to break through their front line and enter Yonabaru. Admiral Ota felt so bad about this that he promised to throw in a number of infiltration units to support Yamaguchi. My classmate Sunano, who always helped when needed, volunteered to organize two infantry companies and lead them to Yonabaru by midnight. We

---

of the Japanese at news of President Franklin Delano Roosevelt's death on April 12, 1945, some six weeks earlier. Japanese speculation about the new president's good fortune may well have generated clichés about "a Truman bonus."

also took Ozaki's battalion of the 2nd Infantry from the defense of Sueyoshi and returned them to their original position in front of Yonabaru, where we also sent one infantry company out of the 36th Signal Regiment.

In addition to the above troops, the 7th Heavy Artillery Regiment and the 23rd Shipping Engineer Regiment were sent to the 24th Division commander to repulse the enemy at Yonabaru. These reinforcements were assigned to Colonel Kanayama's 89th Regiment, and he was designated commander of the battle line. Major Nawashiro, senior operations officer of the 24th Division, was sent along as liaison.

These reinforcements moved to recapture Yonabaru in the evening of May 24. We waited all night at the division command post to hear the battle results. Major Nawashiro returned at dawn on May 25, so exhausted he could barely speak, and told what happened. "The night attack failed. The untrained reinforcements ran blindly onto the dark battlefield, out of control, and were crushed by enemy mortar fire. We made a second attack with the same result, while the enemy advanced and secured their gains. Kanayama's regiment found it difficult to hold Untamamui hill. Amagoimui hill has already fallen, and the enemy now occupies its summit. It was impossible even to maintain the battle front, let alone to recapture Yonabaru."

The division leaders were losing confidence in Kanayama and Higuchi, but it was wrong to blame them for the failure. Our exhausted right flank was bound to collapse. No one was to blame. Even before the Yonabaru crisis we had already decided to withdraw and had made preparations for fortifying the rear area. The battle situation on both the right and left flanks had led to the withdrawal decision. During the Naha battle our forces had made a brief withdrawal. We had believed that if we could maintain our right flank in Yonabaru, then we might continue to fight on the Shuri line a while longer, but even this faint hope was about to vanish.

12

Retreat and Attack

The battle situation on the Shuri line had been deadlocked for more than two months, but now it was about to change sharply. The moment had arrived for more drastic battlefield operations.

It was time to conduct a retreat-and-attack plan against the enemy, who was breaking through Yonabaru and penetrating the right flank of our army. I had been studying maps and observing troop deployments. The 24th Division and Mixed Brigade controlled most of the battlefield, while the 62nd Division deployed some troops in front of Shuri. The main strength of the division, however, was centered around fortifications inside the city of Shuri, and they were preparing for the next assault. We had to use the main strength of this division as much as possible.

The 62nd Division had now to advance to the southwest of Yonabaru, by way of Tsukazan, head northeast along the path that the enemy had used to break through the line, and then assault the enemy. The right flank of the 24th Division should assist this effort by proceeding to the south. Thus the enemy would be hit from both sides.

An important consideration at this time was the arrival of the rainy season. For the last few days Okinawa had been drenched. Mountains, hills, and roads were slick with mud. Tanks were unable to move, and it became extremely difficult to get ammunition and provisions to forces at the front. Bad weather prevented regular reconnaissance flights by the enemy. In land and sea artillery bombardments, their guns fired almost blindly.

We still had to pursue our local offensives as planned. Every evening they were unsuccessful, and there was the ugly likelihood that they would continue to fail. If we could only reduce the threat of having the main strength of our flank attacked on the way to Kiyan Peninsula, it would make our army withdrawal action safer and less complicated. This would be a great gain!

As for myself, when this plan for an "offensive retreat" was formulated, I was wildly overjoyed. Like a child I fantasized comparisons —Napoleon's battle of Marengo, France's counter-attack on the Marne in World War I, the Polish army's counter-attack against the Soviets in 1920. This would be something to boast about! Nagano, Yakumaru, and the others spontaneously pushed their concurrence; and the Chief of Staff and the Commanding General gave me immediate approval.

To digress for a moment, the 62nd Division command post, under Lieutenant Colonel Kitajima, was in charge of this operation. Kitajima finally became ill after working without rest for nearly two months. As a replacement for him I thought of my colleague Nagano, but General Cho said he was indispensable and suggested Yakumaru. I knew he was brave and aggressive and that this would be a good opportunity for him, so I followed the chief of staff's suggestion.

With my plan for withdrawal settled, our retreat-and-attack operation was as follows:

1. The 62nd Division would assign the 22nd Independent Infantry Battalion to its present position on the northwest front of Shuri, under the 24th Division commander. The battalion would immediately advance to the southeast of Tsukazan, attack the enemy approaching from Yonabaru, and drive them back to the north of Yonabaru.

    In the area of Ohzato the following regiments would be placed under the 62nd Division commander: 7th Heavy Artillery Regiment, 23rd Shipping Engineer Regiment, Lieutenant Colonel Tsuchida's 3rd Special Regiment, and Colonel Ito's 4th Special Regiment.
2. The 24th Division would assist in the advance and retreat of the 62nd Division. The 24th Division would take over the defense zone of the 62nd Division in front of Shuri.
3. The Shimajiri Area Garrison would immediately send all available troops to Yonabaru, assigned to the 62nd Division.

This retreat-and-attack plan got underway on Friday evening, May 25, when the 62nd Division commander moved into action.

According to the general outline for withdrawal to Kiyan Peninsula, our army and each of its divisions made their preparations in the rear area, regardless of front-line activities.

Each unit had its own designated retreat area. The following plan was made effective on the evening of May 25.

1. Designated Defense Areas of Kiyan Peninsula.
    a. Army front line will be on the line of Gushichan, Yaezu hill, Yoza hill, Kuniyoshi, and Maezato.
    b. The Mixed Brigade will occupy strongholds from the Gushichan area through Yaezu hill.
    c. The 24th Division's right flank will connect with the Mixed Brigade, and they will occupy positions from Yoza hill to Maezato.
    d. The 62nd Division will defend the coastline behind the army, and reorganize troops wherever they may be.
    e. The main strength of the Artillery Group will occupy strongholds east of Maedera[1] and be prepared to concentrate artillery fire whenever necessary. The focus area of their battle preparations will be in front of the 24th Division.
    f. The Naval Base Force will be in the center of army territory and will act as reserves for all army forces.
2. Outline of Retreat from Shuri Line to Designated Positions of the New Defense Zone.

    Our general retreat policy, following the principle of regular retreat operations, was aimed at a total retreat toward fortifications at Kiyan. Our war objective, however, remained a war of attrition, looking toward the decisive battle in mainland Japan. We intended to carry out a German-army–style, local prolonged resistance, taking advantage of the rugged terrain and numerous caves along the twelve kilometers between the Shuri line and the new front line.
    a. The main strength of the 24th Division and the Mixed Brigade would withdraw from the present battle line on the night of X-Day. Some troops would remain in their present position in order to keep secret the retreat of our main strength and block enemy pursuit at the present battlefield as long as possible. The remaining troops would retreat on the night of X-Day plus two.

---

[1]Variant spellings include Medeera and Maedaira.

b. The Artillery Group would withdraw on the night of X-Day minus one. Part of the group would be deployed deep in the retreat area; they would assist the main strength of the army in retreating safely. At the same time they would collaborate in local resistance with the front-line troops of each division.

c. The Naval Base Force on Oroku Peninsula would occupy the Kokuba River's south bank line, west of the high hills north of Nagado. They would assist in the retreat of the army's main strength. The commanding general of the army would designate the time of their retreat at a later date.

d. The 24th Division would deploy its troops along the west-east line of Tsukazan and along the Noha River to delay enemy pursuit. These troops would link closely with naval forces on the army's left flank to prevent any gaps in the line. To make certain of the link between the main strength of the 62nd Division and that part of the 24th Division which occupied the west-east line of Tsukazan, we would build an army intelligence collection center in Tsukazan. Tentatively, those troops of the two divisions would withdraw on the night of X-Day plus four. The commanding general of the army would designate a definite date later.

e. The 62nd Division would continue its present mission and, if possible, repulse the enemy in the Yonabaru area. They would make every effort to block pursuit by the enemy.

f. The boundaries of retreating troops were to be as follows: 62nd Division and 24th Division—the Miyahira-Kochinda-Yonagasuku line (which belongs to the 24th Division); 24th Division and Mixed Brigade—the Matsugawa-Kokuba-Kakazu-Kugusuku line (which belongs to the Mixed Brigade). The area south of Kugusuku would be shared by both the 24th Division and the Mixed Brigade.

g. Army headquarters would first withdraw to Tsukazan on the night of X-Day minus two, and would withdraw to Mabuni hill on the night of X-Day.

h. X-Day was May 29.

13

Army Headquarters

The presence of young, pretty girls in our headquarters cave had made it seem like a spring garden adorned with beautiful flowers. Now that the girls were gone, the cave was a desolate wilderness in a cold winter. Some of the younger officers and men sat around looking disconsolate, but I was able to ignore the dullness and misery of the despicable cave and forget about the absence of women. There was a serious battle to be fought.

By the end of May the rainy season had finally arrived. We had been waiting for the rains because enemy tanks could not move well in the mud, and their planes could not fly much in bad weather. In 1945 the spring rain came later than usual. I wished it had come two weeks earlier to help our operations. Once started, it seemed the rain would never stop. Water seeped into the cave from everywhere, and it was soon flooded. Brooks flowed in the tunnels, and the cave became a confused babble as we all worked raising beds and building dams. Life in the tunnel kept getting more dismal.

We heard machine guns from south of the headquarters cave. Enemy mortar shells, with their sharply curved trajectory, dropped near the tunnel entrance facing Hantagawa valley and exploded. Enemy ships off the Itoman coast fired naval guns at our cave. This tunnel entrance was once a precious oasis safe from enemy bombardment. Now we risked our lives even to bask in the sun for a few minutes.

The battle situation worsened each day, but morale in the headquarters cave remained high. No one showed signs of despair. Everyone knew that he shared the same destiny with our commanding general, other officers, and fellow soldiers. Our front-line soldiers had been fighting valiantly for two months, and the battle situation was literally deadlocked. No one here believed in a sudden collapse, and this belief kept morale up, even though our last stand would no longer be at Shuri.

General Cho had been busy writing. When he finished he called us in and said, "Today I prepared your fitness reports, and will send them while we still have telegraph communications." He then read each report aloud: "Senior Staff Officer Yahara was wounded while inspecting troops on the front line, but he carried on dutifully. He supported the chief of staff with his superb knowledge of tactics and good judgment. His war plan and its application have been masterful. . . ." He read another report: "Assistant Senior Staff Officer Nagano has provided excellent support to Colonel Yahara, working day and night drafting operation orders and various other reports expeditiously and precisely. . . ." We were embarrassed by Cho's generosity.

General Ushijima, quiet as ever, was busy rewriting merit certificates drafted by Staff Officer Miyake. General Cho said that he awarded a certificate to all men in his command, which kept him busy every day.

The 24th Division command post was located in the heart of the cave, where the heat was so exhausting that I feared a decline in morale and command responsibility. I tried to relocate the post, but there was no other place in the cave. The commander remained there to the last and never uttered a word of complaint.

Army headquarters had moved out along with the 24th Division, but Kidani, the division chief of staff, and officers Nawashiro and Sugimori were ordered to remain in the staff officers' quarters. In the final effort we all had to take care of each other. Each night, after midnight, Kidani and I had long conversations before falling asleep.

One night Major Ogata, of the 22nd Regiment, showed up unexpectedly. He had been ordered to move to Tokunoshima, but the battle started before he could leave, so he remained on Okinawa. We were classmates and had shared many good times. Exhausted from his journey, he quickly went to sleep on a cot next to mine. Lights were out except for one on my desk, and everyone else was huddled in sleep. Before dawn Ogata wakened and began sipping from a bottle of *sake*. I watched him walk silently from the cave and knew it would be my last sight of him.

Many comrades visited the cave, and when they left it always seemed that it was our last farewell. Corporal Katsuyama, a man of few words, asked Staff Officers Nagano and Yakumaru to do everything possible to win the battle. This depressed me because normally a subordinate would never dream of making such a remark to his superiors. Katsuyama had served me well and was very concerned when I was ill and could not eat. He wanted me to be healthy so that we might win the battle. He had married just before joining the army, and I felt sorry for him.

Meanwhile, Major Jin had left Shuri some ten days earlier for Japan, to seek vital air support for Okinawa. He was still awaiting a seaplane at Mabuni, but the waves were too rough for landings. Staff Officer Miyake had at first advocated sending Jin to Tokyo but now realized it was too late to get effective air support, and he suggested that we cancel the plan. I ignored his advice.

14

Farewell
to Shuri

On the night where the moon shone beautifully over Shuri hill,
I think of death, as I throw grenades.

As the sun was setting on May 27, I bade farewell to Shuri hill, the place I had thought would be my last stand. Soldiers left the cave in four groups. The first headed directly south for Mabuni. The next group headed for Tsukazan to await further orders. In the next group, led by General Ushijima and me, as senior staff officer, were fifty soldiers. The last group consisted of General Cho, his deputy Nagano, and another fifty men.

At the same time the command post troops of the Mixed Brigade headed for Shikina. The next day, May 28, the command post of the 24th Division set off for Tsukazan. Staff Officers Kimura and Miyake remained in Shuri for the night to close out the offices and then left directly for Mabuni the next day. Our splendid headquarters cave had been equipped with facilities of all kinds, but the rains now flooded it knee-deep throughout its length. The few remaining lights saved us from complete blackout.

General Ushijima carried a folding fan as he left his quarters. Adjutant Yoshio and I followed immediately, leaving Kimura and Miyake in the staff officers' area. They sat guzzling beer, saying that drinking was their only remaining duty. The adjoining room, which had housed the brigade command post, was completely empty. Before leaving, I destroyed documents to keep them from falling into enemy hands and arranged furniture neatly to leave a good impression.

My clothing got soaked as I splashed through the cave tunnel. Kidani was still working alone in the intense heat of the 24th Division command post as I passed and waved farewell to him. At the fork of tunnels number 4 and number 5 a downpour of water was still flooding the cave. I climbed down the ladder of the number 5 tunnel and found the area jammed with

87

soldiers waiting to leave the cave. We staggered departure times to keep confusion to a minimum. Our schedule was disrupted because we could exit only in the intervals of enemy shelling.

The soldiers were fully armed and carried as much as they could because at Mabuni there was no ammunition, provisions, or other necessities. For a strong man this averaged sixty kilograms (about 130 pounds). They waited patiently for the departure order, not knowing when it might come, standing in water up to their knees. I made my way through the crowd shouting, "This is Senior Staff Officer Yahara. Let me pass." At last I reached the entrance of the no. 5 tunnel and could see General Ushijima. The area was so crowded that I had trouble reaching him over a distance of ten meters.

When the bombardment stopped briefly, he went resolutely out of the cave followed by a number of soldiers. I elbowed my way to the cave entrance just as mortar shells landed and twenty or more soldiers went back into the cave. I regretted not departing the cave with him and hoped that he was safe from the mortar shells. I went back to a spare room near the entrance, where General Cho and his deputy Nagano sat, along with General Suzuki and his subordinates. They were eating dry bread and discussing departure times. After studying the artillery bombardment schedule they concluded that the intervals averaged fifteen to twenty minutes. Thus Cho and the others should leave the cave at 2010.

At a break in the bombardment, Nagano jumped out, followed by me, Sakaguchi, and General Cho, in that order. We at once turned left and climbed a gentle slope for about thirty meters. We had almost reached the top when a massive explosion shook the hill. We ducked into the bushes and hit the dirt. I looked back at Sakaguchi, who was saying, "Quick, Sir, come up here," as he helped General Cho up the slope. Cho passed me without a word.

While lying there, I thought about my traveling with this group of soldiers. There was no great rush involved in reaching Tsukazan; what difference did a few seconds or minutes make? So I let the soldiers pass by. I then returned to the cave, followed by Katsuyama, Nagano, Kojima, and a few others who turned back from the confusion. We were all slightly embarrassed as we returned, and General Suzuki joked, "Hey, brave Yahara, are you back again?" Suzuki was scheduled to leave at midnight.

I had spent so many days in the cave that I was unaware of the situation outside. I was badly shaken by it all. An hour later, at 2110, I had recovered my composure and did not hesitate in leaving the cave. I ran up the slope in a single dash. Enemy shells were falling on top of Shuri hill and on the Shikina plateau, but here in Hantagawa valley all was still.

Through the clouds I saw the outline of the moon, and through the gun smoke appeared the solemn outline of Shuri Castle hill. Goodbye, Shuri Castle.

Kojima, Katsuyama, Nagano, and I continued on. The duty soldiers knew a safe route to Tsukazan, because they had been there before to deliver luggage, so they were our guides. We called to each other to maintain contact. The muddy roads were slippery. It was difficult to walk. As we squished through the mud, I could not believe that the 62nd Division was retreating under such conditions.

About three hundred meters into the valley of Hantagawa we saw a dead soldier, fully armed, at the side of the road. It reminded me of my first such experience, with the 1st Division in China. It is gruesome and dreadful to see hundreds of dead soldiers, but it is especially heartbreaking to see a lone soldier dead by the side of the road.

Enemy flares rose incessantly, high over the skies of Shuri, Shikina, Oroku, and Tsukazan. Tactically I could see no reason for such an excess of flares; it seemed like a meaningless waste. At the same time enemy ships were firing their big naval guns, and some shells hit nearby. There was a strange psychological effect that made it feel as though the shells were pursuing us on the battlefield. I really hated the mortar shells, and it was reassuring to be out of their range.

What a feeling it was to breathe once again all the fresh air I wanted and relax a little. Among various people we encountered were Takahashi, our staff secretary, and Nakatsuka, the duty officer. They joined us.

On our way up Hantagawa valley the road leveled out. Walking was easier. We had to avoid crossing Ichinichi Bashi (the "Bridge of Death"), which had drawn heavy enemy gunfire. So many bodies had piled up there that we could not dispose of them. Instead, we planned to go about a hundred meters upstream to cross the Kokuba River and reach Tsukazan. As we advanced we heard heavy enemy gunfire from the Yonabaru battleground, where our troops were taking a terrible beating. The enemy was within two kilometers of Tsukazan. The 62nd Division had been providing support there since May 25, and I had thought there was no need for concern.

The gentle slope of the road led to the bottom of a basin where, incredibly, we found a farmhouse completely intact. We rested there and sat against a stone wall smoking cigarettes. Enemy shells fell two hundred meters away, but we were safe for the time being, and the air was clean. I relaxed to enjoy a glimpse of the moon, which shines only briefly in the rainy season. The others urged that we leave, but I had no intention of moving from this happy place. My happiness was short-lived, however. Exploding shells along the basin edge soon came closer. Three shells burst directly in front of us and I thought surely we were hit. None of us was injured, however, because we were sitting against the wall. The shell fragments flew overhead. It was a miracle that no one was even wounded. We roused our weary bodies and moved on.

Looking at Tsukazan hill, we saw that the enemy artillery fire was becoming more intense. The guns were firing from Kerama Channel, Nakagusuku Bay, and the Shuri line. Shells came flying from all directions. There were no dead angles. It seemed extremely dangerous, but I saw very few corpses along the road. Someone must have disposed of them. Arms and equipment were scattered everywhere. We knew for sure we were in the Tsukazan area, but the jagged hilltops made it difficult for us to find our way in the twilight. Our party was scattered all over the area.

I followed the dark shadow of someone in front, stumbling down into a deep valley. We then climbed another slope and found a cave entrance but could not be sure that it was our Tsukazan destination. I entered and saw soldiers deeper inside. As I moved forward, someone called my name. It was Staff Officer Yakumaru. Then I saw General Arikawa sitting cross-legged on a bed in the tunnel. This was our destination. Farther in I found Katsuyama and our guide.

Farther along we came to the ordnance section where Colonel Umezu, veterinary chief Colonel Sato, and Major Wada were seated in chairs. They looked comfortable and safe. The enemy had already broken through Yonabaru and were coming closer to Hill 85, which was only fifteen hundred meters east of Tsukazan. We were concerned that Tsukazan might have fallen. Tsukazan communications had temporarily lost contact with army headquarters, which was expected soon, and the three section chiefs were awaiting its arrival. We knew that the 62nd Division was heading for this area and would also concentrate here.

A few meters farther into the tunnel a tall, mature, beautiful woman was sitting on a bed. She seemed dismayed at my presence. The light was dim and my fogged glasses prevented my seeing her clearly, but I believe she had been in a Shuri *geisha* teahouse late last year. She left behind a poem:

> Deep in autumn
> I left the town of flowers

I passed her without speaking and proceeded through the labyrinthine cave for another hundred meters to my assigned room.

Nagano and I went next door to visit General Ushijima. He was eating with General Cho and Colonel Sato. Cho looked up and said, "I'm glad to see you again. When I didn't see your face I was worried. I was just telling these gentlemen that if anything happened to you, I would have to do your work."

I congratulated them on their safe arrival and expressed my regrets that I had not accompanied them. Then I retired to my room, which was about four square meters. There were two beds and a table. One candle lighted the room. I changed my muddy, sweat-soaked clothes. Tsukazan was a supply depot, so we had ample equipment and provisions. I placed my new army boots neatly outside my room.

It was past midnight when Nagano brought *sake* and three cans of pineapple. I was adequately fed. After the hazards of the journey I was glad to be here. We could expect a tremendous fight in the Kiyan fortifications. Although the battle situation was worsening, our retreat thus far had progressed smoothly. Usually, I do not drink much, but that night I enjoyed *sake* with Nagano. This brilliant young officer ate heartily, drank heavily, and spoke in abundance. He even ate part of my food.

A pretty, young girl came to serve us and told us of her recent experiences. She had been living with her mother in Argentina until a few years ago. They had come to Tsukazan where her mother was housekeeper for the bank manager. After the village was burned out, they had lived in a foxhole for a while and then had come to this cave. The bank manager had arranged with the army to permit them to live here. Their room was opposite General Ushijima's.

Nagano and I talked and drank until late at night, and into the early morning. I discussed the army's triple offensive on the Shuri battle front, and the alcohol made me voluble.

"It was wrong to think that air power would be decisive in the outcome of this battle. Sure, we had some victories in the Greater East Asia War because of powerful aerial assaults in the beginning, but it was naive and overconfident of our leaders to think that such victories could be repeated over and over again.

"Only fools and madmen dream of victory in battle against a superior enemy. Where we had only two and a half divisions, the enemy had six. While we had no way of replenishing troops and supplies lost in battle, the enemy has a constant resupply of soldiers and ammunition. The enemy divisions are being continuously reinforced by sea and by air.

"Our army should have faced the fact that we could not win this battle. We should have concentrated on a strategy of attrition for the defense of Japan."

I even carped at Nagano, "Even you, my assistant, never really accepted my plan. You were always influenced by the theories of those madmen. It was a disappointment."

Nagano, who was clever beyond his years, retorted, "No, that is not true. Before the battle I said that we should hang a 'WAR OF ATTRITION' banner in the commanding general's quarters. For the last two months I have been in the middle between you and General Cho. You ought to appreciate my dilemma."

I understood what he was saying, and softened my reply, "Our two generals were obsessed with the idea of the offensive because that is what Imperial General Headquarters and the Taiwan 10th Area Army wanted. They were forced into it."

Suddenly the two generals were standing at the doorway of my room, as if they had not overheard our candid conversation. One said, "Is everything okay with both of you?" They were too gracious to show their displeasure at my candid outburst, and their pretended unawareness made me blush. I begged off from further discussion, saying that it was nearly dawn and there were intelligence reports for me to check. I retired and went to sleep to the lullaby of distant gunfire.

15

The Tsukazan Command Post

Construction of the Tsukazan command post was begun early in the summer of 1944 by the Army Construction unit, the 2nd Field Construction unit, and a large number of civilians. It was originally scheduled to be army headquarters. Toward the end of the year, however, army headquarters was transferred to Shuri Castle. Even so, all army troops except the medical section remained at Tsukazan. Unfortunately, Major Hirayama, the construction unit chief, was killed in action at the end of March during the pre-invasion bombardment.

During the construction I often visited Tsukazan to encourage the workers. Young civilians, including many boys and girls, had been conscripted to work on the tunnels and the airfield. Deep in the tunnel on one of my visits I found several girls repairing a water leak. When I praised their effort, one girl stood and said sweetly, "We'll do our best until the end." I was deeply touched by their devotion to duty.

Inside a cave there is no night and day, of course, but it was well after dawn when I awoke. The explosions that shook this cave were farther away than the ones I experienced at Shuri. Nagano must have gone to the office, because I did not see him around. I looked outside the door for my new boots, but they were gone. Who would steal boots in the middle of a war? I smiled bitterly, put on my old boots, and went out.

On the way to the tunnel entrance I passed a kitchen where young women were preparing food. From the entrance I saw an enemy reconnaissance plane circling the area, despite a light rain shower. I looked toward Tsukazan, which had been the home of some three thousand people. The village had been reduced to cinders. Nothing stood but crumbling brick walls and charred skeletons of once-green trees. Connecting passages between the headquarters command post and those of each division were still under construction.

Lieutenant Colonel Sunano of the Artillery Group command post sent a report by messenger: "Our command post has completed the retreat from Nagado. We are making every effort to concentrate our firepower on the enemy in front of Yonabaru." Lieutenant Moriwaki from the Mixed Brigade command post arrived to report. There was no change in the battle situation in Naha.

The brigade commander proposed the following plan to me. "According to the army plan, if the brigade main strength retreats from the present battle line toward the left bank of the Kokuba River on the evening of May 29, it will be impossible for the remaining troops to hold the present battle line until the evening of June 1. If that battle line collapses sooner than scheduled, it will present difficulties for the general retreat. I suggest that the main strength of the brigade maintain its present position until the night of May 31, and then retreat all at once to Kiyan Peninsula." Tactically, it was desirable to move the main strength of the brigade as soon as possible. General Ushijima approved the plan immediately.

Enemy intelligence was coming in so slowly that we could not confirm enemy moves. The offensive action of enemy tanks, planes, and ships was so slowed by Okinawa's heavy rains that we were getting concerned as to whether the 62nd Division's retreat-and-attack plan would be successful. I asked Staff Officer Yakumaru for his report.

In order for the plan to succeed, the right flank of the 24th Division and Colonel Higuchi's Ohzato Detachment had to attack the enemy front from both sides. Taking advantage of the inclement weather, we needed to attack before enemy troops could go on the offensive. Our vanguard 64th Brigade, however, was still in the Tsukazan area and would not be leaving until two days after the start of the retreat-and-attack operation. They were still on the defensive there, and still bringing rear-area troops up to the front. Why?

The main strength of the division was the 64th Brigade. Instead of going completely around the castle walls of Ozhato to attack the enemy, they went only halfway around, and met in the area southeast of the Tsukazan River. Why? It now became clear that the division would not be able to launch an organized attack the next day as intended. Our main force was ordered to carry out the retreat on the evening of May 29. If we could not inflict decisive damage against the enemy, who was now breaking through our lines, we might lose forever the chance of a successful retreat-and-attack operation.

In reporting the battle situation, even high-spirited Yakumaru was pessimistic. He said sadly, "I am afraid that an offensive at this time is hopeless."

I suspected that the 62nd Division did not really want to go into offensive action; they deployed their troops only to be ready for a retreat. Army headquarters, at one time determined on retreat, now ordered offensive action on the way south. Our own 62nd Division was not what it once was. Most of its seasoned troops were dead, and the officers were totally exhausted. From my experience the previous night, I knew how difficult it was to retreat. I was informed that Staff Officer Kusunose, a most courageous soldier, had started ahead of us for the Kiyan fortifications and had been killed by enemy bombardment.

Sunano gave me a message: "The Artillery Group has lost many guns. Our ammunition is almost depleted. We want to support our troops at the Yonabaru line, but cannot provide appropriate and effective assistance."

It is said that one soldier cannot prevent the collapse of an entire army. We had to give up our futile dream of retreat and attack. All we could now ask of the division was to block the enemy from sneaking up behind us. That would help our entire force to retreat safely to the south. My great retreat-and-attack dream was dead.

American accounts of the battle later commented on this operation. General Simon Buckner learned from aerial reconnaissance that Japanese troops were moving toward Yonabaru. Unaware of our retreat plan, he asked Major General Arnold of the 7th Division, who was in charge of breaking through the Yonabaru line, if he could repulse them. Buckner knew the importance of the Japanese counteroffensive there and he was nervous about it.

Incidentally, what had become of the Naval Base Force? According to information available on May 28, their main strength had, unexpectedly, already retreated to the Kiyan Peninsula the previous day. Ignoring army plans, they had occupied all fortifications there. Only a few small units remained in the Oroku Peninsula, and it was reported that they had destroyed all batteries and machine-gun emplacements.

The navy's withdrawal from Oroku was to have been a matter for the army to decide later. It was vital to the success of the operation. Had they misunderstood the army order? Should we ignore this, or should we ruthlessly order them to return? An immediate decision was essential. Nagano was furious. He drafted an order for the naval forces to return to Oroku and presented it to me for approval. I was perplexed, fearing the chaos that might result, but I approved it.

On Monday evening, May 28, we were served a hearty meal. There I finally got together again with Lieutenant Colonel Kuwahara of the Accounting Section. We had been colleagues in April when we established 32nd Army. I told him frankly, "The troops here are altogether too easygoing. I feel that we must be prepared to retreat at any moment. Just back from the front, you deserve to rest, but if we don't order them out now, an orderly retreat will be impossible." He caught my meaning, and said resignedly, "Whatever happens, we must not die like dogs."

When time allowed I made an examination of the cave. There was poor ventilation in the narrow tunnels. Bunk beds lined the walls. Every space was jammed with people. In one office someone was working with an abacus. I asked for the man in charge of the Ordnance Section and learned he had been killed in action a few days earlier. That night the sound of gunfire from Yonabaru was louder than ever. I felt that the deafening guns were sealing our fate. One officer said, "This may be the end, our final day." I felt the same.

Tuesday, May 29, it was still raining.

A telegram came from Kimura and Miyake, the two staff officers who had gone ahead to Mabuni: "Mabuni cave is not at all suitable for use as army headquarters." General Cho and I were disturbed by this message. Perhaps they meant to say that communications were not good, but I felt they were criticizing our whole operation plan. That place was our last defense fortification. No one could afford to complain. The 24th Division command post had retreated as planned to Tsukazan. According to Staff Officer Sugimori's report, all was going smoothly at the rear of the division, and ammunition at Nagado and Miyahira was being transferred to the retreat area.

We lost contact with the 62nd Division for a while, but it was resumed. Arikawa's brigade on the left flank sent support troops to the line of the 3rd Special Regiment. Nakajima's brigade on the right flank was now receiving troops coming in from north of Takahira. They formed a joint line. Kaya's battalion began an aggressive move from Majikina toward Ohzato. Our retreat-and-attack plan was now hopeless, but we were ready to block enemy penetration of our rear flank, and to support the retreating army. Our headquarters was preparing to leave that day, and the cave was a disaster. This Tsukazan cave was a rear-area organization that prepared ammunition and provisions for the entire army. There was plenty of both, but thus far rations had been limited to two meals per day. Now they would begin to join the front lines and head for the final stand.

The ranking headquarters officers intended to leave the cave at 2100 hours on May 29, riding in two trucks. The soldiers, carrying heavy packs, would leave at sunset. Soldiers left one by one in the dark, and the cave was soon quiet and ghostly.

16

Tsukazan
to Mabuni

It was midnight when the trucks arrived at the outskirts of Tsukazan to pick us up. We wanted to make preparations to ensure General Ushijima's safety, but he went ahead, walking down the dark slope alone. We fanned out and ran after him. I got thoroughly bruised and scratched falling into a deep ditch but managed to reach the waiting trucks. Enemy shells dropped lazily on the surrounding hilltops, and a tall tree burst into flames.

We stood impatiently against a crumbling stone wall waiting for the truck engine to get started. When it did, we climbed on board. It was a very old truck, but we had an excellent driver. We rolled through the inky night without headlights. At Kochinda we caught up with our southbound companies and platoons. They walked silently in good order; it was a proper retreat. This was the 24th Reconnaissance Regiment, which had fought on the army's right flank with the 89th Regiment. They had been in a desperate position to attempt a retreat, but here they were and it was going as well as I had planned it.

The enemy focused their artillery at Yamakawa bridge and tried to block our retreat. The area was strewn with shell craters and soldiers' corpses. An unbearable stench reached us even on the truck. Explosions surrounded us as the shelling became more intense. Katsuyama, standing behind me, kindly put a blanket around my shoulders. At the bridge we met several trucks of the 42nd Transport Regiment heading in the opposite direction. The bridge had been damaged by the shelling, and it took some time for the trucks to pass. We waited anxiously for them to clear. When we at last managed to cross the bridge, the engine stalled again. Someone said, "This truck is temperamental." Adjutant Sakaguchi said, "Here I can be together and die with our honorable commanding general and be the happiest man in the world." The engine finally started and we moved on. Enemy shells continued to fly overhead, and one demolished a nearby house.

When we reached the saddle-shaped hill at the boundary of Yamakawa and Kochinda, the truck again became temperamental and stopped. This was clearly another enemy target point, so we all jumped from the truck to head for a safer place. We climbed down a slope to where a group of soldiers was resting. They belonged to the artillery. Not far away I saw seventy or eighty charred bodies. I was sickened by the sight of one charred corpse sitting upright against a rock. Just outside of Kochinda we encountered scores of defense conscripts heading north, carrying heavy packs of ammunition on their backs. I saluted them respectfully.

We also passed a number of young women as we entered what remained of Kochinda village. At a fork in the road we turned right and came to Shitahaku, where the Artillery Group was once located. The village had been devastated by artillery bombardment. The stench of corpses stung our nostrils again. Many civilian refugees were scattered on the ground, their belongings all around them.

Here we were beyond the range of enemy artillery shells from Shuri, but now the enemy ships off Itoman fired their frightful naval guns. The road was littered with munitions. A sugar cane factory still stood nearby. Our rear-area troops had been hit by enemy air attack, and the situation was even worse at the fork in the road leading to Itoman. Two trucks were overturned, and a horse aimlessly pulled an empty wagon. Big shells were exploding all over the area, raising billows of smoke.

In the ravaged battlefield I heard a crying child. As our truck came closer I saw a girl of seven or eight carrying baggage on her head. Her tiny hands cupped her face and tears streamed down her cheeks. I tried to ask if her mother was dead, or merely lost, but my words were lost in the noise of guns and her sobbing. I started to lift her into the truck, but the others said, "No, don't do it." Indeed, she might find her parents nearby and, even if we got her to Mabuni, we could not care for her.

The truck had engine trouble again near Ohzato Primary School. We jumped off and huddled against a wall for protection from incoming shells from off the Itoman coast.

We joined hundreds of troops in ranks crossing a bridge near a spring. The moment we crossed it, the bridge was hit by huge shells causing tremendous explosions. Everything turned red around us, and we ran back to the truck, calling out to each other through the darkness. General Ushijima and his aide were missing. Concerned and frightened, we searched, fearing that they might be dead. We could not remain in the area. We had to move on. Then, off in the distance, we spotted them walking through some trees. Cho called the aide by name and shouted, "You fool! What's the matter with you? We have been anxious about you. Why didn't you tell us you were going to walk ahead?" I was glad that Cho shouted at him.

From this area onward there were few bomb explosions. At the far left, near Yoza hill, we saw a barrage of enemy shells, and that was all. We encountered our own big guns being moved north. They had passed us at Shitahaku, and I asked why they were retracing their steps. An officer replied, "We are ordered to occupy strongpoints in Shitahaku and support our retreating troops." I remembered having given that order to the Artillery Group and thought of the resolute fighting spirit of my classmate Sunano.

At last we entered our planned defense territory. All over the road supplies were piling up, camouflaged by high grass and trees. Some infantry troops were busy digging up sweet potatoes and preparing dugouts in the virgin woods. Communication units were setting up cable lines. Almost all the villages in the area were destroyed, but groves of pine trees remained standing.

In early May we had ordered Shuri civilians to evacuate to this area. Now I saw a number of them. When the army decided on the retreat plan, we had directed the civilians of Kiyan Peninsula to evacuate to the Chinen area, because Kiyan would soon be a battlefield.

We passed one village in flames and then entered Komesu. The primary school was reduced to rubble. The only thing still standing was a solitary school gate.

Mabuni was three kilometers away. The sky cleared. A cool night breeze blew on my face. At this point we all decided to walk. It was the first time since battle began on Okinawa that I could walk and enjoy the earth without the threat of enemy shells. The soil here was different from the soil at Shuri. The wet road was not slippery, and some thought it was too solid to dig foxholes, but that was not so.

I encountered a young woman in Western dress carrying a heavy bag on her shoulders. She seemed confused about where to go, and I advised her, "There will soon be a fierce battle here. Please head immediately for the Chinen Peninsula." She was dazed and paid no attention to me.

At last we reached Mabuni. Remarkably, we found the village completely intact. In the garden of one home our men had made a bonfire to dry their clothing and prepare a hot meal. It was a peaceful moment.

Following a guide we climbed Hill 89, which stood high and solemn in the dawn. Its lower half was cultivated with vegetables, and above that were bushes.

On top of the hill was our new headquarters cave, which had three openings. One looked down on Mabuni, one faced west, and the central shaft was overhead. We climbed down the ladder of the central shaft to a level passageway. After walking sixty or seventy meters, we turned right and were at the western cave opening. In some places it was difficult to squeeze past the rock formations of this natural cave. Low-hanging stalactites dripped water, and it was dangerous to walk without a helmet. It was an awful place.

Adjutant Katsuno's group had already been there a week, preparing for our arrival. I went to my room in the staff officers' section north of the shaft, where the two generals were also quartered. The rest of the cave was for adjutants. Nagano and I sat across from General Cho. Sharp stalactites prevented us from sitting up straight. Nagano and I shared a bed. If I rolled over in my sleep, he would fall out of bed into a muddy pit.

General Cho shouted at Katsuno, "What's the meaning of this? You came here to prepare for our arrival, but nothing has been done." With pained expression, Katsuno said, "I'm sorry, sir. We just couldn't get enough furniture and equipment."

I, too, was disappointed, but tried to be cheerful. "This cave is a hell of a place, but we do have plenty of fresh air to breathe. We can keep up our spirits by hard work." Cho agreed, saying, "We must get ventilation in here. Also, you staff officers cannot be comfortable in the same room with General Ushijima and me. You cannot talk freely. We will move to other quarters."

At daybreak I went to see the hilltop view. Soldiers and civilians were moving along a narrow, sandy road stretching from Gushichan in the east to Komesu in the west. At the end of gentle slopes rising northward to Shuri were Yaezu hill in the northeast and Yoza hill in the northwest. Beyond Yaezu hill I could see Itokazu hill standing high on the Chinen Peninsula, as if to intimidate us. From Mabuni through Gushichan to Minatoga stretched a deep cliff that dropped off toward the water. At the foot of the cliff were dense bushes as far as the eye could see.

In the distance to the west I saw the Kerama Islands through the mist. Waves crashing against the reefs formed a billowing arch that rippled along the coast. At the end of the arch stood Kiyan Point. On Kiyan Peninsula there are three hill ranges that point toward Yoza hill. At the north end of the range the land drops off sharply to form escarpments ideal for use as natural fortresses.

Kiyan Peninsula is eight kilometers from east to west and four kilometers north to south. It was to be the place of our final showdown. I prayed to the holy spirits of the hills and rivers who would witness the last battle of the 32nd Army. An enemy reconnaissance plane appeared in the skies over Yoza hill, but there was still no sign of the enemy fleet in the open sea to the south. Because of our swift retreat and the enemy's slow advance, we briefly enjoyed this paradise, which would soon become a violent battlefield.

From the opening of the cave entrance a narrow path went along the cliffs and down to the coast. We used that opening as a rest area, just like the Shuri headquarters cave opening that faced Hantagawa valley. We sat there on rugs and chairs to enjoy the fresh air. Seventy days of cave dwelling had taken a toll on my health. After sitting in the sun for a while I felt so lethargic that I had to return to the darkness of the cave to regain energy. I said that I felt like a mole. General Cho chuckled. "Hey, we are not moles," he said. "We are *geisha* girls. By day we are lifeless, but in the darkness we come to life." And he laughed loudly.

At the foot of the cliff, tucked inside a limestone alcove, was a natural spring, about ten meters in diameter. Our kitchen was in a cave beneath a huge rock, not far from the spring, which was our only source of drinking water. If the enemy closed in on this area, it was doubtful that we could maintain a lifeline between our headquarters cave and the spring.

17

Civilians at
the Last Stand

Long years after the war I could remember the misery of the civilians on that road from Tsukazan to Mabuni. According to available information, there had been many civilians living there, and the army had evacuated many more to that area. I really did not want to put these people through another hellish military evacuation. When the army decided on a retreat plan, we told the civilians to withdraw to the Chinen Peninsula, where they would be outside the battle area. It became clear, however, that at Chinen they would be captured by the enemy. Of course, we did not want civilians to fall into enemy hands, but in our present situation we also could not be concerned about caring for civilian refugees. We had to close our eyes to their plight and abandon them to enemy care. As with the civilians in the north, however, we directed that army provisions be left for them in the Chinen Peninsula as a parting gift.

General Ushijima immediately accepted this directive, which his troops issued to all civilians: the local police organizations, the Blood and Iron for the Emperor service units,[1] and neighborhood groups in the caves. In this way we made every effort to contact the civilians, even in the chaos of the battlefield, but it was not enough. They headed for Chinen as directed, but as soon as they saw the enemy they headed back to Gushichan. It was re-

---

[1] These were paramilitary groups of young Okinawan men, organized by the army. Despite only rudimentary training, they were pressed into service and used as auxiliary troops as the battle developed. Losses were heavy among them, despite their bravery.

grettable that many women and children were sacrificed at the southern end of Okinawa.[2]

Even descendants of Ryukyu's Sho dynasty were victims of the battle. On the evening of June 7, when the battle became intense, an aged baron and a dozen or so of his family failed to escape. They had tried to go to Yamaguchi but came under enemy shell fire just as they reached Mabuni, and the baron's daughter was seriously injured. Her mother and sister carried her to our cave and asked General Cho, a close friend, to provide medical treatment. She bravely suffered the amputation of an arm and even thanked Dr. Kakazu, who performed the operation. When they were able to leave, General Cho gave them provisions. They headed for the family home in Mabuni.

A few days later, Governor Shimada and Police Chief Arai visited our headquarters to say goodbye. The once sprightly governor, renowned for his banquet performances of youthful songs and dances, was clearly exhausted. So was the police chief. General Ushijima urged them to flee, saying, "You are civilians. There is no need for you to die here." I still remember my farewell look at them leaving the headquarters cave.

---

[2]In these last stages of the battle, thousands more of Okinawa's civilian population were killed by gunfire. Others continued to seek death by suicide, mindful of the Japanese army's repeated warnings that death, rape, and torture awaited those who fell into American hands. Many were prevented from surrendering to U.S. forces by die-hard Japanese soldiery. True to his own military indoctrination, Colonel Yahara has little to say about this destructive propaganda work on the Okinawan people by the Japanese military.

18

Retreat and
Rear Guard Action

Our commanding general gave us two cautions about retreat operations. First, we should closely follow the movements of all retreating troops and control them to prevent failures. Second, we should avoid strenuous resistance to the enemy so that we could retreat quickly to make strong defense preparations.

A general army retreat directive categorically controlled all troop dispositions, battle lines, timing, and strength for each line of resistance. It was impractical, however, to devise a detailed retreat plan for every battle line south of the Kokuba River. Undependable communications made it difficult to control daily actions by direct orders. Therefore, we had assigned Captain Sayamoto and ten of his men to intelligence chief Yakumaru and left them behind in Tsukazan. Sayamoto was entrusted with troop coordination, especially with the remaining strength of the 24th Division and the main strength of the 62nd Division. They held out at Tsukazan until June 2.

That evening the intelligence group returned to Mabuni. I had caught a cold, was running a temperature of 39°C, and was not satisfied with the job Yakumaru had done. I spoke harshly to him, saying, "You were so preoccupied with attack that you ignored defense." General Cho, who was sitting next to me, nodded agreement. Yakumaru was doubly hurt, and I felt sorry for him.

During the retreat we were also concerned that the enemy might launch a landing operation on the southern coast of Okinawa. In deciding on the retreat to Kiyan Peninsula, we knew that an enemy landing on the cliffs would be difficult, but not impossible. If our main strength did not reach assigned positions before the enemy landed on the coast, it would mean the

end for us. Major General Suzuki, of the Mixed Brigade, repeatedly asked
that we reinforce the 62nd Division to gain time enough for them to occupy
the Yaezu-Gushichan line. We disapproved that request because we had to
be prepared for the threat to our rear.

In spite of such difficulties, our retreat operation was more successful
than expected. By dawn of Tuesday, June 5, our entire army was safely occupying new fortifications on Kiyan Peninsula. We were successful because
we had decided quickly on the retreat plan and had time enough to prepare
for it. Still, the enemy pursuit was cautious and deliberate, except for his 7th
Division, which moved swiftly to the Chinen Peninsula. We understood these
tactics and reacted appropriately. The retreat was successful because our
commanding officers acted calmly and coolly in directing their subordinates.

The American commanders had concluded that we would make our last
stand at Shuri. Therefore, General Buckner wanted to break our defense line
quickly at Yonabaru, approach our rear area, and destroy us under siege.
At a conference on May 28, I later learned, he had said, "The Japanese
decision to move south was made too late." Three days later he added: "The
enemy's next line of resistance will be Naha and the Oroku Peninsula. They
will deploy troops at Baten Port in the east. But General Ushijima's withdrawal decision was made two days too late." It later became clear, however,
that he had underestimated us. Our high command had been insightful about
the move from the Shuri battle line. We had decided on our retreat plan a
week before it began. We were smarter than the enemy thought.

Thanks to the care and caution of Colonel Nakamura, his 24th Transport Regiment still had eighty trucks. They performed perfectly. It was no
surprise, therefore, that they were the first unit of the 24th Division to receive
the army's certificate of merit. They deserved much of the credit for the
success of our retreat.

At Kiyan Peninsula we had enough general provisions to last a month.
In addition, all troop units and individual soldiers carried food supplies of
their own. By cutting allotments in half we could even survive for two
months. If enemy pursuit and attacks continued, we would still be able to
fight until the end of June and not be starved into surrender. If the enemy
took us under siege and did not attack, we were confident that we could
survive for a long time on just sweet potatoes and sugar cane. We had lost
most of our ammunition but knew that we could carry on by limiting expen-
ditures to actual combat situations.

We were very concerned about casualties in the rear areas. In the last two months of the Shuri fighting, our casualties had come to thirty-five thousand. Traditionally, the ratio of dead to wounded averages about 1 to 3. In the battle of Okinawa, however, the numbers were reversed because many wounded soldiers died from improper treatment. As a result of the enemy's "horse-mounting" tactics, most of our soldiers caught in caves were killed. Under enemy siege, many wounded soldiers committed suicide.

Thus, by the end of May, our total wounded in the field amounted to nearly ten thousand. The transportation of the seriously wounded was a great concern. They urgently needed treatment, but there was neither time nor transport for providing it.

The army should, of course, make every effort to carry the wounded to safe areas and prevent their capture by the enemy. The fact was, however, that we were unable to care for such large numbers. How to handle this situation? By Japanese tradition the solution was suicide, but we could not force wounded men to kill themselves. Civilized nations do not consider it a disgrace for the wounded to be captured, and a wounded soldier is supposed to be given proper treatment even by the enemy.

The army directive on this matter stated: "In facing an emergency, every Japanese soldier should act proudly." In fact, many wounded soldiers shouted, "Long live the Emperor!" as they took their lives with hand grenades, satchel charges, or cyanide. In other cases, doctors injected patients with cyanide. Captain Kataoka, our veterinarian, became ill at headquarters and, not wanting to bother fellow soldiers, took his own life at Tsukazan.

Not all wounded soldiers committed suicide. Some, with miraculous courage, made their way to new fortifications. One man, whose feet were badly injured, crawled ten kilometers on his knees, over a muddy road, to join his comrades. At the Shuri battle line there had been some accommodations for the wounded, but there was nothing for them in our new locations. I proposed that we move the wounded to Kiyan Point, a tactically worthless location, but my colleagues merely laughed at this suggestion.

19

Kiyan Peninsula

When we retreated from Shuri to the Kiyan Peninsula, our most important tactical question was how many troops we could concentrate in this area. We received daily casualty reports from every unit, but the situation was a terrible mess. The troops were divided into numerous platoons occupying many underground caves and continually moving back and forth. This made any reports wildly inaccurate. In the 62nd Division, for example, the senior operations officer said there were three thousand troops; the intelligence officer counted six thousand.

At the time of our retreat, I estimated our troop strength at forty thousand. We lost ten thousand during the retreat, so we had about thirty thousand at the Kiyan Peninsula, divided approximately as follows:

24th Division	12,000
62nd Division	7,000
Mixed Brigade	3,000
Army Artillery Group	3,000
Others	5,000
Total:	30,000

Thirty thousand is a large number of men, but the army's real power was now greatly diminished from its original strength. Its actual strength must be considered in components, as follows:

1. *Soldiers.* The army's main strength—24th Division, 62nd Division, and the Mixed Brigade—had lost 85 percent of its original comple-

ment. Regiments, battalions, and companies now consisted mostly of untrained, rear-area soldiers and Okinawan defense conscripts.

2. *Officers.* Among company commanders (junior officers and below) the loss rate was about the same as soldiers. There were very few losses among battalion commanders (field grade) and above. That is why we were able to direct orderly operations and maintain a reasonable command system.

Officers surviving the retreat included:

24th Division: five battalion commanders
Independent Battalion: two commanders
62nd Division: one staff officer, four battalion commanders
Mixed Brigade: one battalion commander, one independent
    battalion commander, one artillery battalion commander
27th Tank Regiment: one commander
26th Shipping Engineer Regiment: one commander
3rd Special Regiment: one commander
4th Special Regiment: one commander
AA Artillery Group: one commander
26th Sea Raiding Squadron: one commander
29th Sea Raiding Squadron: one commander

3. *Ordnance.*

Automatic infantry weapons reduced to one-fifth.
Heavy infantry arms reduced to one-tenth.
Artillery Group arms reduced to one-half. All they could
    muster in the new defense zone were two 15-centimeter
    guns, sixteen howitzers, and ten antiaircraft guns.

4. *Communications.* Cable and radio communications were reduced to nothing, but because the battlefield was small, we no longer had to rely on them.

5. *Miscellaneous.* All construction equipment was lost, so we were unable to construct more fortifications in the new territory.

Our defense policy was to fight to the end with all our strength at the main defense fortifications of the Yaezu and Yoza hills. If the enemy launched landing operations on the southern beach, we would destroy them there. Each area had troop deployment problems:

1. *Mixed Brigade area.* Major General Suzuki asked what was meant by fortifying Yaezu hill. Our reply was, "We must maintain Yaezu hill by all means, and deploy our troops deeper into the right flank of the hill."

Hiraga, the Special Regiment's commander, was to occupy Yaezu hill, and the rest of the Mixed Brigade's main strength was to occupy the Yoza-Nakaza area. We later learned that the all-important Hiraga regiment did not occupy Yaezu hill directly, but rather stationed itself at the foot of some escarpments northeast of it. We were not sure why they occupied the fortifications against the escarpments; perhaps for lack of water supply at the top, or perhaps because the hilltop was an easy target for enemy bombardment. In any event, Yaezu hill was empty. By attacking the opening between Yoza and Yaezu, the enemy could easily capture this area. I urged that Hiraga occupy the hilltop, but Brigade Commander Hiraga sent only 110 men of Katsuta's naval battalion.

At Gushichan there is a natural cave large enough to accommodate several hundred soldiers. This made an ideal defense fortification, but it was located in an isolated area. We made it into a front-line stronghold. General Suzuki deployed Ozaki's battalion into this cave and ordered him to defend it to the end.

Colonel Higuchi's Ohzato detachment was pursued by the enemy. They withdrew from the Chinen hills and were placed under General Suzuki's command because their 62nd Division had retreated to Kiyan Peninsula. On Tuesday night, June 5, Colonel Higuchi and his remaining troops retreated to Yoza and Nakaza. The chief of staff and General Suzuki did not care for Colonel Higuchi from the beginning. For this reason Suzuki ordered him to attack the enemy from behind, and on the same night he retreated to the area where the enemy's 7th Division had made its assault. Before leaving, Higuchi telephoned his farewell to headquarters. I was sleeping and did not receive his message.

2. *24th Division area.* At the outset, the main strength of the 22nd Regiment was assigned as division reserve. When the enemy began to threaten the division's coastline defenses with many amphibious tanks, they were assigned to the left flank of the 32nd Regiment and sent to the Maezato area.

3. *62nd Division area.* This division took defensive positions against the enemy landing force on the coastline. They acted as reserve troops for the entire army. They were to support the Mixed Brigade and the 24th Division when necessary. Their two battalions were especially prepared to support the Mixed Brigade whenever ordered.

4. *Army Artillery Group.* The main strength of this group occupied the area at the 24th Division front, to prepare artillery attacks, but because of deployments and water supply, the main strength of the group had to move westward, and the Naval Base Force returned to Oroku Peninsula. The battle began unexpectedly in front of the Mixed Brigade, where the Artillery Group had to direct their firepower. I was to blame for this mistake because I was not sufficiently familiar with the terrain and the general battle situation. I apologized to Sunano, the senior officer of the Army Artillery Group.

5. *Miscellaneous troops.* Army medical, ordnance, and legal units were assigned to the caves around Mabuni. The Accounting Section was located at Maedera and later moved to Mabuni. Ordnance and Legal Sections moved to Yamagusuku.

20

Mabuni Headquarters Cave

Major Jin made every effort to escape from Okinawa and get to Tokyo, but had still not succeeded when our headquarters was preparing to withdraw from Shuri. Staff Officer Miyake, realizing that Jin's mission was futile, drafted another order to cancel it. General Ushijima approved the order, and it was sent to Jin on the southern part of the island. Before the order reached him, however, he had departed from the famous fishing village of Itoman on May 30 and had escaped to the north in a canoe with a fisherman.

Around June 9 a telegram came saying that Jin had reached Tokunoshima. The news shocked everyone in the cave into silence, except General Cho, who shouted, "Call Jin back!" No one responded. It was too late, and the silence continued. This was just Cho's way of consoling the staff officers left behind.

The peaceful atmosphere of Mabuni headquarters lasted only until noon of June 4. General Cho and several adjutants were outside the cave entrance that Monday enjoying the sun when they were surprised by gunfire from enemy patrol boats. Adjutant Sakaguchi suffered a minor wound in his right hand before dashing back into the cave. I found bullet holes in General Cho's uniform jacket, which he had left behind. Enemy patrol boats continued to drift near the coast and fire at the cave entrance. It was no longer safe to be outside.

When enemy forces realized that our soldiers and civilians were hiding in the caves around Mabuni and using the natural spring, they attacked it at random. As a result of these attacks, corpses with canteens began to pile up near the spring, which we nicknamed the Spring of Death. Since we had to have water, we risked our lives during the night to reach the spring. Our soldiers cooked their meals on the coast, well guarded by rocks and boulders, and then carried the food up to the caves. These missions were as dangerous as a suicide charge, and soldiers engaged in them always looked grim.

One day soldiers came under enemy attack while carrying food up the cliff, and one was killed. Katsuyama survived but was so unnerved that he was unable to give us details of the attack.

It came to a point where even our headquarters did not have enough provisions. Lieutenant Colonel Katsuno, the administrative officer, limited each day's meal to a single rice ball. I caught a cold and suffered from diarrhea, so the ration was not a hardship for me. The young soldiers, however, could not stand the hunger. At night they left the caves and risked their lives to gather sweet potatoes and sugar cane from nearby farms. I advised them against it, but they ignored me. Every night Nakamura, Nakatsuka, Kojima, Katsuyama, and Yonabaru went out for food, usually getting small sweet potatoes, which they boiled. They were delicious.

Major Yakumaru caught a cold and ran a fever but was happy as a child. "Sweet potatoes," he said, "are much better than rice balls." General Ushijima shared sugar cane with us and taught us how to eat it. Miyake, who ate more sugar cane than anyone else, chewed it all the time, even taking sticks of it to bed.

Before the battle for Okinawa, we had discussed the matter of food provisions in these islands. A young government civilian observed, "Okinawa is quite different from New Guinea. Because we have sugar cane and sweet potatoes the year-round, there will be no food shortages here when battle comes." We were, indeed, fortunate to have Okinawa's abundance of cane and potatoes.

In the caves there were many young women and schoolboys who were members of the Blood and Iron for the Emperor service units. Among the boys in the staff officers' quarters was a little fellow named Kinjo, who reminded me of my son in homeland Japan. Kinjo would go out at night with the soldiers through showers of enemy shells to gather sugar cane. He offered cane to Kimura and Miyake in exchange for a rice ball. The caves were so crowded that even General Ushijima had no room to stretch his legs. Kinjo, like most of us, had no assigned sleeping place. He slept wherever he found room, sometimes under my bed, like a puppy, sometimes in the muddy passageway. Seeing him brought thoughts of my son. I had heard that everyone in the homeland was mobilized, and I wondered what was happening to my boy. Was he living as we were here in Okinawa?

On Thursday evening, June 7, I heard three young women enter the cave. It was too dark to see faces, but I recognized their voices and knew them from Shuri. Lying in my bunk I heard them tell Nagano and Miyake that, after withdrawing from Shuri, they served near Maedera in the field hospital of the 24th Division. They spoke through tears, "We were accustomed to seeing seriously wounded soldiers, but the caves became flooded during the rainy season, and we saw people drown. We spent many nights standing in water up to our waist. We ran short of food and began to feel that it would be better simply to die. We are here now because a kind officer at the hospital ordered us to go to headquarters. We shouted, 'Please let us stay to die with you. We will all share the same fate wherever we are.'"

Because of our food shortage, Adjutant Sakaguchi did not really want them to remain in Mabuni. General Cho, however, said that they could live in the cave, and Sakaguchi, of course, did not oppose the chief of staff. So the girls stayed on in the Mabuni cave.

On Friday evening, June 8, enemy gunfire ceased. I went to the top of the hill and enjoyed a pleasant rain shower. Incendiary bombs filled the sky over Yoza hill and Minatogawa. As the bombs continued to explode, I recognized a man's face off in the distance but lost it the next moment in the complete darkness. Then by light of the flares I saw a column of about thirty people ascending the hill. They were young women, carrying heavy sacks on their shoulders. I let them pass without saying a word. These included the girls that General Cho had called back.

As I had done at Shuri, I banned the girls from the staff officers' quarters. The adjutants' room could accommodate only three: Misses Yogi, Nakamoto, and Heshikiya. The senior adjutant searched for nearby caves where the others could be quartered. With the two generals having moved into newly constructed quarters, Miss Heshikiya served as General Ushijima's maid, and Miss Sakiyama as General Cho's. The cave was so overcrowded that the girls had to stay near the central shaft. I exchanged greetings with them the day after their arrival. The eldest girl, Heshikiya, looked exhausted, but the others were surprisingly cheerful. There was mud on their faces instead of powder, but they still looked beautiful and healthy. They all worked very hard. Some were *geisha* from their quarter in Tsuji Town. I did not approve of that, but what could I say?

General Ushijima was comfortable in his new room and kept busily absorbed in reading books and writing letters of commendation by candlelight. When he grew weary, he would grate dry bonito (*katsuobushi*). Grating dried fish is a good method of meditation.

General Cho, whose room was next to Ushijima's, often called us in for a party. He smoked a big pipe, and when he was not entertaining he read books. After the failure of the May 4 counteroffensive, he would greet me over and over with such remarks as, "Senior Staff Officer, we had better stop this war of attrition. I can't stand this life anymore." Was he joking or complaining? As I said before, he slept directly across the hall from me. I could watch his every move and usually tell what was on his mind. As to this joke or complaint, however, I could not be sure.

One day I announced that I had three lice. He quipped, "The lice must be fond of you." I replied, "A great sage once said, 'The thing I enjoy most is picking lice out in the sun.' I agree with the sage, there is nothing quite like picking lice."

The next day General Cho shouted, "Hey, Yahara! I have lice too, and more than you. I have five!" Everyone laughed. Of course, they were all busy picking lice themselves. We often made night attacks against the enemy, but it was worse to fight lice in the dark.

Through the efforts of the field maintenance unit, electricity became available in the cave for the first time. After living in the dark for so long we were as happy as children to have the power, but it lasted for only a few days. The water-powered generator was located near the Spring of Death. Our electric wires were hit and severed by gunfire from enemy patrol boats. That was the end of our electricity, and the cave was plunged into darkness again. We were short of candles, so they were used only when we had to draft an order or read a telegram. Occasionally we spent scarce fuel to run a gasoline generator and light a few lanterns to brighten the cave.

When Nagano wearied of his bunk and moved elsewhere, I was finally able to stretch my legs. Katsuyama made a blanket canopy to catch the water dripping from the stalactites. That helped for a while, but the blanket soon became soaked. When the two generals moved to new quarters near the central shaft, I took General Cho's bed to get free of my uncomfortable bunk. Major Nishino and Captain Matsunaga moved to my bunk room but soon tired of it.

While I struggled with a bad cold, Nagano efficiently handled my duties. He often fumbled and stumbled in the dark to answer the phone but never complained.

When the battle situation was calm, we enjoyed friendly conversations. Nagano told me proudly that he had been the best student in his famous high school. He spoke of his falling in love, getting married, and of their happy honeymoon. Talk of such pleasant memories reminded me that our two generals never spoke openly about their private lives. General Ushijima once mentioned that his son had been sent to New Guinea, but nothing more.

Staff Officer Kimura used to plague the rest of us with Buddhist chants, but he finally quit. Now when his duties were done he would lie in bed, leaving only to go to the latrine. For days at a time he would not say a word. Then for a few days he would sing all the songs he knew in his fine tenor voice. Once when he was silent I asked him for a song. He replied, "Using my voice makes me hungry, so I will not sing."

When Miyake was not eating sugar cane, he kept busy sending and receiving messages on our makeshift radio system. It was difficult to reach Taihoku (Taipei), and even more difficult to contact Tokyo. Enemy bombardments often interrupted our telephone lines, despite valiant repair efforts by our communications people.

We even had difficulty in contacting the 62nd Division's command post in Yamagusuku, sometimes because of downed wires, but also because we had trouble understanding the stations. Sometimes when the lines were operating, they did not receive our transmission. Intelligence Officer Yakumaru was always busy reporting our battle situation to 10th Area Army in Taiwan and to General Headquarters in Tokyo. He also collected enemy intelligence. As General Cho insisted, his daily reports pulled no punches.

When Major Jin left for Tokyo, his place was taken by Major Matsubara, who was assisted by Major Nishino and Captain Matsunaga. Their task was to report the results of *kamikaze* air attacks and compile weather reports for the aviators. Captain Sayamoto's job was to observe enemy attacks from the top of Mabuni hill, but he was killed by enemy mortar shells on June 11. If he had still been alive on June 22, the enemy would not have had such an easy time taking that hilltop. Months later, after the war was over, comrades found his body and buried the remains.

In the narrow tunnel between the staff officers' room and the central shaft, Captain Wasai, Lieutenant Horiuchi, and a few soldiers carried out their duties. They pitched a tent because of a bad overhead leak and slept in shifts for lack of room for all to lie down at the same time. In passing this dismal section of the tunnel, and seeing what they endured and how hard they worked for our homeland, I always bowed my head in respect.

21

The Battle
for Kiyan

As our 62nd Division retreated to the vicinity of Kiyan, the enemy's 7th Division broke through our Yonabaru defenses and, sooner than expected, closed in on our Mixed Brigade. In an effort to gain time, we left our forward units behind, but that did no good.

The Gushichan-Hanagusuku-Asato action intensified on June 7 and 8. Then the enemy began shelling Minatogawa, and it soon became their main port in the east. Our 100th Independent Heavy Artillery Battalion tried to use their two remaining guns to fire on the ships, but these weapons were damaged during the retreat from Shuri, and it was impossible to fire them.

The brigade put up a good fight against the combined land, sea, and air forces of the enemy, but our right flank could not even dig foxholes in the coral rocks. Our casualties increased by the minute. Enemy offensive tactics were much the same as they had been at Shuri, but here they used tanks much more extensively. Our defenses had disintegrated so badly that enemy tanks could move at will.

Our brigade had only a few big guns remaining. Our Artillery Group was supporting the brigade, but they had only tens rounds per gun to fire each day. Even worse, they were able to fire only in the morning and evening, when enemy planes were not flying. They posed no real threat to the enemy. The brigade sent an urgent demand, "We are unable to counterattack against fifty or sixty M-4 tanks. We need artillery support and satchel charges immediately. Our Artillery Group can fire only at random, and they are shooting blindly. We need the Artillery Group to fire on enemy tanks."

I relayed this request to Sunano, who replied, "I am well aware of their situation, but they must realize that the Artillery Group's strength is greatly reduced. We have no effective communications. It takes two hours for our observation posts to contact artillery emplacements. We cannot rely on radio contact, but must risk the lives of messengers. Captain Yamane, commanding our heavy field artillery, reports that he is fighting alone against incendiary bomb attacks on his Yaezu hill observation post. We try everything possible to meet your needs, but we simply cannot do it."

Colonel Hiraoka, in charge of ordnance, reported that he had more than ten tons of explosives available for satchel charges, but enemy tanks still ran rampant through our area. Fortunately for us they withdrew at night, and we could then rebuild our stronghold defenses.

On Sunday, June 10, the battle situation in front of our Mixed Brigade began to collapse rapidly. The enemy seized Gushichan, and we lost all contact with Asato, which was completely isolated.

A snappy noncommissioned officer came to the cave headquarters around midnight on June 12. I asked what he was doing there. "I lead a machine-gun detachment of the Ozaki Battalion. In withdrawing from Gushichan I lost contact with the battalion. It took me three hazardous nights along the coast to reach you here. I am not alone. Six of my men are waiting outside, and I have a machine gun. We have not eaten for three days. Can you help us?"

For not having eaten in three days this man looked healthy. When I asked about his battalion commander, he replied, "I lost him not far from here." It seemed unpardonable for him to have lost his commanding officer and then retreat from his command post, but I was glad he had kept the machine gun. I said, "Have your men come inside before they get blown up." They had a hearty meal.

After this more and more strange-looking soldiers began straying into the cave. One time when I was working on tactics, a soldier appeared, staring blankly as he stood silently beside me. Another time I saw a strange soldier in the muddy tunnel, sleeping like a log. These poor men were all victims of combat fatigue. Some had lost their way. Others were deserters. When I spoke, they were silent and seemed not to understand. They had wandered into the cave without knowing at all where they were. Some of my colleagues thought they might be spies. Ruthless as it may seem, I had to order that all strangers be kept away from our quarters. The very sight of them made the war more depressing.

On Oroku Peninsula, American marines were blocked by our Naval Base Force. Unable to march directly south, the enemy was trying a flanking movement by way of Kochinda. Our division still had powerful artillery units, and they were assisted by the Army Artillery Group until Sunday, June 10. The enemy avoided our front line to save losing their soldiers in vain.

Our front and left flanks held their positions, but the right flank and the Mixed Brigade were near collapse because of a tactical blunder. General Cho and I were greatly concerned. Whatever it took, we had to prevent the collapse of our right flank, so we reinforced it with the following units:

11th Sea Raiding Squadron, under Lieutenant Colonel Ohki, supported
    by fifteen hundred Okinawan conscripts, with bamboo spears
36th Communications Regiment, two companies
Army Artillery Group, two companies
Field Construction Force, less one company

In addition we assigned to the Mixed Brigade all guns in front of the 24th Division and part of the field artillery of the 42nd Regiment. Our new infantry units were poorly trained. For want of antitank weapons, we had to use Okinawan conscripts armed with bamboo spears. They were all destroyed in one day. The war situation had changed so drastically that the enemy had no opposition. It was frustrating to see our men being killed by a well-equipped enemy, while we had nothing left to fight with.

On Monday evening, June 11, Sunano phoned and said angrily, "About ten enemy tanks, accompanied by two or three hundred troops, are advancing on Yaezu hill by way of Asato. Part of our Artillery Group is trying stubbornly to stop them, but I see none of our brigade infantry here. What is going on? Why haven't you sent your brigade to help us? Yaezu hill is the most crucial artillery observation post in the eastern area. We can't afford to lose it. Please take decisive action as soon as possible."

It had been agreed that Yaezu hill must be held at all cost. Nevertheless, Hiraga's regiment had deserted the hilltop, taking up positions to the east and thus causing a disaster. Yaezu not only belonged to our Artillery Group, but was the center of our entire operation. That's why we had put all available forces there to die in battle.

I felt unjustly accused and phoned Staff Officer Kyoso to ask if Sunano's report was correct. Kyoso answered calmly, "We received the same report, and sent a scout there. He found no sign of the enemy on Yaezu hill. Indeed, the enemy is trying to break through from the east, where, as I told you, we have deployed the 44th Brigade. The 1st Mortar Regiment, under the brigade commander, is stationed in front of Yaezu hill, so please relax." I was confused as to whether the report of the Mixed Brigade or the Artillery Group was correct, but at least I knew we were clearly losing Yaezu hill. I decided to send in the 62nd Division and issued a prearranged order for two battalions of the 62nd to be placed under Major General Suzuki and moved east to secure the army's right flank. Fortunately, it appeared unlikely that the enemy would land at Mabuni beach in the near future, as we had originally feared.

The Mixed Brigade commander, General Suzuki, put the newly assigned 13th Independent Infantry Battalion (IIB) on the right flank of the 15th Infantry Regiment along the coastline, and he put another newly assigned unit, the 15th IIB, on the left flank of the brigade at Yaezu hill. Colonel Hara's 13th Battalion, moving quickly, reached the assigned line that very night. The 15th Battalion, however, did not move from its position south of Yoza hill, even two days after the order was issued.

Unfortunately, the Artillery Group's report on the Yaezu hill situation proved correct. The brigade command post was unable to fix the position of Hiraga's regiment. Furthermore, they were falsely influenced by the battle situation at Yoza and Nakaza villages. They could not offer any help to Hiraga. On June 14, I received a phone call from mild-mannered Kidani, the 24th Division chief of staff. His tone was now very harsh.

> Hundreds of enemy soldiers are approaching Yaezu hill. Why can't your Mixed Brigade do something about it? The right rear flank of this division is in danger, and we can no longer hold our front line.
>
> Accordingly, although they were not under our command, we forced the 24th Reconnaissance Regiment, located south of Yoza, to attack the enemy at Yaezu. Preparing for the worst, we ordered the 89th Infantry Regiment, on the right flank of the center of Yoza hill, to retreat south to Maedera and take defensive positions. We asked the 15th Battalion to join the 24th Reconnaissance Regiment in its counteroffensive against the enemy, but they would not do it. This is totally incomprehensible!

General Ushijima then issued a direct order to Major Nagameshi, the 15th Battalion commander: "Advance immediately to Yaezu hill and take offensive action." When General Suzuki later voiced his objection to this order, I told him we had to do it. There was no alternative. I learned afterward that Nagameshi had been critically ill, unable to walk; but he gave the necessary commands from a stretcher. I felt bad about this, but knew that orders had to be carried out—even unreasonable ones.

22

The Naval Base Force Is Wiped Out

By direct order of 32nd Army headquarters, Admiral Minoru Ota's Naval Base Force returned for the second time to its original fortifications on Oroku Peninsula. On Monday, June 4, while they were still preparing defenses, the enemy's 6th Marine Division made surprise landings on Oroku Peninsula and stormed inland, cutting the road between Naha and Itoman. The high hills of Nagado, near the Kokuba River, had already been captured by the enemy when our main force retreated from Shuri. On June 5, with his force isolated and completely surrounded, Admiral Ota radioed General Ushijima:

> Under your command our naval forces fought bravely to the last man at Shuri, as you are well aware. They aided your successful retreat from Shuri to Kiyan Peninsula. I have discharged my duties, and have nothing to regret. I will command my remaining units to defend Oroku Peninsula as brave warriors unto death. My deepest gratitude, Excellency, for all you have done for us. May our fortunes in war last forever.
>
> > Though I die on the desolate battlefield of Okinawa,
> > I will continue to protect the great spirit of Japan.

We had been preparing to deploy the Naval Base Force in the Kiyan Peninsula fortifications, so it came as a great shock to learn that Admiral Ota was determined to defend his old Oroku territory to the end. Strategically the defense of the Oroku Peninsula was worth the expenditure of many lives, so it was understandable that the navy would want to fight to the death. We felt, however, that when the time came, our army and naval forces should perish together. I could not bear to think of the navy being crushed in isolation, while we stood by as mere spectators.

General Ushijima replied:

> I must express my heartfelt gratitude, Admiral Ota, for the honorable perfor-
> mance of your duty. The naval forces under your command and my army troops
> have fought together audaciously and contributed greatly to the Okinawa cam-
> paign. We truly admire the completion of your naval mission and your fight to
> the death to defend Oroku Peninsula. I cannot bear, however, to see your forces
> perish alone. It is still possible for you to withdraw. I hope that our forces may
> be joined so that we may share the moment of death.

Admiral Ota, however, was firmly determined to remain at Oroku.
When he showed no intention of withdrawing, Ushijima sent a personal letter
urging him to retreat. For all our efforts, he never changed his mind.[1] At the
start of the Oroku action we believed the situation to be hopeless and felt
that Ota's forces might be crushed at a single blow. They fought remarkably
well at Kanegusuku, Tomigusuku, and in the Oroku hills, however, and daily
reports to our headquarters cave made it seem that a counteroffensive might
succeed. But it was impossible for our limited naval troop strength to match
their fearsome opponents. The enemy was closing in.

Late on Monday evening, June 11, came a message from Admiral Ota:
"The enemy has begun an all-out assault on our headquarters. This is our
last chance to contact you. 2330, June 11." What a tragedy! Faces came to
mind of Admiral Ota, Captains Tanamachi, Haneda, and Maekawa, and the
many good times we had shared together.

The previous Tuesday, June 5, Lieutenant Nakao, a naval liaison officer,
had started for Mabuni headquarters with a paymaster to discuss how the
Naval Base Force might withdraw to Kiyan Peninsula. It was so dark they
did not find our cave but reached instead the entrance to the medical corps
cave, where they were seriously wounded by enemy mortar shells. They were
treated immediately, but the paymaster died. Nakao survived but was unable
to move. When Major Nishino heard the news, he rushed out of our cave
through a heavy bombardment to see Nakao. They had become friends when
Nishino was on temporary duty with the Naval Base Force. In fact, later,
when Nishino heard of the naval capitulation, he wanted to rush to Oroku

---

[1]Here we see another example of the consensus system disastrously at work. Once an
original operations plan was abandoned—or needed revision—Japanese military commanders
generally resorted to varying degrees of persuasion, rather than giving subordinates a direct
order. Particularly in cases of army-navy joint action, persuasion rarely worked. As in Okinawa,
each service preferred to die defending its own right of way, so to speak.

with weapons, but General Cho and I stopped him from thus wasting his life.

Another friend Nishino had met at Oroku was Lieutenant Commander: Miike of the 5th Sea Raiding Squadron. Early in May he had escaped by canoe from Kerama Island after its capture by the enemy. He made it to Oroku. There he was wounded and hospitalized in late May and shared the fate of the Naval Base Force.

23

The Last
Battle

While we were trying desperately to regain the lost territory of the 44th Mixed Brigade, one of the strongest positions of the 24th Division started to crack. Through skillful artillery tactics and fearless suicide attacks, the division had inflicted great damage on the enemy day after day. By June 13 it seemed that our army, with the 24th Division as its nucleus, was overwhelming the enemy assault. Back in May, during the Shuri battle, the 62nd Division, as the center of our army, had fought splendidly from its formidable fortifications. Now the 24th Division, at Kiyan, had become the army's main strength, but it was declining. (See map on page 130.)

Despite the strenuous efforts of our headquarters and the 24th Division, the 24th's right flank at Yaezu was starting to collapse. Iizuka's battalion was stalled, and the recapture of Yaezu hill was now impossible. To back up the 24th we sent Hara's 13th Independent Infantry Battalion, but it collapsed when Colonel Hara was killed in action. By mid-June only a few Mixed Brigade soldiers remained fighting in the losing Yoza-Nozaka battle. We received a last message from Major General Suzuki, the brigade commander:

> Flowers dying gracefully on Hill 109,
> Will bloom again amid the Kudan trees.[1]

In the last ten days we had thrown a force six-thousand-strong into the Mixed Brigade front line. Most of our soldiers had only small arms and

---

[1]Kudan is the section of Tokyo where the Yasukuni Shrine is located. This Shinto institution was the traditional spiritual resting place of Japan's military men, whose souls were said to hover over the precincts. It continues to be venerated.

129

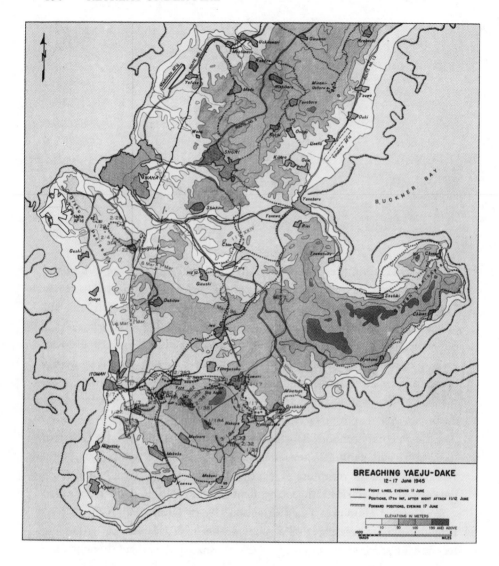

BREACHING YAEJU-DAKE
12-17 June 1945

bamboo spears against millions of shells from the enemy's formidable fleet, planes, and tanks. They never had a chance. All vanished like the morning dew. It was a bitter pill to swallow.

On Friday evening, June 15, I had an unexpected visit from Major Kyoso of the Mixed Brigade. This once vigorous and healthy man now looked completely drained. Lines of sorrow and suffering showed through his dirt-laden face. He reported the battle situation and then, lowering his voice, continued furtively, "The brigade is finished. Our right flank has collapsed. We can fight no more. I regret to report that unit commanders are crying aloud as they watch their men dying in vain. Whatever we do we cannot stop the enemy. Imperial Headquarters never gave us adequate support. Our commanding officers are asking if Japan will follow the fate of Okinawa. Why? Is there no alternative?"

Kyoso used the word "alternative," an ambiguous word, but I understood clearly and felt miserable. He was saying that we should not die for nothing. He changed the subject, "In March I urged Lieutenant Moriwaki to leave infantry school and come here with me to teach antitank strategy. I cannot let him die here. I want him to return home safely. Will you please help me, Colonel?" There were tears in his eyes. I remembered when Major Jin was about to leave Shuri for Japan, how Moriwaki had pleaded with him to teach him to fly, so he, too, could escape.

I had often asked Kyoso to do unreasonable things, and he always cooperated, so I approved his request, as did General Ushijima. Kyoso was pleased at our granting his wish. His eyes sparkled with tears of joy. Happily he ate some canned pineapple and drank a bit of *sake.* I noticed that he wore no helmet and asked why. "I am prepared to die at any moment," he replied, "and no longer need it." He disappeared in the pre-dawn darkness.

Because our brigade was on the verge of defeat at the front line, headquarters sent reinforcements. On June 15 Lieutenant General Fujioka, 62nd Division's commander, took command of the Mixed Brigade and attached units to stop the enemy offensive at Yaezu hill, which had been the central key position of the Mixed Brigade. Fujioka deployed the 24th Division's main strength along the Yoza-Maedera-Mabuni hills. He ordered Lieutenant General Nakajima,[2] of the 63rd Brigade, to take charge of the Mixed Brigade and maintain its key positions.

Fujioka's action was not at all responsive. We wanted his division to assist the Mixed Brigade in battle, not take a defensive position. The 62nd Division was too cautious about moving to the front line. It was strange that Fujioka stayed next to 32nd Army headquarters while his command post was in Yamagusuku, far distant from Mabuni. The 32nd Army order first reached Yamagusuku through a broken transmission system and then reached Lieutenant General Nakajima of the 63rd Brigade, who remained next to our headquarters. That command channel was absurd. Therefore General Ush-

---

[2]Like some other officers, Nakajima had been promoted during the battle, in his case to Lieutenant General.

ijima put the 24th Division in charge of Yamagusuku so that the 62nd Division could move to Mabuni.

We were well aware of the situation at 62nd Division headquarters. Among the staff officers, Kusunose had been killed in action, and although Kitajima's wounds were healed, he still walked with a limp. The division chief of staff suffered so from neuralgia that, since the retreat from Shuri, he could get about only on a stretcher. It was rumored that the division was in the hands of two young officers. The 62nd Division was exhausted, but then so was our entire army.

Division headquarters at Mabuni was uncomfortable, and we put up with many inconveniences. I felt especially sorry for General Fujioka. He had first wanted his final resting place to be at Shuri, then at Yamagusuku, and now it would be Mabuni. We should not be in a hurry to die but should make the most of our life to the very end.

Despite all our efforts to back up the eastern Yaezu front, the 62nd Division was now drained of its strength. Most of its men had been killed in action. We finally deserted Yaezu and withdrew to front lines around Yoza, where General Fujioka had earlier chosen to deploy his forces. The 62nd Division command post was moved to Mabuni on Monday evening, June 18.

The enemy's 7th Division approached Yaezu from the east, and from the north they penetrated the high ground between Yaezu and Yoza. The 89th Regiment, the 24th Reconnaissance Regiment, and the 24th Engineer Regiments—all from the 24th Division—were sandwiched between the enemy from the north and southeast. They fought to the last man, and the enemy captured the Yoza hilltop on June 17.

When the 24th Division's right flank was on the point of collapse, the 32nd Regiment was in the center and the 22nd Regiment was on the left flank. The battle intensified on June 12. By June 15 the enemy marines charged, and the battlefield was total chaos. For a couple of days after that, Kunishi Ridge changed hands repeatedly, with the battle situation in doubt. We knew, however, that the enemy was moving along the coast making continuous small-scale attacks. A radio transmission reached us that the 22nd Regiment command post southeast of Maezato had been attacked with hand grenades and satchel charges. Colonel Yoshida's troops were wiped out. This simple message conveyed all the agony and pain of his soldiers and stunned the high command. The situation was hopeless.

I had first met Colonel Yoshida in Thailand on December 8, 1941, at the start of the Greater East Asia War. He came to Bangkok, commanding a detachment of the Guards Division, to engage the Thai army. I was assistant military attaché in the embassy at that time, with additional duty on the operations staff of the 15th Army. My task was to hold off any confrontation between our Guards Division and Thai troops defending their capital, while we completed diplomatic negotiations with Thailand. Mild-mannered veteran that he was, Yoshida restrained his younger officers so that everything went successfully. Strange chance had brought us together again to fight in Okinawa, and now he was dead. What a shame.

On Monday, June 18, enemy tanks attacked the Mixed Brigade command post and overran a low-lying hill some fifteen hundred meters east of Mabuni to engage the 12th Independent Infantry Battalion.

In the 24th Division area, enemy marines broke through the lines of the 89th Regiment and appeared at Makabe village, northeast of the 24th Division command post. We heard a radio message that enemy tanks had penetrated deep into our defense zone and were rolling into Komesu village. From what we had already experienced, this news came as no great surprise. It meant that the collapse of our entire army was imminent.

It was only a matter of days until our war would be over. Explosive blasts of machine guns outside reminded me of the final days at Shuri. Our telephone lines were out and radio messages reached us only intermittently. We had to send orders by messenger. Reports reaching the dark corners of our cave gave the names of commanders killed and battalions annihilated. It was grim and disheartening, and my blood curdled at each such message.

We had done everything possible. Now there was not a single soldier left. Our Kiyan Ridge situation was fragile beyond imagination. When our headquarters had retreated to Mabuni, Colonel Umezu had me issue the commanding general's special instructions to raise army morale. Police Chief Arai said to me, "Army morale was high at the Shuri battle, but since the retreat it has plummeted." Naturally, morale is low at the end of a battle, but we had never experienced anything like this. The odds were tremendously against us at Kiyan Ridge, but we did our best.

When he saw that both flanks of our army had collapsed simultaneously, General Cho said, almost to himself, "So much for that. I should be satisfied." At last relieved of his heavy responsibility, he seemed happier that his mission was accomplished.

The battlefield was in such complete chaos that it was impossible to send out final orders, but General Ushijima wanted them drafted for issue to each unit. Nagano cradled in his arms, almost lovingly, the two large volumes of orders issued since the battle had begun. Trembling with anxiety, he said to me, "As senior staff officer, don't you wish to draft this final order yourself?" I replied, "You have drafted so many orders. This should really be your job. Please do it for me."

Acknowledging that this momentous task was something that he could and should perform, he wrote this draft for the commanding general:

> My Beloved Soldiers:
>
> You have all fought courageously for nearly three months. You have discharged your duty. Your bravery and loyalty brighten the future.
>
> The battlefield is now in such chaos that all communications have ceased. It is impossible for me to command you. Every man in these fortifications will follow his superior officer's order and fight to the end for the sake of the motherland.
>
> This is my final order.
> Farewell.

After reading this, General Cho dipped his writing brush in red ink and added:

> Do not suffer the shame of being taken prisoner. You will live for eternity.

Silently, as always, General Ushijima added his signature. With the issuance of that final order, I felt a sudden bliss at being free of all worldly burdens.

The landing beach on Okinawa, after the U.S. naval bombardment. Here one can see amphibian tanks advancing inland, as landing parties continue to head toward the beach. Various landing ships have been unloaded on the shore. (Mainichi Newspapers)

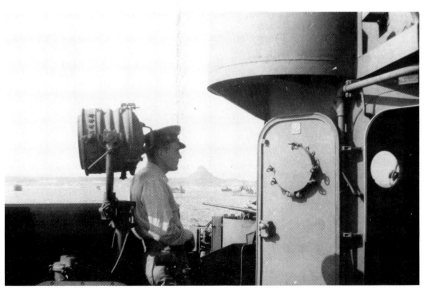

Looking out over Nakagusuku Bay with Sugar Loaf Hill in the background. (Courtesy of Charles Odam)

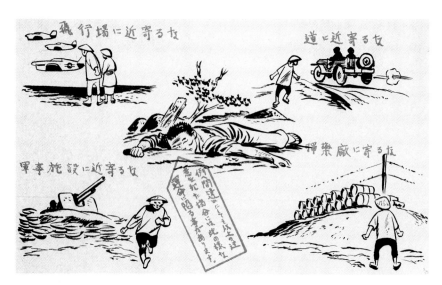

Propaganda leaflet titled "Notice to Refugee Civilians" dropped by U.S. aircraft on Okinawa in the wake of the 10th Army landing. The captions, reading clockwise from the top left, are "Keep away from aircraft!" "Keep away from the roads," "Don't go near ammunition dumps!" and "Keep away from military positions." The sign in the middle, below the picture of a wounded Okinawan, reads, "Even if, by accident, you overlook any of the warnings set forth above, you may meet with a sad fate."

The marines in Shuri. Here a U.S. Marine Corps patrol is shown cautiously walking through the ruins of Shuri city, shortly after the Japanese main defense line there was breached. (Mainichi Newspapers)

Col. Hiromichi Yahara.

Col. Yahara with his wife
and two children.

Lt. Gen. Mitsuru Ushijima, commander of Japan's 32nd Army.

Lt. Gen. Isamu Cho, chief of staff of the Japanese 32nd Army, shown here as a colonel in the late 1930s, while he was on the staff of the Kwantung Army. (Mainichi Newspapers)

White flag at last: Survivors of a Japanese unit holding the white flag, peacefully surrendering after the breakdown of resistance on Okinawa in the latter part of June. (Mainichi Newspapers)

Lieutenants (jg) Kenneth Lamott and Frank Gibney (right) in Tokyo, six months after the Okinawa campaign ended, where they had been assigned to do further intelligence work after the war's end.

Children of war. These two small children were found, fortunately unscathed, in a tomb in Shuri city on the border of the Shuri defense line on April 23rd—the tomb was just fifty meters from the front line. (Mainichi Newspapers)

Japanese Navy personnel surrender. They were among the few survivors of the navy landing forces' last stand on the Orote Peninsula, South of Naha, in mid-June. (The boy with hands up is an Okinawan "youth corps" draftee.) (Mainichi Newspapers)

Japanese prisoners of war photographed with U.S. Army guard. These Japanese troops were among those taken prisoner in June after resistance had crumbled. (Mainichi Newspapers)

More Japanese prisoners: Here a few wounded Japanese prisoners, surrendering, are helped out of their cave by U.S. soldiers (June 24). (Mainichi Newspapers)

24

Cave Fantasies

Enemy artillery, naval, and air attacks increased daily against the heights of Mabuni. The gunboats below seemed to think that ordinary bombardments were not adequate. They used mortars to blast the limestone cliffs on the ocean side of Mabuni. Day and night the American fleet off Minatoga and Itoman struck our forces. When the big bombs and shells exploded on the Mabuni cliff, our entire cave shook as in a great earthquake. The cave was not as impregnable as our Shuri headquarters, but the hill terrain was so solid that small bombs bounced back like beans on a hot skillet.

To make matters worse, the enemy dropped drums of gasoline [napalm] from the air for incendiary attacks. The fuel seeped through cave openings, caught fire, and caused many casualties from burns and smoke inhalation.

When we first reached Mabuni, the area had received little war damage. There were only a few large ground craters where random bombs had fallen. The fields had still glistened with beautiful shades of green. Two weeks of fierce battle changed the scenery completely. Hills were flattened and re-shaped by tanks and bombardments. It was now a wasteland, the darkened terrain exposing a gateway to hell.

Early one morning I left the cave and saw dark clouds rolling turbulently across the sky, with gun smoke creeping across the land. For a moment the roar of the guns ceased. I was overwhelmed by the ghostly sight of the battlefield that had sucked the blood from thousands of soldiers. As a wise old man once said, "Even the demons of the world would mourn at this sight." The hilltop was covered with corpses.

Messenger Sunano said to me, "Many of our soldiers lie dead near the headquarters cave. That is so bad for morale. Why don't we dispose of them

135

quickly?" I was touched. But I was unable to answer or even look him in the eyes.

American propaganda was transmitted from small craft offshore. There were daily broadcasts in fluent Japanese: "Okinawan civilians. We will guarantee your lives. We will give you food and medicine. Please move toward Minatoga before it is too late." Alternatively: "Japanese soldiers. You fought well and proudly for the cause of Japan, but now the issue of victory or defeat has been decided. To continue the battle is meaningless. We will guarantee your lives. Please come down to the beach and swim out to us."

Thus the enemy struck not only with broadcasts and shells, but also with countless propaganda leaflets dropped from the sky. None of it showed the viciousness so typical of propaganda. They said candidly that Japan's defeat was inevitable. They spoke of Japan's leaders and their indifference to the lives of subordinates. I was concerned that the leaflets might affect our soldiers in the caves and further lower their morale, but no one seemed bothered by that. Most of them simply said, "Americans always talk nonsense." I received reports, however, that some people were swimming out to the enemy boats. There were no indications whether they were soldiers or civilians.

On Sunday, June 17, a message from General Simon Buckner, the enemy commander, to General Ushijima came to our headquarters cave:

> The forces under your command have fought bravely and well. Your infantry tactics have merited the respect of your opponents in the battle for Okinawa.
>
> Like myself you are an infantry general, long schooled and experienced in infantry warfare. You must surely realize the pitiful plight of your defense forces. You know that no reinforcements can reach you. I believe, therefore, that you understand as clearly as I, that the destruction of all Japanese resistance on the island is merely a matter of days. It will entail the necessity of my destroying the vast majority of your remaining troops.

General Buckner's proposal for us to surrender was, of course, an affront to Japanese tradition. General Ushijima's only reaction was to smile broadly and say, "The enemy has made me an expert on infantry warfare."

Lying on my bed in the dark room, I thought about the history of military surrenders. In modern warfare in the West, defeated commanders usually surrendered gracefully to the victors. This was generally true of white-race societies—from Napoleonic times, the Franco-Prussian War, the American Revolution and Civil War, down to World Wars I and II. Top commanders would generally be held responsible for defeats. And where commanders were killed, units below them were generally allowed to surrender on their own. To my limited recollection, there existed no cases of Western armies fighting to the death. When an army's value as a fighting force was obviously spent, they would take the course of surrendering.

In Japan, on the other hand, it was not uncommon for a losing commander and his subordinates to commit suicide.

In Japan, from the thirteenth century until the Meiji Restoration of the mid-nineteenth century, there are many examples where every soldier was killed in defense of the castle. In some cases only the lord of the castle committed suicide, while the soldiers (*samurai*) lived. In the early years of Meiji, Tokugawa supporters readily surrendered to the new Imperial Army. Since the Meiji Restoration, through the Sino-Japanese War, the Russo-Japanese War, and the China Incident of 1931, Japan had never lost a war. We also had never waged a war in which large forces were isolated from mainland support. Thus, not to be taken prisoner became a fixed principle—part of our military education.

Since the middle of the Greater East Asia War, most Japanese garrisons in the Pacific islands adhered to this supreme Japanese principle: "Never surrender to the enemy." Officers and men usually committed suicide, as a last resort to avoid the ultimate "shame" of capture. Our 32nd Army was now faced with this situation. Must one hundred thousand soldiers die because of tradition? From this point on it was but a battle to kill the remaining Japanese soldiers for nothing. We could cause the enemy little damage; they could walk freely on the field of battle. The war of attrition was over, and we would simply be asking the enemy to use his formidable power to kill us all.

Indeed, it is a high ideal to fight to the end to maintain national morale. But were our leaders worth the sacrifice of an entire people? With the end of the war in sight, they shout at us: "Millions of people must die for our nation." Why? Are they really aware of the entire war situation? It was foolish to force everyone to die, simply because Japan had never before lost a war.

The Japanese believed that, as in every other war, they would win this one, even at the cost of millions of lives. In one sense Japan's leaders continued the war because they were afraid of losing their status and power. Why did they not surrender with dignity when they had no prospect of winning? Why did they not follow the European practice of surrender? Our fate was at an end.

General Cho ordered us to write up our opinions about the battle, for the sake of Japan's future. He would send his own candid comment on the battle to Imperial General Headquarters. From the beginning he had refrained from complaining and did his very best to be loyal.

The young staff officers urged me to write my opinion of the situation, but I could not bring myself to do it. It was natural for us to be concerned about our nation's future. Japan might be able to prolong the conflict for a year or so by a war of attrition in the home islands, as at Okinawa. But, just as in Okinawa, this would also have meant the total destruction of Japan. Japanese leaders should rid themselves of their ridiculous pride that Japan had never been defeated. The decision to surrender should have been made as quickly as possible, at least before Okinawa was lost.

General Cho said, half-jokingly, "I have many followers in mainland Japan, and I have powerful friends in the Imperial Household. Should I mobilize them all to achieve peace?"

25

Final Days
at Mabuni

One day a soft drink bottle containing a letter drifted ashore at Mabuni. The letter, written in mid-May by a Japanese officer, detailed the situation on the Kachin Peninsula. The enemy had them under heavy siege, and he was just awaiting death. If anyone should find the bottle, he hoped that it would be sent to Imperial General Headquarters. From the Kachin Peninsula, where it was tossed into Nakagusuku Bay, this bottle had floated more than forty kilometers. After nearly a month it arrived at Mabuni, where the writer's commanding general was located. Was this fate or a miracle?

About that same time, our intelligence officer asked Imperial Headquarters to send planes to Okinawa to help us fight the brutal enemy. Our aircraft flew over Kiyan Point and dropped a quantity of ammunition, but what we needed most were antitank satchel charges and mortar shells. Imperial Headquarters did its best, but we received very little of what was needed. The fact that headquarters at least sent planes gave us hope—tremendous hope.

Staff Officer Kyoso had requested permission to send Lieutenant Moriwaki to mainland Japan. Before leaving, Moriwaki reported to headquarters, his face flushed with excitement. He was advised on how to break through enemy lines. There were only two possibilities: the sea route that Major Jin had taken, or by land. Since we had no boats or fishermen to take him by water, he would have to go overland. This seemed impossible because the enemy occupied the land completely, and he would have to pass thousands of enemy soldiers. Nevertheless he was optimistic at having at least a chance to escape. He left in high spirits. We learned later that he found a boat but got no farther than Komesu. We felt that he had failed and pitied him. After the war, however, I learned that he had made it home.

139

When it became obvious that the end was approaching for our army, General Cho also gave permission for Kyoso to head for mainland Japan and was hopeful that he could make it. We never heard anything more of Kyoso.

On Tuesday evening, June 19, I heard a rumor that Major General Shigeru Suzuki, commander of the 44th Independent Mixed Brigade, had given up the idea of an all-out suicide attack at Hill 105 and retreated to a cave in a hill near Mabuni. A few days earlier Suzuki had sent letters to General Cho and me. Mine read: "I command all surviving soldiers to penetrate the enemy lines and advance to the Kunigami area in the north. We will join forces there, and continue to fight as long as possible."

I thought this plan absurd but offered him the following encouragement: "While you are under the command of General Ushijima, it is absolutely wrong to shift your field position. After his death, however, you are permitted to do what you wish."

General Cho showed me his letter from General Suzuki, which was much the same as mine. Cho must have had conflicting thoughts, but he never told me his reply. Nor did I reveal mine.

Intelligence Officer Yakumaru set up a plan for us to follow after the collapse of Japanese military resistance. Every officer would penetrate enemy-held areas, work with our small remaining forces, and engage in guerilla warfare. There was little chance of penetrating enemy lines successfully, but every officer must make the effort. One out of three would survive, and the survivors would continue guerrilla war until death. He whispered to me, "You are an exception, you don't have to die." All staff officers silently agreed to his plan. I did not feel like disagreeing. General Ushijima approved the idea.

On Monday morning, June 18, Staff Officers Kimura and Yakumaru left Mabuni. Kimura was to engage in guerrilla warfare in the southern part of Okinawa, Yakumaru in the northern area. Two other staff officers—Miyake and Nagano—were to return to the homeland, report the Okinawa situation, and continue to serve the nation. I received a similar order. General Cho wrote them out individually on paper the following day and gave one to each of us.

To celebrate the sortie of the staff officers, a final banquet was held that evening, attended by General Ushijima, General Cho, myself, Staff Officers Kimura, Yakumaru, Yoshino, and Mazaki. Majors Matsubara and Nishino, who were attached to the staff, were included with a few others for a total of thirteen. We dined in the staff officers' room, which was big enough for all of us. Half of us had to stoop inside the room because of the stalactites; the others stood in the passageway. Two candles dimly lit the room. We were served fish, canned pineapple, an Imperial gift of one bottle of *sake,* and *awamori* (Okinawan rice brandy).

General Ushijima and General Cho each gave a short and simple speech, nothing impressive. Strong words would have moved us all to tears. Cho even tried to provide levity for the occasion. I ate very little because I had been ill for some time, and my appetite had dwindled. Seeing this, General Ushijima shaved a piece of dried fish and offered it to me, saying that it was tasty.

At the height of the banquet, General Cho suddenly stood up, faced to the east, and clapped his hands three times. This ended the festivities.

The staff officers prepared to set out the next evening, Tuesday, June 19. Each was to act on his own initiative, and each officer was assigned two attendants. These were sixteen- or seventeen-year-old students from the Blood and Iron for the Emperor service units. The officers planned to disguise themselves as civilians, some in Okinawan garb, others in short pants. They all looked and felt awkward out of uniform. To deceive the enemy, they assumed false names and occupations. Miyake posed as a *kendo* (Japanese fencing) instructor; Nagano as a truck driver. Yakumaru chose not to use a disguise, saying if he got caught he would die. Each man carried a small bag of white rice, two dried fish, a two-day supply of dried bread, canned fish, salt, and a first-aid kit.

After considering the situation in enemy-held territory, they started for Gùshichan. Further plans as to whether they would head for Chinen or Yaezu would be decided by circumstances. The coastal road led to Gùshichan, but the problem was how to reach the road. The path down the cliff went past the Spring of Death, which enemy patrol boats constantly watched. They could shower it with gunfire. Another escape route ran along the north slope of Mabuni toward the east for about one kilometer, until a hill path led to the ocean. This was the better way to reach the coast, where the enemy was more likely off-guard. Either route was risky, however. This was all enemy-held territory, and we would be exposed to danger.

On Tuesday evening heavy gloom hung over the staff officers' quarters. There was little talking, and then only in low, hushed tones. As soon as the staff officers had reported to Generals Ushijima and Cho, they changed clothes and prepared to leave. I was determined to stay and witness the suicide of the generals, then, if I still lived, to leave the cave on my mission. The young officers, anxious about leaving the generals behind, asked that I please take good care of them. I wished them all good luck and urged them, whatever happened, to do their best.

It was now time to go on their mission, but they still sat on the beds, as stationary as boulders. That evening the enemy guns thundered more violently than ever, and shells struck Mabuni hill from all directions. The cave walls trembled with every hit. The candles were flickering their last flame. Nagano, youngest of all, as if to shake off fear, shouted, "I'll take the lead! Long live the Emperor!" and marched out of the cave. Miyake, Yakumaru, and Kimura followed. In a matter of moments they were gone.

The cave was suddenly as silent and empty as it had been thousands of years ago. I was alone, and my heart felt frozen. Already I missed the familiar voices and footsteps. Unable to stand the silence, I called the noncoms—formerly prohibited from this room—and told them to use the empty beds. I wrapped myself in a blanket and went to sleep.

Postwar investigation showed that Miyake was killed at the eastern foot of Yaezu hill. Kimura was killed west of Yonabaru. Nothing is known about the fate of Yakumaru and the others.

At midnight on June 19, Lieutenant Colonel Ohki, the shipping chief who was assigned to the Mixed Brigade, reported that he and his remaining soldiers were at the northwestern edge of Mabuni village. At the same time, several Artillery Group commanders, who were supposed to remain in their fortifications, rushed into the headquarters cave. I showed them the army order and told them to do their best.

At dawn on June 20 the guns were momentarily silent. I saw hundreds of civilians in small groups heading from Mabuni toward Minatogawa. Everything looked so tranquil that it did not seem like a battlefield, but this peaceful scene would not last. That day there were many firefights. Soon more than twenty enemy tanks made their lumbering way up Mabuni hill. They fired shells onto the hilltop, and this was followed by hand-to-hand combat. Enemy tanks also swarmed into the villages of Maedera, Komesu, and Odo. There was such complete confusion that I could no longer distinguish enemy forces from our own. The enemy tanks withdrew from Mabuni in the evening and moved east.

Sunano came to see me just after sunset. I admired his wonderful spirit, bringing good cheer even in trying times. Despite the general gloom of our final days, he looked around and asked, "What happened to everybody?" I told him my story and added that General Cho wanted to speak with him. He returned shortly and showed me General Ushijima's order to Lieutenant General Kōjo Wada, the 23rd Artillery Group commander. It read:

> You will send Commander Sunano and two other officers to mainland Japan to report the local battle situation, after which they will join in the final decisive battle for Japan.

Sunano asked if General Ushijima would order our final destiny or leave the matter up to us. I told him we would follow the army's final order, but after the general's death, each command post would be free to decide. He laughed heartily, saying, "Considering the terrain of Mabuni hill, enemy tanks can approach only from the east, where our artillery command is located. Thus we will be the first victims."

I said to Sunano, "After the old men commit *hara-kiri* in the cave, we shouldn't bury them here where the enemy can find their corpses. Don't you think it better that they die on top of the hill? We can drop their bodies into the East China Sea."

"I don't think much of the idea," replied Sunano, "but there is no alternative."

I then explained the all-out suicide attack plan in which our soldiers would charge down the hill to Mabuni. The generals would witness this scene just before they died peacefully on the hilltop. I was glad to hear Sunano add, "Our artillery can't contribute much to such a finale, but somehow we should move some guns to Odo village. From there they can contribute to the scene, by firing guns like fireworks. It will be spectacular." I was heartened to hear his plan.

We went on to discuss Japan's future, about which we were deeply concerned. It was clear that Japan would inevitably fall after Okinawa. Our leaders had chosen this path to destruction. They did not care that hundreds of thousands of soldiers would die. They seemed to care only about preservation of their own status, prestige, and honor. We talked from our hearts of many things. As he left the cave, Sunano said flamboyantly, "I may never see you again, but should we meet again we will have another good conversation."

I had just dozed off when Commander Ono, the chief code clerk, ran into my room shouting, "A telegram of commendation has come from Imperial Headquarters." Beaming with pleasure he handed it to me. I, too, was elated.

The Okinawa operation had been doomed from the start, but I knew that we had far surpassed Imperial Headquarters' expectations. I had read many such messages since the start of the China Incident. I really hated them. They always contained the same flowery praises and hollow compliments. Nevertheless, every word, phrase, and sentence of this message was fresh and meaningful, consoling and impressive. I hurried to General Cho's quarters with the telegram. Moving through the narrow passageways, I saw desperate and exhausted soldiers huddling miserably together. Still their faces lit up as I passed, saying, "We've got a message from Imperial Headquarters."

General Cho was lying on his bed in the dark when I reported. He stood up, lit a candle, and had me read the message. General Ushijima sat up in bed and said, "I'm listening." So also were the adjutants, guards, young women, and everyone else in the vicinity, listening closely as I read:

> Under command of Lieutenant General Mitsuru Ushijima, you have fought courageously for three months against a formidable enemy, ever since his landing on Okinawa. You have destroyed the enemy in every battlefield, causing great damage. You have truly displayed the greatness of the Imperial Army. In addition you have restrained the enemy's overwhelming naval power. You have also contributed greatly to our air raids against enemy fleets.

Slowly reading the message, I did my best to hold back my emotions. When I had finished, the two generals closed their eyes in silence. I knew they were content.

Standing at Cho's bedside, I took a message form, borrowed a pencil, and drafted this reply:

> Against the overwhelmingly powerful enemy, with our survivors at hand, as we are about to make an all-out suicide attack, we received the commendation letter bestowed by your excellency. Nothing can surpass this glory. We are supremely moved. The soldiers who have died shedding their blood on these islands of Okinawa can now rest in peace forever. The remaining soldiers at this final stand are encouraged to fight to the death. With all our strength we will fight bravely so that we will come up to your expectations. We are very grateful.

General Cho, still lying on his bed, had me reread the message twice, then asked me to add after "bestowed" a paragraph saying that we would always be loyal subjects of the Emperor; and after "fight bravely," to add, "and respect and revere the Imperial wishes." I had Warrant Officer Chiba make copies of the letter for delivery by liaison officers to all units, no matter what the risk.

Thursday, June 21, was a total disaster. Enemy tanks swarmed into Mabuni at daybreak and advanced northwest to attack our forces in Odo from the rear. Strangely enough, a group of several dozen infantrymen followed closely after the tanks and penetrated into Mabuni, where they seemed to be digging in. None of us believed the reconnaissance report. It was unthinkable. We sent other scouts to verify the report, and it appeared to be true. After the war I checked and learned that they did not fortify the area, but they did bury dead Japanese and also cared for the wounded.

Lieutenant Colonel Katsuno was in charge of our headquarters cave defense. He was planning to send Lieutenant Matsui with a platoon to retake Mabuni village. Matsui, a graduate of the elite Hitotsubashi College in Tokyo, was always a source of entertainment in the cave. He was determined to deal harshly with any Japanese who worked with the enemy. Leading his platoon, he retook Mabuni without firing a bullet, because the enemy had withdrawn from the village. On learning this, and fearing that they might come to attack our headquarters, I had the cave entrance facing Mabuni sealed off. In the cave were many rocks blasted loose during construction. I mobilized all available soldiers to seal the entrance with these rocks, and the work was quickly completed.

After sunset, Sato, the paymaster general of the army, and his chief accountant, Major Masai, came up from their cave at the bottom of the cliff to visit our headquarters. They took over empty beds in the staff officers' section and made themselves comfortable. Sato, a distinguished gentleman with white hair and mustache, had been a classmate of General Cho. They often played chess and had shared many friendly conversations. When I told him that his dear friend and General Ushijima were going to commit suicide, he was overwhelmed. He sat silently for some time. I admired the stolid acceptance of his friend's death. Then he spoke in a quiet but determined way, "It is my destiny to accompany him." Trying to change his mind, I said, "The enemy will not kill an old man like you. You could disguise yourself as a civilian and escape to the north."

He smiled and replied, "I had a hell of a time just now climbing this cliff. Old men like me don't want much anymore. The best thing I can do is to die here." Then he gave me his bag of rice, salted fish, and canned food. He also gave me all the money he had, saying that it would help me get through the enemy lines. He appeared totally indifferent to death. He talked about his family, his son in school, and his three happily married daughters. He was content and had no regrets.

That same evening we received a farewell telegram from General Korechika Anami, Imperial Army chief staff, and General Yoshijiro Umezu, the minister of war. It read:

> For three months 32nd Army has fought bravely under General Ushijima, a commander with great nobility of character. They killed the enemy commander, General Simon Buckner, and delivered deadly blows against his eight divisions of troops.
>
> Your troops struggled hard, preparing superbly for decisive battle. As the enemy strength increased, your troops—officers and men—responded with vows to destroy that strength.

Last night the letter of commendation; tonight the telegram. Everyone in the cave was overjoyed.

The death of General Buckner, the enemy commanding general, was the greatest news of the entire operation. We had managed to kill the enemy leader before our own commanding general committed ceremonial suicide. It seemed as if our forces had actually won a victory. General Cho was elated, but General Ushijima was not pleased. He looked grim, as if mourning Buckner's death. Ushijima never spoke ill of others. I had always felt he was a great man, and now I admired him more than ever.

At dawn on Friday, June 22, a messenger from the 24th Division came to report that his headquarters was under heavy enemy attack from the north, east, and west. Nearby friendly guns were still active, however, so they could hold out for a while. The messenger also carried a letter for me from Staff Officer Sugimori. It was scribbled in large characters on a scrap of paper:

> The end is near. I must express my gratitude for all your good work and sound advice. I will see you at Yasukuni Shrine.

He had been a student of mine at the Military Academy. I responded with a brief note telling of conditions at headquarters and my fondness for him. I wished him unlimited good luck, sent parting words, and enclosed a short poem:

> Kiyan guns may soon be silent,
> Only the dreams of lost warriors remain.

As soon as it was dark, the messenger returned to his headquarters and the waiting jaws of death. I do not know which destination he reached. One by one our remaining soldiers left the cave. Nishino's mission was to penetrate enemy airfields, collect data on enemy air strength, and report to Imperial General Headquarters. Captain Matsunaga and his suicide squad survivors were to break through enemy lines, invade the airfields at Yomitan and Kadena, and destroy the aircraft there. On departing, he looked in my eyes without saying a word. I shared his thoughts. With five of his intelligence officers, Captain Wasai set out to wage guerrilla warfare. He said simply, "I'll do my best." The two paymaster majors, Masai and Kojima, left to return home and report on the Okinawa situation.

For several days General Cho kept saying, "We must have thousands of young soldiers still alive here, Yahara. I wish we could send them all home."

As the soldiers left on their missions, the cave became even lonelier. I said to Lieutenant Ikeda, "Everyone is leaving. What are you going to do?" He replied firmly, "I'll stay here until the last moment."

On my way to see General Ushijima, one young officer shouted, "Make way for Colonel Yahara!" He need not have shouted, for everyone was gone.

26

The End of 32nd Army

At dawn on June 22, after three hours of violent machine-gun fire, Mabuni village was silent. That meant the end of Lieutenant Matsui and his platoon. I heard nearby tanks rumbling over the savaged earth. They bombarded our headquarters cave, which was empty and still as we waited to die. Colonel Sato visited General Cho, and Lieutenant Akinaga came to chat with me. Just before noon there was a tremendous explosion at the staff headquarters entrance. Smoke and dust blew inside and soldiers came rushing back to me. It was a phosphorous bomb, and we all put on gas masks. The entrance was still open, and I heard footsteps and arrogant laughter. The enemy was approaching the entrance, and I shouted to Lieutenant Akinaga, "Hey, it's okay here! Defend the central shaft!" He ran to the shaft.

Katsuyama brought a memorandum I had left behind and, gasping for air, reported, "The hill is completely occupied by the enemy. They exploded a satchel charge at the main shaft, and there are many casualties around General Cho's quarters."

Akinaga dashed off to the main shaft. Ten minutes passed, and I thought he had been killed. If the enemy could pass through the shaft, they would get Generals Ushijima and Cho first. The rooms of the staff officers and adjutants would be cut off, and we would have no escape.

I approached the shaft cautiously, with flashlight in hand. Smoke and dust filled the air. There was no one to talk to—they were all dead. The smell of blood was everywhere. I shone the light at the base of the shaft, revealing a pile of ten soldiers. Expecting more assaults through the shaft, I hurried to leave the area, stepping on bodies as I went. There was a groan of pain. One still lived.

General Cho's room was completely blown up. He sat silently on a bed next to General Ushijima. Soldiers stood guarding them. Alone in a dark corner sat Miss Nakamoto, pale-faced, clenching her fists to fight back tears.

What had happened was this. As soon as Lieutenant Akinaga and his men reached the hilltop, they threw grenades at the enemy and were shot down. Lieutenant Ikeda and his men then tried to reach the top, but they were all shot and fell to the bottom of the shaft. To make matters worse, several grenades accidentally went off, causing more damage. In the medical room two girls were lying on beds among the wounded soldiers. They were unrecognizably disfigured. Our doctor, Lieutenant Colonel Kakazu, had cut into one girl's arm to expose an artery and give her a cyanide injection. They were Misses Yogi and Sakiyama. Alas, the fragrance of the flowers was gone. Since I had ordered the staff officers' room off limits for women, they had had no place to go but the shaft entrance. I was to blame for their deaths.

The enemy finally occupied the hilltop. They might penetrate the shaft at any moment. The only remaining entrance, the one facing the ocean, was now within their reach. Generals Ushijima and Cho knew well that their time was up, but they had not yet given the word about *hara-kiri*. They now ordered troops to retake the hilltop by nightfall and make a suicide charge on Mabuni the next morning. The generals would then commit suicide on the hilltop. I entrusted to Colonel Katsuno the task of retaking the hilltop. I stepped over the pile of corpses one more time and went to my room. It seemed empty, but one by one my men appeared out of the darkness.

Exhausted, I wanted only to rest. I lay on the bed and closed my eyes. A host of distracting thoughts filled my head. Mortification and regret tormented me. Generals Ushijima and Cho had generously ordered me to return home and join the final battle of Japan. Could a senior staff officer abandon two great generals and thousands of comrades and escape to Japan? It was a heavy responsibility. If I did return successfully to the homeland, what would people say? They would surely give me the cold shoulder. Should I give up the homeland mission and die gracefully with my comrades? No, no, I could not die so easily.

Reflecting back on the Okinawa battle, I knew it was my operation plan, made of my blood and soul, that had been trampled in the first place. The ideas of the generals on warfare were far different from mine, yet it was I who had to absorb the failure of the operation. General Ushijima had said that I should concentrate on escaping to the homeland. I looked at the aviation watch Captain Matsunaga had left hanging on the wall. It was the evening of June 22.

General Cho had said that I did not have to watch over the final days of our headquarters. He told me, in effect, to "get the hell" out of there. I decided to hold out until the very last moment, to remain in the cave until the generals were dead. If I lost my chance to escape, then fortune was against me. I would stay for the night and let fate decide.

About sunset a guard came in, his body covered with mud. Early in the morning he and his comrades had ambushed enemy tanks on the east slope of Mabuni hill and blasted two of them. But he had lost all his buddies. I was riveted by his exploit and felt helpless listening to the details. He was on a life-and-death mission, while his commanding generals considered suicide.

According to him, the communication unit commander, who had helped blast and seal the cave entrance facing Mabuni, had been killed on his way back to headquarters. It was rumored that all soldiers of the Mixed Brigade and the Artillery Group had made suicide attacks the previous night. There was no way of knowing if the 62nd Division command post was still fighting. In the dark recesses of the cave, they had already started their last supper, rice balls steamed in muddy water.

Everything was so quiet now in contrast to the recent hand-grenade battle. Our comrades had fallen. Soldiers who a few minutes ago had been laughing were now dead. There were no sounds of laughter or crying. All we wanted was to reach the top of the plateau, to take our last free breaths.

The communication detachments that were serving our staff and liaison officers had already left for their own units. As our assault time neared, five girls and noncommissioned officers from the staff officers' room joined the adjutants. The remaining staff officers left in our room were Majors Nishino, Yonabaru, Chiba, Katsuyama, Arakaki, and myself. I had the five majors guard the north entrance to the cave. Walking to the adjutants' section, I found the two generals sitting cross-legged, quietly smoking. Paymaster Sato, sitting beside General Cho, smiled at me. Adjutants Yoshino and Mazaki, Privates Nakatsuka and Nakamura, Miss Heshikiya and the other women remained seated, dreaming their own dreams. At the entrance facing the ocean were two rows of soldiers, armed and ready for the expected assault. Several women were folding clothes in a corner of the cave. It looked like a funeral scene.

At the entrance, a tall senior adjutant was giving commands for the final assault. I watched in silence so as not to disturb their high morale. The moon had not yet risen, and the pitch-dark valley below presented a ghostly scene. Two enemy patrol boats drifted in the distance. This corner of the battlefield was ominously still. My men guarding the shaft would start the assault.

Their orders were to climb the hill and meet the enemy. The assault team, led by Major Ono, consisted of ten soldiers, ten adjutants, and one detachment of the 24th Engineering Regiment. Major Ono would send the final telegram to Imperial General Headquarters. The adjutants would dispose of the bodies of the generals.

Our headquarters cave assault team and the soldiers around Mabuni hill were scheduled to make a joint suicide attack. I expected no great achievements. There simply was not much they could do at this point.

Under the orders of the senior adjutant, the engineer detachment team crawled on elbows and knees and disappeared one by one into the dark. There was no naval gunfire from the ocean, nor any hand-grenade attacks from the hilltop. The senior adjutant and I clenched our fists in silent encouragement. Several shots rang out above, but there was no noise of machine guns or grenades. I figured the enemy was avoiding a night battle, as usual, and had retreated from the hill. A soldier came to the cave for more ammunition, however, reporting that the enemy was hiding overhead. Lieutenant Yasuda said, "I'm going to reconnoiter," and went out with his men. They did not return. Still, nothing seemed to be happening on the hilltop. We began to feel uneasy. Finally, Major Matsubara ordered all units to attack.

He took the lead and advanced without looking for cover. Next out was Lieutenant Tsubakida, brandishing his sword high in the air. Lieutenant Yabumoto, a master swordsman, followed them and encouraged his men by shouting "Charge!" Operations secretaries Takahashi, Kato, and Koshino saluted me and departed. We had shared happiness and pain for over a year. I will not forget them. A few meters ahead of them the darkness of death awaited. It was a cruel and heartless suicide attack.

As the moon rose in the east, the ocean beneath my feet gradually became clearer, as in a dream. The hills still shed dark shadows into the valley and cast devilish figures. There was sporadic gunfire. I felt the desperate struggle of our soldiers trying to reach the top of the overwhelming cliffs.

Major Matsubara sent a report saying that he would avoid a frontal attack and instead would strike from behind the cliff. I knew, however, that it was impossible to reclaim the hill today. The enemy had occupied it skillfully, and our soldiers were too exhausted to counterattack successfully. We had been too involved with menial tasks inside the cave. I put the matter in the hands of the senior adjutant and withdrew into the cave. Adjutant Sakaguchi showed me thirty-by-ten-centimeter tomb markers bearing the names of the two generals and said solemnly, "Colonel Yahara, no matter what happens to me, I will dispose of the bodies of our generals and set up their tombs. I will leave the other bodies, including yours, as they are."

I reported to General Cho that it was impossible for us to recapture the hilltop. Intoxicated with *sake,* he was in good spirits. Paying no attention to my words, he offered me a drink, saying, "We drank in Saigon before the war started. Do you remember the beautiful movie we saw at the theater across from the Majestic Hotel? It was *Daniuvu no kazanami* [*Waves of the Danube*]. You and I always behaved properly. We shared much pain together, and now we face our final day.

"Ever since my arrival in Okinawa I said you would not die here. I am happy to have kept this promise. You must break through the enemy lines and succeed. Be cautious, and do not make any rash decisions if you can help it. I will give you this pill in case you become ill. Take it and you will recover." So saying, he gave me a pill that looked like *Rokushigan* [a Chinese medicine]. He said it was important. He also handed me five hundred yen.

General Cho's and my ideologies were poles apart. He always insisted on an aggressive offensive, I on a war of attrition. Until the May 4 counter-offensive, I had managed to oppose his strategy. We could hardly be good friends, yet our human relationship was warm. Arrogantly, he had once struck a brigade commander in the face, but he had never even threatened me. To me he had always been generous.

It was this generosity that now brought tears to my eyes. He was about to die the death of a supreme warrior. Unable to conceal my emotions, I headed for my room. There Major Nishino and five soldiers sat silently around a single light bulb dangling from the ceiling. I lay on my bed and wondered if this was a dream or reality. Overhead I heard soldiers walking around, or were they fighting? I was isolated from the outside world, but my ears picked up every sound, no matter how slight, within the cave. Perhaps enemy troops were tapping our cave noises with listening devices. This was an icy, silent war.

At midnight on June 23 we abandoned any effort to recover the hilltop. Generals Ushijima and Cho scheduled their *hara-kiri* for the morning. Both were fast asleep. The paymaster had yet to return from General Cho's room. I stared helplessly at the stalactites—like them, devoid of all energy and emotion. Time ticked away.

At 0300 General Ushijima summoned me to his room. Dressed in full uniform, he was sitting cross-legged. General Cho was drinking his favorite

King of Kings whisky, and he was very intoxicated. They were surrounded by familiar faces. I solemnly saluted them but said nothing. Cho offered me whisky and a piece of pineapple that he extended on the tip of his sword. This startled me but I ate it. Cho said, "General, you took a good rest. I waited patiently for you to waken, for time is running out."

Ushijima: "I could not sleep well because you snored so loudly. It was like thunder."

Cho: "Who will go first, you or me? Shall I die first and lead you to another world?"

Ushijima: "I will take the lead."

Cho: "Excellency, you will go to paradise. I to hell. I cannot accompany you to that other world. Our hero, Takamori Saigo, before committing *hara-kiri*, played chess with his orderly, and said, 'I will die whenever you are ready.' As for me, I will drink King of Kings while awaiting death." He laughed heartily.

At mention of Takamori Saigo everyone looked at General Ushijima, because subordinates often referred to him as Saigo.

The two generals exchanged poems back and forth. I could not hear them clearly, but I recall their mention that Japan could not exist without Okinawa. Later, I learned their final words.

General Ushijima's last poems:

> Green grass of Yukushima, withered before autumn,
> Will return in the spring to Momikoku.

and:

> We spend arrows and bullets to stain heaven and earth,
> Defending our homeland forever.

General Cho's last poem:

> The devil foe tightly grips our southwest land,
> His aircraft fill the sky, his ships control the sea;
> Bravely we fought for ninety days inside a dream;
> We have used up our withered lives,
> But our souls race to heaven.

Time was running out. Everyone in the cave formed a line to pay their last respects. Major Ono, a man of innocent face and indomitable spirit, returned and reported that the final message had gone to Imperial General Headquarters. It read:

Your loyal army has successfully completed preparations for homeland defense.

Ono, who had been a code clerk for many years, laughed bitterly. We have used those same words, he said, ever since the capitulation of Attu Island in the North Pacific. General Cho and I nodded agreement.

Officers and men who had shared the hardships of war, as well as Miss Heshikiya and the other young women, came to pay their respects. The young women were scheduled to descend with the remaining soldiers and reach the caves along the cliff before daybreak. General Cho's orderly, Nakatsuka, gave them his canteen of precious water, saying he no longer needed it. Cho's personal assistant said, "Excellency, I am sorry I must leave before offering incense at your funeral." Cho gave a wry smile.

General Ushijima quietly stood up. General Cho removed his field uniform and followed with Paymaster Sato. Led by candlelight the solemn procession headed for the exit, with heavy hearts and limbs.

When they approached the cave opening, the moon shone on the South Seas. Clouds moved swiftly. The skies were quiet. The morning mist crept slowly up the deep valley. It was as if everything on earth trembled, waiting with deep emotion.

General Ushijima sat silently in the death seat, ten paces from the cave exit, facing the sea wall. General Cho and Sato sat beside him. The *hara-kiri* assistant, Captain Sakaguchi, stood behind them. I was a few steps away. Soldiers stood at the exit, awaiting the moment.

On the back of General Cho's white shirt, in immaculate brush strokes, was the poem:

> With bravery I served my nation,
> With loyalty I dedicate my life.

By first light I could see this moral code written in his own hand, in large characters. General Cho looked over his shoulder at me with a beautifully divine expression and said solemnly, "Yahara! For future generations, you will bear witness as to how I died."

The master swordsman, Sakaguchi, grasped his great sword with both hands, raised it high above the general's head, then held back in his downward swing, and said, "It is too dark to see your neck. Please wait a few moments."

With the dawn, the enemy warships at sea would begin to fire their naval guns. Soldiers at the cave entrance were getting nervous. Granted their leave, they fled and ran down the cliff.

People were still nudging me toward the cave exit when a startling shot rang out. I thought for a moment it was the start of naval gun firing, but instead it was Sato committing suicide outside the cave. When that excitement subsided, the generals were ready. Each in turn thrust a traditional *hara-kiri* dagger into his bared abdomen. As they did so, Sakaguchi skillfully and swiftly swung his razor-edged sword and beheaded them. Ushijima first, then Cho.

Like a collapsed dam, the remaining soldiers broke ranks and ran down the cliff. I sat down outside the cave with Captain Sakaguchi, who declared with solemn amazement, "I did it!" His ashen face bore a look of satisfaction. Utterly exhausted, we watched the brightening sky. What a splendid last moment!

It marked a glorious end to our three months of hard battle, our proud 32nd Army, and the lives of our generals. It was 0430, June 23, 1945.

The Okinawa Defense Forces had lost some sixty-five thousand dead in battle. In addition there was a vast loss of civilian life and property. Enemy battle casualties amounted to about forty thousand on land and ten thousand at sea, with nonbattle casualties of about twenty-six thousand.[1]

In closing this chapter, I wish to add that we had many fiascoes in the Okinawa battle but, as historians have noted, our accomplishments deserve great praise. This praise properly belongs to the soldiers of 32nd Army, the famous *kamikaze* pilots, and the brave civilians of Okinawa. To all deceased comrades, I dedicate the words of Hanson Baldwin, the distinguished American critic and military historian, concerning Okinawa:

> In the Pacific War, the defense forces at Okinawa fought most courageously of all.

---

[1] The exact numbers of U.S. casualties were as follows:

10th Army	7,613	killed or missing
	31,807	wounded
	26,000	nonbattle (sickness, combat fatigue, etc.)
U.S. Navy Units	4,900	killed or missing
	4,824	wounded

The death toll among Okinawan civilians exceeded 100,000.

Part IV

Exodus

Yahara's attempted escape

27

The Mabuni Departure

Because of the inevitable enemy mop-up operations, Lieutenant Colonel Tatsuno and Captain Sakaguchi urged me to get out of the headquarters cave. They advised that I would be much safer in one of the many natural caves that pockmarked the lower face of the cliffs. I had decided, however, to stay in the main cave, merely moving back into the staff officers' section. As I nodded farewell and headed toward the rear of the tunnel, the eyes of my friends reflected their compassion and sympathy. They assumed that I was resigned to die.

I shared this lower section of the cave with Nishino, Chiba, Katsuyama, Arakaki, and Yonabaru. The other staff officers and soldiers had already moved down to the caves near the beach. The enemy was thus free to enter the big headquarters cave either through the topside central shaft or through the main entrance overlooking the ocean. The mopping-up assaults of the enemy could come at any moment, so we prepared for the worst.

It was my plan to lie low in this secret hideout for several days if necessary, awaiting a good chance to escape. With this in mind I had urged the others to bring blankets and what food they could. One by one we had squeezed through the tiny opening into an out-of-the-way pocket, where there was barely space for the six of us. We then sealed the entrance with rocks, confident that we would not be discovered. As long as we could survive in these cramped quarters, we would be safe from the enemy.

The interior of our shelter was unbelievable. Overhead loomed a petrified shower of stalactites mirrored in the ground by a carpet of jagged stalagmites as sharp as a saw. These inhibited our every move. We were unable to sit up, lie down, or even stretch our arms and legs. We were literally

clamped in these fierce jaws of Mabuni hill. There was scarcely a level place
to put a candle. The blackness consumed us. Occasionally I would strike a
match to glance at my watch and keep some track of the slowly passing time.
That was about all I could do, as we crouched corpselike in the darkness.

Within this cocoon of our rugged earth and limestone fortress we were
sheltered even from the ceaseless thunder of enemy guns. Only the long-
forgotten sound of quiet and tranquillity reached our ears. For brief moments
it was as though the war did not exist. Then the precious silence was broken
by an unremembered sound. Yonabaru and Katsuyama had fallen asleep
from exhaustion and were snoring. I nudged them awake because the enemy
might hear their snoring, and we would end up as prisoners of war—a disgraceful thing.

Then I got an idea for an alarm against being surprised by the enemy.
I crept from the hideout and piled things in front of the entrance—chairs,
desks, and whatever else—to make a barricade. On top I strung empty cans
as a security alarm against enemy approach.

My secure feeling ended shortly when I thought I heard enemy scouts.
Had we been discovered? Was my mind playing tricks? No, now I was sure
I heard the whimpering of army scout dogs, the sound of holes being dug for
explosives, and the scuffling of heavy boots up on Mabuni hill. The enemy
must be directly above us.

I tried to talk myself out of a growing anxiety. The cave headquarters
was protected by rock solid and strong enough to withstand a 15-inch pro-
jectile. Yet I knew that we could not hide here forever. My destiny was at
hand. Any lingering reservoir of hope was dripping through my fingers.

Shortly after noon a scout dog came to the ocean entrance. My string
of cans was disturbed. We held our breath and listened. The dog went away
and we breathed a collective sigh of relief.

I sent Warrant Officer Chiba out to reconnoiter the cave entrance. He
returned to report that Major Yamazaki and ten or so of his subordinates
were alive but that the staff officers had committed suicide. At this shocking
news a great wave of guilt swept over me. Should I have taken my life with
them, or before them? No wonder the supposed enemy had not penetrated
the cave. What I thought were scout dogs must have been Yamazaki's men.

At sunset I decided that we could come out of our hiding place. By the
pale light of a candle I made out the chaos of the officers' quarters. It was
disgusting to think that I had lived in this filth and clutter for nearly a month.
In addition, the place was intentionally littered with abandoned clothes and
weapons to make the enemy think the cave was deserted.

We were overjoyed to be free from our claustrophobic hideout. A breeze of elation engulfed us. The psychological effect was overwhelming. We brought out our meager rations of dry bread and dried bonito and devoured them. We had been without water for more than two days but felt that we could still get by for a while longer.

Arakaki, who had been on guard at the north entrance, reported that he heard a strange noise. Listening closely I detected a staccato sound overhead. It must be a jackhammer digging into the rock. Again I felt like a cornered animal. The penetrating noise increased my helpless feeling and inflamed my nerves. With the butt of my rifle I jabbed violently against the ceiling. The drilling stopped and then began again. I sent Major Nishino to scout the cave entrance. He returned to say that Major Yamazaki and his men had already set out for a cave at the foot of the bluff. We decided to follow. The narrow footpath along the bluff was dangerous because it was completely open to enemy gunfire, but it was the quickest way to the base of the cliff.

The terrain of the east coast would be the easiest and safest to cross. We could hike down the bluff and take the "safe" route along the beach, behind the enemy line at Gushichan. We had to avoid contact with the enemy. If that were successful, we would have clear sailing. Then we could disguise ourselves as civilian refugees, mingle with them, and continue on our mission.

We were such a large group of soldiers that it would not be easy to blend in with civilians unnoticed. Accordingly, we decided to proceed independently and rendezvous at Haneji, Arakaki's hometown in northern Okinawa, by the end of July. After recuperating there we would get a small boat and head north for Yoron Island. This was our basic strategy, and we moved quickly to carry it out. Nishino and Yonabaru had an escape plan of their own, and we all set out at the same time.

I tried on a civilian suit that had been stored for a long time in my military bag. It was far too neat and dapper to permit me to pass as a refugee. An old golf jacket I had worn years ago in the United States seemed more suitable. I filled a pair of socks with cooked rice and tied them around my waist. I also took a couple of dried bonitos and a 32-caliber Belgian Browning pistol. If we ran short of food, sweet potatoes and sugar cane were available throughout the island. Arakaki and Yonabaru, who were Okinawans, looked natural in native garb. The rest of us appeared and felt quite awkward.

Eager to get away from the menacing din of the overhead drilling, we moved cautiously toward the exit of the eerie cave. Chiba led the way through a section where there were a dozen or so corpses. Four of them were covered with white sheets, from which their legs protruded. Chiba recognized them as adjutants. I paused only long enough for a silent prayer. Near the bed was another group of bodies, some of them women, but I was too sickened to check on them. I walked to the cave opening and peered out for possible enemies.

It was an hour before midnight on June 23, a Saturday. A full moon floated silently in the cloudless sky. Toward Kiyan Point stretched a long chain of dark bluffs. Beyond all this was the sparkling ocean, shimmering like an endless field of gold and silver. Scattered enemy searchlights pierced the night sky, and the merciless ravages of war were at my back, but I looked on a sight as lovely as a dream.

From the dark depths below I heard shouts of a *banzai* charge. It was probably Major Ono's men making an assault on the enemy among the giant boulders on the shore. Then all was silent again.

The continuing stillness of the night became fearsome and ominous. I pictured innumerable demons in a ritual dance of death, with sharp glistening fangs, waiting to engulf me. As I waited for the right moment to leave, my feet would not move. The night silence seemed to accentuate the frantic beating of my heart. Suddenly seized with hunger pangs, I went back into the cave and asked if any cans of pineapple remained. We searched but found none.

There had been no enemy fire for some time, so it seemed like a good idea to escape under cover of darkness. Chiba and Katsuyama argued against starting at this time, but I decided to go ahead.

Although the men were clearly opposed to my departure, I collected my rations and bade them farewell. I wished them good luck and reassured them that we would meet in Haneji. I inched cautiously out of the cave with my pistol cocked and ready.

The night air was crisp, but I was sweating as if the midday sun were blazing on me. I hunched close to the ground to make a small target. My adrenaline surged like a rushing river as I concentrated on getting to the foot of the hill. Stepping right and left I tried to rush down through a sudden open way. The incline was much steeper than it appeared in the romantic moonlight. I missed my footing and fell, tumbling headlong down the slope, suffering bruises at every bounce. I tried to slow my descent, but instead seemed to be gathering speed. Stones and pebbles tumbled after, pelting me and adding to my pains. I lost hold of my pistol. It fell from my hand and went off accidentally. As if that were not enough, enemy gunfire began blazing at me from all directions.

Frightening as this was, it was also quite ludicrous. Here I was, tumbling down Mabuni hill in the dead of night, my body battered, my weapon gone, and an enemy barrage intent on killing me. In that instant I became resigned to death. Closing my eyes while millions of blurred images appeared, I continued to tumble in darkness.

Miraculously, I suddenly stopped, having landed on a small ledge in the middle of that steep incline. My skull felt as if it had been cracked by a sledgehammer. I put my hands to my head and they came away drenched with warm blood. Spiritual immortality became a reality at that instant. The moment filled me with dread, but I felt sure I would survive.

My clothes were in shreds, my body bruised and bleeding, my socks of rice gone. I had lost everything, but my senses slowly returned. On hands and knees I moved to the shelter of a large rock. I was out of danger for the time being. I heard the clattering of stones and looked up the hill, hoping my men would soon find me. The chances were very slim.

I leaned back against the cool surface of the rock and wiped my bloody head with a handkerchief. I thought of the men left behind just a few minutes ago, missed them, and wished they would appear. Waves gently lapped at the nearby shore. The salty ocean smell was pleasant. I breathed deeply of the breeze and considered my next move. Should I wait for my men or move on? With no one in sight, I decided to move on.

If I were to reach Gushichan, I must get going. Slowly and unsteadily, I got to my feet and limped eastward along the bluff. Weaving my way through the towering boulders, I stopped to take a last look at the crest of Mabuni hill. American soldiers were firing flares down into the valley. Twinkling sparks fell gently at my feet. As I turned my head I saw the outline of a man approaching. My heart skipped a beat, and I froze. Was it an enemy? I waited for the figure to come closer. Ah! it was Katsuyama. My spirit soared to see that my friend had escaped and found me.

Katsuyama's pace was slow and unsteady; his face looked like a ghost. He appeared crushed and beaten. From my own desperate state moments ago, my heart went out to this pitiable man. He did not respond in the slightest to my words of encouragement. While I tried to explain that daylight was coming and we should find a hiding place, Arakaki suddenly appeared. His nonchalance was amazing. Eager to help, he led us to a nearby cave.

We wiggled through the small opening into a chamber no more than ten feet square. There before a tiny fire sat a scrawny young soldier rubbing his hands together. Behind him sat an Okinawan girl who said not a word. I recognized her as a clerk from the Shuri accounting office. Far back in a corner were two soldiers; one dead, one severely wounded.

Engineer Nagaya had killed himself. His face was in repose, with no sign of anguish or torment, only a mask of peace and eternal rest. As I uttered words of prayer, the girl watched me and sobbed. The wounded man sat dazed and despondent, saying nothing, even in answer to my questions.

I turned to the young soldier by the fire. He explained that he had set the fire to smoke out mosquitoes but was glad that it now offered some warmth against the chilly night air. From his cheerful tone it was clear that he was a good-hearted person, but his jovial manner was strangely out of place in this setting. He served us dry bread and boasted of having killed an enemy with his rifle. I thought of how easily an enemy might attack us by morning light. We were a ready target for flamethrowers.

I sent Arakaki to find a better cave. He was back in half an hour, having found a hideout safer from surprise attack. I decided to move at once, but Katsuyama demurred, claiming that he would just be a burden. Back in the headquarters cave I had been able to dissuade him and the others from suicide by holding out the hope that I could lead them to safety. That prospect was now so dim, he no longer had cause to believe it. I cautioned Katsuyama that it was unwise to remain here. He would do better to go back to the personnel section of the big cave where his friends were probably waiting. We would all meet again in Haneji. His eyes showed no sign of hope. There was nothing more to say. Katsuyama was weeping as I left the cave. We would not meet again.

Arakaki and I walked past charred boulders and came to an arched rock where there were several dead Americans. We swiftly passed them. Arakaki led the way another hundred yards to a clearing surrounded by boulders that formed an amphitheater. I angrily observed that this place was not as good as the last one. Without a word Arakaki walked over to a large rock and pushed it aside to reveal a cave entrance.

We groped some twenty feet through a narrow tunnel that gave onto a chamber no bigger than our hideout pocket in the headquarters cave. By the flickering light of my last matches I beheld a group of about ten soldiers clinging geckolike to the rough walls of the cave.

It was weird, but an ideal hideaway, and I had to admire Arakaki's houndlike instinct in finding the place. He certainly was a reliable friend. The "gecko" soldiers were from the 89th Regiment. They had retreated here from Yoza hill several days ago.

I introduced myself, and a Sergeant Sato identified himself as the squad leader. I could not make out his face in the dark, but his voice left no question about his being both quick and clever. He served some cooked potatoes and suggested a place for me to relax. He assured me that there were provisions enough to last us for a couple of weeks and that we need not be concerned about an enemy attack.

Having had no drink in two days, I was becoming dehydrated and asked for water. There was none available in the cave. Just then a drop of water fell on my shoulder. As my eyes adjusted to the dark, I looked up and saw a drop forming on the ceiling. I opened my mouth to catch it. After a few seconds, which seemed longer, the drop fell into my mouth. It was the sweetest drink I ever tasted.

The morning sun peeked through the tunnel opening and deep into the cave. I was still savoring single drops of water when I heard heavy thuds outside. The enemy was combing the area for hideouts. Land transmits sound very well, and I knew that these thuds originated not far from our hiding place. At that moment my recurring cold of the past several weeks caught up with me and I had to cough. I buried my face in a blanket to muffle it. The others held their breath in dread, knowing that the slightest noise, even a whisper, might attract the enemy. My coughing stopped, and shortly we heard a scout dog sniffing nearby. He did not sniff us out.

I realized again that the Mabuni area was the focal point for enemy artillery and the target of a final encirclement. Mop-up operations would no doubt be more severe than we had expected, so we were not safe here. We had to leave the cave and head for the enemy's rear area at Gushichan. Since Sergeant Sato had been defending the Mabuni area and knew the terrain, I asked him for the best route to Gushichan. He offered to accompany me to the north. There was no objection from Sato's men, so we made plans to leave that evening of June 24.

28

Gushichan Cave

Rolling away the rock from the cave entrance, I crawled out with Arakaki and Sato. It was a relief to be out of the damp cave and fill our lungs with fresh air. A bright moon rose high above Mabuni hill, and I could make out an enemy boat patrolling offshore. Heavy gunfire came from the west, probably from Odo or Komesu. The nearby enemy troops scattered along the edge of the reef were firing rifles, but it seemed to be merely for diversion.

I cautioned Sato to avoid the natural spring. Enemy soldiers were probably waiting there for unwary victims attracted by the clean drinking water. To stay clear of the Spring of Death, we hiked toward the reef. The three of us, now adept at night escapes, advanced quickly through a maze of boulders. As much as possible, we took advantage of the terrain and the cover of night. Occasional stray bullets swept through the lifeless skeletons of burned-out trees and hit rocks, but we knew they were not aimed at us. We came across deserted pillboxes and entrenchments, but no friendly faces. The ground was strewn only with destroyed equipment and empty food packages.

Our daring escape turned out to be much simpler than expected. About three hundred yards beyond the deadly spring we came to the beach. This beach was not spread with soft white sand but covered with millions of close-packed coral daggers that made the shoreline something like the walls of a citadel. It was almost impossible to walk on this bed of pointed stones. Here, however, we had the protection of buttresslike rocks which formed huge canopies over the cliffs.

Scattered on the coral reef as far as the eye could see were decaying Japanese corpses. Their sickly stench assailed our nostrils. One corpse floated back and forth with the tireless tide. One was washed up on the reef, his face on the rocks, his legs dangling in the water. Another lay on his back as though basking in the moonlight. A thousand faces of death appeared as we marched through this seaside graveyard.

The horrid decomposed bodies were repulsive on land, but here on the coral reef my deceased brothers seemed purified by the tide and whitened by the light of the moon. I had to step on the dead but never felt that it was irreverent. Their souls had departed. These soldiers must have tried to break through the enemy siege by way of the coastline and fallen victim to enemy attack.

We met one of our soldiers after another attempting to flee. One soldier in short pants was accompanied by a woman and child. He apparently believed that the enemy would not kill a young family. He said enemy troops were stationed at the corner of a nearby overhanging cliff. He was turning back to avoid them.

I went ahead to check his story. There were a few Japanese deserters standing around, not knowing what to do. I reconnoitered the reported checkpoint; it was an excellent location. Passersby would have to walk through a narrow path between the cliff overhang and the deep defile to the ocean. Upon close inspection I concluded that our informant was imagining things. No enemy was there. All I could see was a patrol boat and a frigate moving slowly through the water. The random gunfire from the top of the bluff was not a serious threat. I returned to my party and, without hesitation, led them along the bluff.

I wanted to cover as much ground as possible until we found a suitable place to rest. The course along the beach was treacherous, and we saw more dead soldiers, but we pressed on. The impossible becomes possible when one is running for one's life. While hiding in the Mabuni hill cave, the pain from my cuts and bruises was almost intolerable, but now I had scarcely an ache as I trekked and scaled the difficult path between land and water. We finally came to a group of refugees and worked our way among them.

One man stepped up to me, examined my face by the dim moonlight, and said, "Sir, you are Senior Staff Officer Yahara." I recognized him at once as Mr. Shimada, General Cho's personal secretary. Akira Shimada was a remarkable character. At our farewell banquet in the headquarters cave at Mabuni, he had astonished me by greeting General Cho with the ceremonial farewell words of Japanese gangsters (*yakuza*)—and in their secret code, no less. (See Prisoner-of-War Interrogation Reports, page 205.)

General Cho had entrusted him with the mission of carrying personal letters to important people of our high command. He had left the cave before me, and yet here he was. I asked what had happened to him.

He replied, "Yesterday afternoon we climbed the bluff over there on the left and hid in a sugar cane field. The enemy searched for us and killed three of our party. The rest of us managed to escape and make it down to here. I burned the general's secret letters to keep them from enemy hands. Before doing so, I opened the envelopes and memorized the contents. The enemy will not squeeze a word of that information from me."[1] I appreciated this report, realized that Shimada would be an asset in our escape, and asked him to join us.

We resumed our journey eastward toward Gushichan as the cool moon yielded the sky to the warming sun. We stopped to confer when we came to a steep cliff. Should we try to climb over this barrier or wend our way around it by unknown paths? While we considered the possibilities, someone at the front of our group shouted, "Enemy! Enemy!"

Knowing that an enemy encounter here was most unlikely, I yelled, "Calm down. There's no enemy around here. Let's get moving." As no one moved, I took the initiative and started to climb up the bluff. Shortly I sensed a nearby movement and came upon several soldiers in the shade of an overhang. They were obviously in great despair. I approached and asked them about the local situation. One man replied sullenly, "In the morning your alarm will be an amphibious tank whose chime will be a dirge composed especially for you."

This gloomy exchange was interrupted by a distraught man who appeared out of nowhere and roared, "Who the hell are you? Where do you come from? You are full of talk. You must be enemy spies. You are troublemakers. Get out of here. Beat it!" The insane shrieking of this troubled man continued until he seemed to run out of words. Then he just wandered off, muttering obscenities. We felt pity for him, but this poor soul was clearly beyond our help.

We continued toward the cliff. I dismissed the intimidating thought of being awakened by the sound of enemy tanks, thinking only of finding a good hiding place for the day. The huge bluff appeared to offer no easy solution. Incessant enemy gunfire was a constant reminder of what might be around the next corner. But we could not give up; we had to persevere.

---

[1]See Prisoner-of-War Interrogation Reports for Shimada's interrogation report and the description there of what happened to him.

Because our large party of soldiers traveling together made an easy target for the enemy to spot, we decided to separate from Shimada and his men in climbing the bluff.

At the top of the bluff we found a footpath running along the thin outer rim of the cliffs. As we headed farther eastward, we encountered isolated soldiers who had been neutralized by enemy assaults. Then, once again, the air was offensive with the smell of rotting corpses. It was becoming as pervasive as the sound of enemy guns. The right flank of our 44th Mixed Brigade must have fought a hellish last-ditch battle here.

We came to a huge rock shaped like an Egyptian sphinx. At its base was a cave occupied by about fifty refugees, mostly elderly women. They appeared comfortable and relaxed. A baby cried. It seemed to me that there were also some soldiers in the group. I was delighted. It was like coming upon an oasis in a desert.

Thinking twice about this peaceful scene in the midst of a war made me feel it might be an enemy trap. Or it might be an enemy refugee camp. There was the sound of a radio broadcast in the Okinawan language, which was unknown to me. Was it propaganda? I became uneasy and asked Arakaki to translate for me. He said that it was not a radio broadcast at all but merely the sound of voices amplified in the huge cave. My nerves were getting the better of me.

The gloominess of the cave so depressed me that I went to the entrance where I found a smooth rock about three meters in diameter. I sprawled out on it and went to sleep. I was awakened by the bright sun of a glorious morning. It was the first time I had seen a sunrise since the battle for Okinawa began almost three months ago. People emerged slowly from the cave to enjoy the sunshine.

These Okinawans were the real victims of the war. Their land was devastated, their homes burned to the ground, and countless innocent civilians killed. For the moment, however, the sun was shining, and they were out of the reach of bombs and grenades. Some of them stared at me in curiosity, but there was no sign of hostility. They each went about their business, indifferent to what others were doing.

Reassured by their casual attitude, I spread my clothes to dry, relaxed under the warm sun, and plucked lice from my skin. A native conscript, a husky old man with cold piercing eyes, lay down next to me on the rock.

Women, young and old, in ragged clothes spread mats and blankets to air in the sunshine. A middle-aged woman wrapped the limp corpse of a little girl in canvas and carried it away. An elderly couple were eating breakfast. A leper, with his left ear wasted away, walked in and out of the cave. Occasional enemy planes flew back and forth at low altitudes to attack the area. We must have been plainly visible, but strangely they showed no interest in us.

In my headlong dash and tumble from the headquarters cave I had lost all my provisions, but Arakaki and Sato got some rice from the mess kit of a dead soldier and shared it with me. Sato also shared some roasted beans given him by one of the refugees. While we ate, a tall, pretty girl appeared at the cave entrance. Sato indicated that she had given him the beans. I told him not to reveal my identity to anyone and to call me "uncle" for safe measure. It was clear that this was not an enemy trap, but I did not want to take chances.

In the afternoon Sato and Arakaki went out to scout the enemy situation and look for an escape route to Yaezu hill. They returned at dusk and reported no sign of the enemy around the crest of the cliff, but they did see heavy traffic at the intersection of the roads to Yoza and Nakaza. At a well not far from the top of the bluff they had found a heap of more than fifty charred bodies, victims of flame-throwers. Since there seemed to be no imminent danger of attack, we decided to stay here while we regained our strength. We would need every ounce of it to reach our destination.

While I pondered our next move, the dark of night descended. The rainy season was past, and stars blinked in the quiet sky. I looked at the galaxies and wondered if battles raged up there, too. A different kind of illumination appeared here on earth. Enemy flares arose from the edge of the escarpments, and the staccato of gunfire crashed through the night. Another enemy siege was on. Many of our soldiers would be trying to escape from this area, but escape would be difficult under the menacing, revealing flares. A few lucky ones might make it to the northern villages of Kunigami.

I wondered what had happened to Shimada, the secret messenger, and his party. Were they still alive? By the light of the moon I could make out a raft with about ten men rowing eastward along the coast. They were probably headed for Chinen. The moon was so bright that an alert enemy could easily spot them. I hoped they would get through.

Dawn broke on my second day in the caves. It was now June 26. These two days on the rocky terrace had been like a small slice of heaven for me. But now my mood had changed and it was time for action. I could no longer stand this Spartan existence without either blankets or a change of clothes.

We discussed the next step toward escape. As a creature of logic and reason, I was disinclined to act upon mere instinct; yet the insightful intuition of my men in recent days had been most helpful. They now advised that we go beyond the escarpment and head for Yaezu hill by way of Nakaza and Yoza.

Shortly after our discussion, the morning calm was broken by enemy airplanes directly overhead showing signs of attack. I moved toward the cave as someone yelled, "Enemy attack!" The earth shook as exploding bombs threw the whole cave into pandemonium. A refugee running into the shelter screamed that the enemy was on the hilltop. It suddenly occurred to me that I had failed to check the cave in detail. I did not even know if there was an opening onto the beach. I raced headlong into the depths of the cave and suddenly came to an exit leading directly to the reef.

The tide was in. Waves lapped at my legs as I stood in the opening, cursing aloud at my own stupidity for not having thought earlier of this possible escape route. At the moment I was unaware that an American soldier was rounding the rocks with a machine gun. As our eyes met he hollered, "Hey, come on! Come out!" and leveled the gun at me. There appeared to be no way to escape, but I still resented being cornered and backed reflexively into the shadow of the cave. What could I do? Trying to think rationally, I could hear only the swish of the tide, over and over. Then came the crack of gunshots and the sound of the enemy soldier sloshing through the water as he approached step by step. Instinctively, without any kind of plan, I turned and fled upward into the cave.

Again I was with the refugees who were all sitting huddled together. There was no place for me to turn. Looking up I saw another American soldier standing high above in the upper cave entrance. Like a broken record he kept shouting, "Come out! Come out! Come out!"

An excited Japanese soldier stepped out from the group of refugees. "I'll kill that damned American if he comes closer," he yelled. This show of bravado seemed to inspire a young woman, perhaps his lover, to step forward. Wearing a tight headband, her sleeves tucked into a sash, she began flailing the air wildly with a bamboo broom. The scene was too incredible to be true. I ordered them both to stop the theatrics and sit down.

Suddenly I had become the leader of this frightened and hysterical group, while the American above us at the entrance yelled, "Come out now or I'll start shooting." This was the moment of truth. I decided to lead the refugees in surrender, a plan I had been thinking about for some time.

The refugees were in mortal terror of being raped or murdered if they fell into enemy hands. From my two years of experience in the United States I knew that Americans were not at all brutal. The refugees would be as safe in American hands as in mine. I spoke to them. "Listen, all of you. Listen. The best thing for us is to surrender as the soldiers request. If you agree, I will negotiate with the enemy on our behalf."

An older couple spoke up, saying, "Please put an end to our trouble. Please speak for us all." Their adult daughters began crying.

I said firmly, "Do as I say. Do not make a fuss. If you surrender obediently, no one will be harmed." Speaking for this large group of refugees, I had to be resolute. Fear had robbed them of their faculties.

Standing at the cave entrance there were now several American soldiers. Turning toward them I spoke in English, to the surprise of the refugees, and said that we were ready to come out. I asked them not to shoot us. An American said, "Okay. Put down your weapons and come out."

Repeating, "Do not shoot," I led the way out of the cave and was again face to face with an American. He was calm and appeared kindly. Two soldiers behind him chuckled at my repeated request that they not shoot. There was no belligerence or violence in their appearance; but a group of their comrades stood a hundred yards away, guns at the ready. I could see them through openings in the rocks. Beyond them spread the glistening ocean.

My peaceful conversation with the Americans calmed the refugees and wounded soldiers. They filed out of the cave after me. A number of American soldiers now moved forward from their deployment positions and helped the refugees—taking an old man's hand, carrying children in their arms. It was a touching scene. Hostility and fear were replaced by compassion. My thoughts swept back to one terrible night in Philadelphia when I was in an automobile collision. Two young men came to my rescue and extracted me from the wreck. I knew we would not be mistreated.

Some fifty or sixty people came out of the cave, and I figured that one-third of them must have been soldiers. Two Americans helped a wounded soldier to first-aid treatment. He whispered to me that he was glad to leave everything in the hands of the enemy. The American officer in charge appeared completely satisfied at having taken so many soldiers and civilians without bloodshed. He told me that the war was now over.

We exchanged a few words as we moved toward the beach. As two officers chatted I heard one say, "This Jap fella could be useful to us in the future." "Good heavens," I thought, "I may be in trouble." Fortune was smiling on the refugees, but not on me. I was relieved to hear the other officer reply, "We already have enough English-speaking natives. We don't need him." The last thing I wanted was to become an interpreter and have my identity discovered.

29

Mingling with
the Refugees

When we had gathered at the beach, two patrol boats from the Minatogawa area arrived; we were quickly put on board. A forlorn chubby-faced Japanese officer in my boat recognized me, and his face brightened. He was about to speak when I stopped him with a discreet wink.

Our boat pulled in to Minatogawa, and I saw Ou Island on the right but could not believe my eyes. The land was covered with hundreds of tents stretching to the horizon. Heavy automobile traffic swarmed everywhere. Laid waste by the war and now completely dug up by American engineers, the once lush district of Minatogawa had been changed beyond imagination.

Overwhelmed and perplexed at the sight before me, I stepped onto the temporary landing pier. A tall Japanese dressed in American military clothing spoke to me, "Hello, Colonel Yahara." I thought I was prepared for anything, but this bolt from the blue completely astonished me. Coming closer he whispered, "I was captured a few days ago, and I am now screening Japanese soldiers from civilians."

What? Spying for the enemy? I almost exploded with rage. I managed to control my anger, however, realizing that he probably had no alternative. Besides, he could help me. I confided my plan to him and asked for his assistance. He replied readily, "Certainly, sir. I will do all I can toward the accomplishment of your mission."

I did not expect everything to run smoothly and had already created several alibis in case I was discovered by the Americans. Fortunately for me now, I would not need alibis. I was encouraged by the soldier's promise of help. This new turn of events delighted me, and I thanked him profusely. He was a friend of Arakaki's and promised to treat him, Sato, and me as civilians.

When our screening process began, he succeeded in getting us into the civilian group. I was grateful and happy. American soldiers came in jeeps and lavished biscuits, chocolates, and candies on us. The refugees were no longer afraid, especially the children. They all gathered around to enjoy the welcome gifts. Never had I seen such happy children.

While eating a piece of sweet chocolate, I noticed an elderly lieutenant colonel. He just stood there smiling and watching the children enjoy the sweets. His kindly face beamed with the satisfaction of a benevolent conqueror. He looked familiar to me, but I dared not speak to him. He could never have imagined that he was standing near the senior staff officer of the entire Japanese army on Okinawa, against whom he had been fighting a ferocious battle just a few days before. Now that senior staff officer was clad in rags, munching on a chocolate. Thinking of this twist of fate, I felt a bit sorry for myself.

The captured Japanese soldiers were sent to stockades on Ou Island. We refugees were marched in a long line under guard of armed American soldiers. The setting sun cast a lingering warm orange glow. The old men and women walking with me were delighted by the unexpected goodwill of our captors. In turn they treated me as a defeated hero who had saved them from tragedy at the Gushichan cave. There was little talk as we trudged along. From time to time I stretched my wounded knees. When thirsty, I picked roadside sugar cane to extract its juices, just as I had done at Mabuni.

We were directed into the village of Fusato, south of Itokazu hill. At the stockade entrance we were issued passes. I gave my age as forty-seven, though I was only forty-two. Forty-seven, of course, was too old to be a soldier. The military police clerk wrote my age as given, but he added a note saying that I appeared to be between twenty-five and forty. I chose to believe that Americans think Japanese look younger than they really are.

In our stockade there were more than two hundred Okinawans from all over the southern part of the island. Within the compound were seven or eight barrack-type buildings side by side, each with a capacity of about fifty occupants. The civilians, singly and in families, were assembled with their meager belongings and assigned to these houses. Sato, Arakaki, and I were put in a separate dwelling. My scheme to escape northward disguised as a civilian had taken its first solid step.

I had everything to make me comfortable: a soft bed, warm sunlight, sweet air, and abundant clean water. Seldom in my life had I felt so secure and happy. The waning moon, however, was the only friend with whom I could speak intimately and share my plan. I had heard that the stockade was only a temporary stop, and we were scheduled to move soon to the north. I was still full of optimism but wondered if all would turn out well for Arakaki, Sato, and me. Ocean breezes wafted over the island, as my imagined talk with the moon drifted off into silence.

For several days I took great pleasure in the peaceful atmosphere of the stockade, but then the sun turned scorching hot and I felt restless. A friendly Okinawan woman who worked in the military office loaned me some American magazines. American guards watched with interest as I read the English text, but they simply smiled pleasantly and never seemed at all suspicious.

On the morning of June 29 we were suddenly ordered to leave Fusato. We formed into two lines on a path south of the stockade. There was no mention of our destination, but we were as excited as children going on a picnic. We went through a simple check, and I pretended to be weak and fragile. The guards were sitting on chairs, but the instant I looked at them they sprang to their feet, yelling that I was a soldier, and reached out to grab me. I stepped back to avoid a confrontation, and one guard stopped the others when he said, "This is a woman." They all stopped but seemed uncertain and ready to jump at me again. "Hey, look," he continued, "how can she be a soldier?" They all looked closely at me again and decided from my slender build and light skin, which contrasted so with that of the swarthy Okinawans, that I was a woman. In addition to a slender build, my purple pants and brown golf jacket must have been persuasive. Regardless of their reasons for thinking so, I was glad they concluded I was female.

The hot summer sun and the dry dusty road forced many exhausted refugees out of line as we walked northward. The American guards, also weary, did not pay close attention to their long line of wards. I could easily have escaped at this time, but not wanting to go it alone, I stayed with the civilians.

We walked on in silence, chewing occasionally on sugar cane to quench our thirst. Following along the coast of Chinen Peninsula at a snail's pace, we reached Tanagusuku after more than an hour. Because the battle had not come to that village, many of the houses were still intact. The trees were green and not stripped of their foliage by gunfire. The village atmosphere was pure jubilation because of the cease-fire. Children played happily with American soldiers. Women of the village cheered us up by serving biscuits and fresh drinking water. The general spirit was joyful.

Late in the afternoon, when the unbearable heat had moderated, we resumed our monotonous trek. Turning northward we went to the tip of the Chinen Peninsula and then headed for Nakagusuku Bay. The heels of my shoes were so worn I could hardly walk. How I envied the native Okinawans who were used to walking barefoot! My limping caused even the old women to pity me, and they offered me juicy sugar cane. I was grateful. From the Baten plateau we had an incredible view of Nakagusuku Bay filled with hundreds of American ships at anchor. This spectacular view reminded me of our own proud fleet at anchor in this very harbor after the Marianas sea battle only a year ago.

30

Fusozaki Village

We trudged down the famous Baten slope to Fusozaki on the east side of the harbor. At the edge of the village we rested, awaiting our lodging arrangements. Arakaki must have gotten in with another bunch of refugees, for I did not see him. Sato, however, was in my group. He made a remarkable show of acting as a proud father carrying a child on his back. I never knew how or where he got the child.

At sunset our lodgings were assigned. Two young men, three children, and I were to stay at the Sonan residence, one of the few houses still intact at the eastern edge of the village. The front yard was surrounded by stone walls laced with an intricate network of vines. The back yard gave onto an expansive field of sugar cane. The Sonans were obviously one of the wealthier farm families in the area. Their house consisted of three large rooms with dirt floors and a long veranda. At the end of the main room was an exquisite Buddhist altar. Along one wall were large clay pots filled with a variety of grains.

I learned that our host, Ryoji Sonan, had at first been reluctant to accept us but ultimately agreed to lodge us through the good offices of the village mayor. When we arrived at the house it was plain why he had initially refused. Standing at the entrance we saw a huge crowd of guests sitting in the main room. Indeed, there were already thirty homeless refugees; too many to be accommodated all at once. It took me several days to remember all their faces and names, not to mention their personal tragedies. They were all victims of the bloody three-month battle. Every kind of war casualty could be found here. A mother bereaved of her son, a widow, malaria sufferers, young children crying out in their sleep for their parents, a helpless child found alone on the battlefield. What was their future?

179

The Sonan family of five slept in the main room. Families evacuated from nearby Gochinda and Ginowan were in the next room. The family of Sonan's niece occupied the other room. The rest of us were distributed on the veranda and the adjoining turf, which was my place. At night I worked so hard at fighting off the pesky fleas and mosquitoes that there was little time for sleep.

The next day civilian police and a village official in charge of supplies paid a visit of inquiry. I assumed the name Hiroshi Yagi, one I had used in prewar years on an official visit to Thailand to collect strategic information. I told the police I was an English teacher at a junior high school in my home prefecture of Tottori and that I was on my way home from a visit with relatives in Taiwan when I was shipwrecked, rescued, and brought back to Okinawa. I had been wandering from place to place on the battlefield and was finally captured by the Americans. In short I told every conceivable lie to convince the police that I was a civilian. They interrogated every visitor, young and old. We were relieved when they left.

The next day two military police (MPs) arrived on motorcycles. After a few words they took away three of our number: Mr. Sonan's youngest brother, a former Naha City employee, and the son of a woman who was lodging on the veranda. A heavily bearded distiller from Shuri hid out in the back cane field, but I composed myself and stretched out while the MPs were there; they overlooked me.

After that first surprise visit the MPs returned every now and then to check on sanitary conditions. They found amusement in sprinkling DDT on the young girls infested with lice. We were free to walk around the village and its outskirts, but it was dangerous to go out in the evening because of Japanese guerrillas who still remained in the area.

As soon as the sun set behind the mountains the darkening sky was brightened anew by the sky dance of swaying searchlights. Intermittent gunfire and antiaircraft artillery assailed our ears from the north, perhaps from the air bases at Yomitan and Kadena. In addition to these military lights and noises, I continued my own fierce battle against swarms of bloodthirsty mosquitoes. My few hours of restful sleep came only after the daylight departure of these winged enemies.

During the day Okinawan men, including Mr. Sonan, lounged about engaged in idle conversation. The women, on the other hand, never seemed to sit still. Mrs. Sonan worked continually. She delegated many household chores and saw to it that meals for thirty people were prepared, cooked, and served with amazing efficiency. A keen observer of all that went on, she apportioned food according to the amount of work each person did. We had three meals a day, mostly sweet potatoes, rice, and a soup made with the leaves of sweet potatoes. Every third day she took soybeans from one of the large jars, hand-milled them, and prepared a delicious bean-curd soup. She told me that on special occasions, such as the thatching of a roof, it was customary to invite all relatives and neighbors to a bean-curd soup banquet.

After a few days things became organized so that the refugee men and women were put to work—some on military projects, others setting up barracks for homeless civilians or digging sweet potatoes. Working for the American military turned out to be a prestigious occupation. Workers returned from their jobs in high spirits, triumphantly shouldering their bounty of cigarettes, canned meat, clothing, and abandoned Japanese goods. They became objects of envy for those of us who could not work because of physical limitations. Mr. Heavy Beard was specially admired because he brought back great quantities of things that he shared with the rest of us.

Idling away the days was very pleasant in a way, but I felt ill at ease with our host family because I was not contributing. There was nothing I could do about it, however, because I was not healthy enough for hard labor. I also did not want to be seen by anyone who might identify me. After several more days of doing nothing but listen to my guilty conscience, I went to the village refugee office and asked for a modest job. The middle-aged clerk, who appeared to be an educated man, persuaded me to remain under the care of the Sonans. I could not decide if he was aware of my identity. Encouraged by his advice, my peace of mind returned. I continued to enjoy my leisure days with the Sonans.

Chatty Mr. Sonan was good company, even though he spoke broken Japanese. We discussed the linguistic and cultural differences between Okinawa and mainland Japan. I felt that we could narrow that gap, at least between the two of us. He told that he had once gone all the way to my hometown of Tottori to buy some well-bred bulls. I told him of an embarrassing experience in Okinawa when I greeted a farmer with the word *Konnichiwa* ("Good day") and apparently offended him because he responded with a string of obscenities. His verbal abuse in turn angered me, and I was intent on court-martialing him. Later, however, I found out that the farmer had mistaken my greeting for the word *kuncha,* which means "leper" in Okinawan.

When the others went to work each day, I was the only guest remaining at the lodge. To pass the time I went to a nearby beach with the children and collected shellfish or walked to the edge of the village and sat under a mandarin orange tree for a few hours. On the way to this favorite resting place I noticed two canoes tied up in a creek. I was tempted to get in a canoe and start paddling north, but the vast American fleet was too intimidating.

31

Coolie on a
New Battlefield

The middle of July arrived, yet the promised evacuation of refugees to the north had not occurred. Although I was completely safe in my pose as a civilian refugee, I was also completely miserable. I wanted to meet Katsuyama, Arakaki, and Warrant Officer Chiba in Haneji by the end of July as promised. That time was approaching, but I was unable to obtain information about enemy or friendly positions and dispositions. My patience grew thinner with each passing day. My mission was to learn of enemy positions in Okinawa and convey that information to Japanese Imperial Headquarters, which was now readying itself for a major and final showdown on our own sacred soil.

I hoped with all my heart that Miyake and Nagano had broken through enemy lines and reached the homeland. This was no occasion for me to be wasting time. First I had to learn the local Japanese situation. I tried to find this out by casual questioning of my lodge mates who worked for the American military, but all they could tell me was that the roadsides were lined with tents. I asked for American newspapers they might pick up while cleaning rooms at the military facilities, but I never got any. It would not do for me to be too inquisitive. That might betray my identity.

Around July 17 Mr. Heavy Beard offered the friendly advice that I should go to work for the military base, saying that I might acquire things I wanted such as newspapers, cigarettes, candy, and even rice. The jobs there were simple and did not require strenuous work. He offered to help, so I went with him the next morning.

We finished breakfast at four o'clock and went to the meeting place at Yabiku, with lunch boxes tied to our waists. I wore worker footwear (*jika-*

183

tabi) and a tattered kimono borrowed from the Sonans and tied a kerchief around my head for a cap. The laborers were dressed in such a wild variety of garb that we looked like a grotesque fashion show. I felt that I was the most conspicuous model of all. We were to meet officially at eight o'clock in the morning to be chosen for the limited number of jobs on a "first-come, first-served" basis. That is why we showed up earlier than the official opening time and waited. As dawn broke I was in line smoking my second Chesterfield of the day, provided by Mr. Heavy Beard.

By eight o'clock hundreds of people had gathered. Most of them were either younger than eighteen or older than fifty. The area was patrolled by military policemen in white helmets and civilian police in red helmets. Inside the camp were many tents and lots of young men standing around waiting for a chance at the daily jobs. Nearby was a Combat Intelligence Center surrounded by barbed wire. A nervous-looking American *Nisei* soldier, who spoke broken Japanese, was in charge of the laborers. Curious as I was to learn about what was going on, it had been a long time since I was involved in such an active situation, and I was uneasy. Yet none of the American soldiers on guard seemed to suspect my identity. I told myself, "Relax, Ya-hara, relax."

The selected laborers were loaded into trucks. I was disappointed at not being on the same truck with Sato and Arakaki. I was excited about doing something new but anxious about possible disaster. The laborers were all cheerful as we headed for our unknown destination. The trucks drove in a line along Nakagusuku Bay to Yonabaru on a smooth new road. I had thought this terrain was familiar, but now it was a strange and foreign land. The towns of Shinzato, Tsuhako and Itarashiki had vanished completely. The only village I recognized was Sashiki, because several homes there had not been burned.

Otherwise I saw only an endless series of tent houses stretching for miles along the road. Atop one large tent house, presumably the commanding officer's quarters, a huge American flag fluttered against the clear blue sky. The sight of it gave me a sudden chill as I recalled my own strategic writings about how to fight the Americans. My words had been distributed to all soldiers of 32nd Army: "The key factor of the upcoming battle is completion of cave fortifications. If we fail in this we will surely lose the battle, and end up as tragic corpses under the Stars and Stripes."

Without stopping at Yonabaru, our trucks continued west toward Naha. Just beyond Yonabaru was the bloody battlefield where our soldiers had fought to the last man at the end of May, until 32nd Army headquarters retreated to the south. In every direction I could see that the mountains and fields had been battered by savage bombardment. All of nature, except for a few blackened trees, seemed to have been incinerated. Untama hill rose in the distance, lonely and shivering in the summer heat, as if mourning the death of Mother Earth. So complete was the devastation that the most gifted poet could not have expressed the desolation of this Okinawa. It was beyond description or belief.

We passed Haebaru, where hundreds of U.S. Army tents covered the long hills sloping down to the road. It was "chow time." Enemy soldiers were standing in line for breakfast. It reminded me of Fort Benning where, as an exchange student, I had often stood in chow lines with American soldiers.

On a farm north of Haebaru we saw more than a hundred civilian workers stacking packages of bean paste, barrels of soy sauce, and other foods. These provisions had been stored in Japanese fortifications. They were now were being prepared for distribution to hungry refugees.

I caught unreal glimpses of the villages of Tsukazan and Shuri as in a dream world. It seemed as if blood and iron had covered the mountains, changing them into new and different mountains. In my fantasy world there existed no American tents, no soldiers, or even any Okinawans. I was entirely by myself, alone. When reality returned, I was still on the truck and we were passing through Kokuba on the outskirts of Naha City. The roads had all been rebuilt by American engineers. The scenery, too, had been reconstructed. Madanbashi, the famous stone bridge over the Kokuba River, had been totally destroyed by American bombardment. Only its crumbled stones remained, a ghostly relic of the past.

Oroku Peninsula, south of Manko Creek, where our navy had fought bravely against the American 6th Marine Division, lay devastated in the glaring light of the sun. We passed Kufanga and entered Naha City. The roads were lined with massive piles of junk and litter from our army. Many corpses still lay strewn about, and the offensive smell of death pervaded all. The city had been reduced to ashes by the massive air raid of October 10, 1944, and for the past eight months there had been no reconstruction.

At Naha pier we stopped in front of a Western-style building that had managed to survive the October bombing. After some repair it became the headquarters of Lieutenant Colonel Hiraga's Shipping Engineer unit, until the enemy invasion in April. The enemy had repaired the building and was using it as a transportation center. We were told to get off the trucks.

The area was bustling with American traffic. A group of pale-complexioned American nurses looked at us with curiosity. Small planes skimmed overhead, landing and taking off at Naha airfield. Surprisingly, Naha Port was not yet in full operation. Many Japanese ships lay damaged and lifeless in the water, another grim reminder of a once-proud navy.

An energetic, smiling American soldier came out of the office and put us to work carrying debris from the office entrance to a cleared ruins area a hundred yards or so distant. This good-natured soldier talked about souvenirs we would collect and joked about women, but he did not really pay much attention to our work. By lunchtime we had not done very much, but we were served C-rations, two cans of beans, and biscuits and cakes. I got my food from a soldier who smiled and winked at me as if he were happy to be surprising me with far more than I had expected. During lunch we exchanged words with the Americans in Japanese and English, with many explanatory gestures. I pretended not to understand a word of English.

I bartered Okinawan trinkets for an American leather belt, three packs of cigarettes, and two cans of cocoa. Okinawans bought cigarettes and canned meat with Japanese currency. The kind American soldier promised we could come back the next day and continue our easy work in exchange for many more American supplies. Our work, which was little more than child's play, stopped at four o'clock in the afternoon.

Meanwhile, I continued to prepare my escape plan. Naha City was an ideal place for escape because the American soldiers did not keep strict watch over the civilians. Among the ruins were many good hiding places, and there were only a few American campsites between the port and the distant river mouth.

We piled onto the same trucks for our return to Fusozaki. In Yabiku we stopped at a distribution center where three smiling Okinawan girls were issuing rice. As I stepped up for my share our eyes met, and one girl looked startled. She did not speak but must have recognized me because she turned her face away. I was even more startled but did not betray any sign of it. The unwary bear the brunt of danger.

We were on our own after getting the rice. I walked toward the Sonan home, passing new cemeteries in Yabiku and at Fusozaki with hundreds of grave markers. Most of the dead were children or elderly. Many civilians who had survived the three months of battle perished from wounds and malnutrition after the fighting ended.

In the Yabiku cemetery a personable little boy told me the story of his short life. While his family of seven sought shelter in Hantagawa valley, his father and four brothers were killed by enemy naval gunfire. He was wounded slightly, his mother seriously. They fled from one place to another and were finally captured by the Americans. They were staying in Yabiku until she was well enough to return to their home village. The boy was too young to work for the American army, so he did civilian labor to get his daily share of rice. This tragic story saddened me. A beautiful summer sunset and cool evening breezes seemed only to add to my melancholy.

The Sonan family welcomed my safe return. Following the custom, I distributed cigarettes to the men and served sweet cocoa to everyone. I did not go to work the next day or for some time thereafter. I wanted to regain my strength and also to preserve my identity. I helped Mrs. Sonan by pounding rice, tying straw bundles, and performing other chores around the house. I soon began to feel normal again. She was generous in providing me with her husband's garments, and she even bought rice for me on the black market. I gave her a crocodile belt.

The villager in charge of supplies provided me with army clothes stamped with a large C.W., which stood for civilian worker. My life improved each day, thanks to the kindness and generosity of the people around me.

A gracious elderly lady visited us one day to retrieve two young boys I had helped to rescue from caves at Yoza and Nakaza. She thanked me profusely and returned several days later with rice, cigarettes, money, and more thanks. I had heard that Okinawans were ungrateful and without heart but learned from experience that this was totally untrue.

Not long afterward I was able to assist in reuniting a young girl with her mother. Another stroke of luck came when I met again the elderly gentleman whose acquaintance I had made in Nakaza. He too was pleased to see me, and we chatted on the Sonan veranda.

Idle gossip turned to rumor, and the rumor became reality as word came that we were being moved to the northernmost Okinawan villages of Kunigami. This saved my having to act independently on the next stage of my escape plan. It would be much simpler for me to advance northward with the refugees rather than move alone through enemy-held territory. This also spared me from continuing to risk working with the American army. All I had to do was to make the right decision at the right moment.

32

Reversal of Fortune

On July 23, a Monday evening, a young Okinawan came to my lodging with word for me to report immediately to the Combat Intelligence Center (CIC). It came as a great shock to think that they might have found out who I was. Nervous and frightened at this prospect, I asked if there was some problem. The youth smiled and said, "Nothing to worry about. All civilians are being evacuated to Kunigami, and civilians from mainland Japan will be screened by the Americans." He added encouragingly that one man they screened had been promptly released. I was still fearful and decided to ignore the CIC, at least for that evening.

Next morning people began preparing for the evacuation. Despite my anxieties I resolved to compose myself and remain calm. The Sonan family was sympathetic about my having to report to the CIC but felt that it was just another routine matter, not to be taken seriously. I gave my remaining cans of meat and cakes to the lodgers on the veranda and made a gift of my last bag of rice to Mrs. Sonan.

The messenger boy had said that the sooner I appeared at the CIC office, the sooner I would be released. Before I was able to go there, however, two military policemen arrived on motorcycles to pick me up. I said farewell to the Sonans and waved goodbye to the children at the gate as I was taken away. That was the last I saw of them.

At CIC there were hundreds of men of all ages. I was eager for the investigation and my release. My turn came on Thursday, July 26. To my surprise, all the interrogators were Japanese. I sat beside two men who were being questioned. My interrogator was young, tall, and very intelligent. I gave him my account of being an English teacher returning from a visit with relatives in Taiwan, that I was shipwrecked near Okinawa, and thus got involved in the battle.

Meanwhile the two men seated next to me were being struck in the face, knocked to the ground, and kicked in the stomach. As calmly as possible I continued my dialogue, mentioning my trouble getting transportation. My interrogator interrupted at this point to say, "Speaking about problems in getting transportation, my senior adjutant was reluctant to issue me a pass. To make matters worse, Senior Staff Officer Yahara was a mean bastard." At these words he glared into my face, turning as pale as I was. When I said, "I am that Senior Staff Officer Yahara," he sprang to his feet and ran to the next office.

He returned with an American officer. They came directly to me. All my plans were ruined and I was petrified; but I was furious with rage at the traitorous investigator and shouted, "*Inu!*"

The officer calmly asked the meaning of *inu*. With trembling voice I answered, "He is a dog."

"A dog? I do not understand you. Please write it down." My hand shook with anger as I wrote the character for "dog."

The American officer took me into his office where I saw the man in charge of the camp and two other influential Japanese. In the brief month since the cease-fire they seemed to have become very Americanized. Should I have expected anything different?

After a brief conversation, the young American officer led me from the room, and we got into a jeep. As we rode he spoke of his family in the United States. His older brother, an officer, had once been stationed in Japan. Still shaking, whether from anger or fear I knew not, I did not feel like talking, so for most of the drive we sat in silence. With each turn of the wheels, myriad thoughts rolled through my mind. Should I kill myself? Should I try to escape?

We passed through mountains and villages that were as disturbed and torn apart as I was. We finally stopped at Goeku, where 10th Army command was located. Strangely, this area had not been bombarded. The foliage was as green here as all of Okinawa had once been.

I was led into the CIC office, where there were several officers. A fat lieutenant colonel asked me questions. When I explained how I had escaped American hands for so long, he said, "You are very clever."

Everyone laughed when I replied, "If I am so clever, why do I stand before you now?"

In further conversation he said—perhaps to discourage any thoughts of suicide on my part—that Japan would soon surrender. Japan surrender?

In the final stage of the battle for Okinawa many Japanese officers had said, "If Okinawa is lost, Japan will certainly fall." I, on the other hand, was one who predicted that Japan's destiny lay in an inevitable battle in the homeland. It was for this reason that I had swallowed pride, refused suicide, and had endured the tribulations of the past weeks.

The colonel's words shattered the very foundation and meaning of my life, which was to live—not die—for Japan. I saved my composure by convincing myself that those words were nothing more than enemy talk.

As I was being driven to my "quarters," I saw General Stilwell's residence, not far from a familiar sphinxlike rock.[1] Our vehicle stopped at the entrance to Goeku village, and the iron gate was opened. Guards saluted as we entered the village, which showed not a trace of battle damage. Houses and trees were untouched by the war.

A guard showed me to my quarters, a small thatched farmhouse where *tatami* mats had been laid. Inside were three blankets and a mosquito net. The surrounding garden was overgrown with summer weeds, and there was a bamboo grove in the northeast corner. Across the bumpy road in front of the garden was a banana field, and beyond the garden another farmhouse.

The head guard was a smartly uniformed lieutenant. The mess attendants—Sergeant Sims and Corporal Richards—were very correct in behavior. Corporal Richards removed everything I might possibly use to take my life. He overlooked, however, the rope for the mosquito net, which was hanging from a beam and swinging in the breeze.

To resist temptation I recited Chinese poems aloud and soon regained my composure, realizing that just now it was pointless to take my life. Better risk it in escaping than to kill myself for nothing. For the time being I had better observe the terrain and the enemy camps around the village and allow time to recover my health and calmness of mind. I could choose my demise when the time was right. I heard predictions that Japan would surrender in ten days and wanted to see if this were true.

Next day I was visited by a naval intelligence officer, Lieutenant (jg) K. C. Lamott, a cordial gentleman, who was attached to 10th Army Head-

---

[1]After the death of General Buckner on June 18, General Joseph A. Stilwell succeeded to 10th Army command. Buckner had been killed by enemy fire while standing at a forward observation post.

quarters staff. He was in charge of liaison matters and said he would visit me each day. Born in Tokyo, he had lived in Japan until the age of 13 and spoke Japanese quite well. He arranged for me to have the services of Azama, a boy from Gushikawa, as my attendant.

I pretended to accept the present situation completely, but inside I was still plotting an escape. My existence here was quiet and outwardly peaceful, but I spent sleepless nights thinking of escape and anguishing about continuing to live.

Then quickly there came a series of shattering events. On August 6 an atomic bomb was dropped on Hiroshima, and three days later one on Nagasaki, accompanied by the Soviet Union's declaration of war on Japan. These were the subject of headlines in the 10th Army newspaper *Buckner*. On August 10, *Buckner* reported that Japan had accepted the Potsdam Declaration, on condition that the Emperor's prerogatives remain intact. Lieutenant Lamott and the guards were ecstatic.

That evening there were gunfire celebrations all over Okinawa. Through the gunfire I heard joyous American soldiers shouting, "We'll go home." There was no longer any doubt. My homeland and its leaders had collapsed before there was need for a final showdown.

No longer would I have a chance to participate in a decisive battle on mainland Japan, much less a life-or-death escape, or even resort to pointless suicide. After my long and anguished journey I decided to live. On August 15 *Buckner* displayed an English version of the Emperor's surrender rescript. The war was over.

On August 23 Captain Ito, commander of the 32nd Infantry Regiment, appeared, accompanied by several American officers. We were equally surprised at our encounter. It is hard to imagine how a commander and his entire regiment could disappear for a couple of months in the middle of a war and then suddenly reappear. Baffling as it seems, that is what happened. It happened also in the case of the Shimura Battalion. It had been defending the fortifications at Maeda. They hid for a considerable time and then reappeared intact. They had an ample supply of provisions and were protected by well-concealed cave fortifications. With units large and small it was not an uncommon occurrence.

One of the American officers with Captain Ito said to me, "You succeeded in escaping from us by screaming through us." Offended by this remark I protested, "What? I never screamed."

He laughed and explained, "No, no. I said, 'screened,' not 'screamed.' " This provided a laugh for us all.

Later, Major General Frank D. Merrill, 10th Army's chief of staff, and Colonel Louis B. Ely, his G-2, came to visit me, and we discussed the Okinawa operation from the Japanese viewpoint. General Merrill told me that he had served as a military attaché at the American embassy in Tokyo before the war.

On August 28 I said farewell to the American officers in Goeku and was moved to Yaka stockade, located at the southeastern edge of Mount Onna, facing Kinmu Bay. There and at Machinato some ten thousand officers, soldiers, and Okinawan and Korean conscripts were gathered into separate compounds. Until the end of the year, remnants of our army continued to appear from caves both in the north and in the south.

All survivors were treated kindly and well. Some were put to work at various tasks, but most spent their time in complete idleness. There was periodic friction between the various groups, but generally life was calm and monotonous. In October Okinawans were transferred to a stockade at Kokuba, and Koreans were repatriated. They were replaced by disarmed soldiers from the outer islands.

On December 30, 1945, the first Japanese troops were repatriated, and hundreds of us sailed for home in the transport *Gable*. We landed safely at Uraga in Tokyo Bay on January 7. Heartbroken, I traveled through the devastation of Yokohama and Tokyo to our former war ministry in Ichigaya and reported to Senior Officer Colonel Nijin.

On July 1 I was appointed to take charge of the remaining business of 32nd Army. About that time the last group of surviving troops from Okinawa arrived in Nagoya harbor on board a transport. They disembarked on the soil and into the streets of our once-sacred homeland and vanished into the mist of history.

The Colonel's Postscript

I have already disclosed all my actions and experiences during the battle of Okinawa, except for the period in late June 1945 when I surrendered disguised as a civilian refugee. Because of my silence concerning this surrender, some have criticized me, saying that I was captured as a prisoner of war. That is an absolutely disgraceful charge to make against a senior staff officer, and it is a completely absurd accusation.

It arose out of a gross misunderstanding of the situation and left me with an unbearable burden. As I have said previously, the truth is that I tried to escape with the refugees for the sole purpose of avoiding enemy capture so that I could get back to Tokyo. There I could report the war situation to General Headquarters.

As revealed in this book, I mingled with the civilian refugees, moving freely among them, and waited for the right moment to escape. In late July, however, a shameless breach of faith by a Japanese led to my capture by the enemy. While I was in enemy hands until Japan's total capitulation (of which I had been informed by Americans on August 10), I never tried or even considered suicide. On the contrary, during all that time I was thoroughly engrossed in planning my escape. I am satisfied that actually I was never a prisoner of war.

When the war ended it struck me that I should have followed our commander-in-chief in suicide. Then I thought about my mission to return to the homeland. But everything was now over; there was nothing left for me to do. In addition to my personal agony, I was upset about the tactics and strategy of the entire Okinawa operation.

I was tormented by the wishful strategic thinkers who dreamed of air-war priorities—not to mention the absurd suicide tactics that were resorted to in our ground actions. While such strategies and tactics had devastated the enemy earlier in the war, they became a futile illusion as the war drew to a close.

Understanding many of our past failures, I had developed the operation plan for Okinawa. That plan was endorsed by Lieutenant General Mitsuru Ushijima, 32nd Army commander, and Lieutenant General Isamu Cho, his chief of staff. Our entire army of one hundred thousand soldiers was ready to follow my plan as one man, and they all labored hard in preparation for the inevitable showdown.

When the enemy began landing at Kadena, however, Imperial Headquarters panicked. In a sudden *volte-face,* Tokyo ordered an all-out assault on Yomitan airfield in the north. What a turn of events! This field had long been abandoned by our army as of little military value. This abrupt change in operational policy left our army in utter confusion. I tried desperately to stop the assault on Yomitan and was partially successful, but my efforts added to the ensuing confusion. The high command's continuing demand for an offensive added fuel to the aggressive character of General Cho.

My entire plan was doomed by our tremendous night assault of April 13, 1945, and our great counteroffensive of May 4. When it became clear on May 5 that our offensive moves were a fiasco, General Ushijima summoned me to say that he had been wrong in carrying out the demands of the high command. He said that my judgment had been correct concerning the whole operation and that he was following my operation plan from that point onward. But he knew that it was too late to make up for the lost battles. We had lost most of our elite veteran force and were out of artillery ammunition. What options we had possessed were exhausted and drained.

It was clear that the foolish ideas of a decisive air offensive and suicide assaults had resulted in irreversible failures. They were bad strategy and bad tactics. Nevertheless, Imperial Headquarters and 10th Area Army in Taiwan had insisted on these senseless offensive moves.

Just before his suicide on June 23 at Mabuni, General Cho confided to me that we had been doomed to defeat, no matter how good our operation plans might have been. He whispered that if I were lucky enough to return home, I must never utter a word about the correctness of our battle plans. Now [1972], after twenty-seven years, I have swallowed my words for too long. It is time for me to tell what General Cho wanted to remain a secret.

While preparing for the battle, as ordered, he had insisted on remaining in our solid fortifications at Shuri. He must have realized the need for our army as a front-line force in the final showdown in the homeland. We could have accomplished much more than we did if only he had stayed with the attrition strategy instead of yielding to offensive tactics. In a battle of attrition we could have saved at least one-quarter and perhaps even a third of our forces until the end of hostilities.

Much has been written on the battle of Okinawa, but most of it has failed to understand the basics of the operational plans. Without solid facts there can be no truth.

There is no room for outdated tactics in modern land warfare. Before beginning to fight, the situation must be examined objectively with insight as to the status quo; one must foresee possible shifts in events and establish a consistent war plan. Then one is ready for battle. To the extent possible, one must remain rational at all times and have respect for human life.

At Okinawa the strategic defensive (attrition warfare) and the all-out offensive (direct confrontation) plans constantly collided, leaving us without a consistent war plan. Only I can reveal the true situation there.

Epilogue:
The Battle Ended—Capture and Return
By Frank B. Gibney

Hiromichi Yahara was discovered and made prisoner on July 15. Because of his rank and importance, he was taken to the special stockade he mentioned—actually a farmhouse made into a kind of VIP prisoners' quarters. I met him there several days later. Ken Lamott undertook a detailed interrogation, at which I assisted. We housed another VIP prisoner in an adjacent building. Akira Shimada, an old friend of General Cho's from his China days and a longtime Japanese intelligence agent, had served as Cho's secretary during the campaign and was privy to all of the major decisions taken. He had been captured a few weeks before. While Lamott interrogated Yahara, I questioned Shimada. We would then compare notes. (Both interrogations are included in the Prisoner-of-War Interrogation Reports.)

By this time POW interrogation on Okinawa had become a big little business. Around June 20, while the two Japanese commanders were preparing for their ritual suicide, their troops had begun surrendering daily by the hundreds—sometimes singly, sometimes in groups. By the war's end, we had taken almost eleven thousand military prisoners, of whom seven thousand were Japanese army and navy regulars. This was an unheard-of number, if compared with past experience. Accustomed to rather leisurely questioning periods at Pearl Harbor, where we sometimes felt more like psychiatrists (or confessors) than military information seekers, we never thought we would see the day when one needed a jeep to go from one end of a POW stockade to another.

Nonetheless, those who surrendered or let themselves be "involuntarily" captured were still a minority. Even with defeat now certain, hundreds took their own lives daily rather than face capture. Soldiers would either die fighting in *gyokusai* suicide charges against American tanks or simply pull out a grenade pin and blow themselves up. Navy men were as stubborn as their army counterparts. As Yahara's narrative noted, several thousand perished in suicides or futile last-ditch attacks in a literal battle-to-the-death inside the navy base entrenchments on the Oroku Peninsula, near Naha Port.

Worst of all were the civilian deaths. Thousands of Okinawan civilians, and as many women and children as men, were ordered to stay in caves with Japanese troops who were preparing a last-ditch "defense." The flower of the island's youth—teenage girl nurses' aides as well as *boeitai* boy soldiers— were sacrificed to the directives of the Japanese army command. In many cases they were forced to hurl themselves from the low southern cliffs into the sea, so they, too, could "die for the Emperor."

Even after entering the stockade as prisoners, many soldiers still regretted their decision to stay alive. This was a backhanded tribute to the cruelly effective indoctrination of Japan's militarists. As sophisticated an observer as the novelist Shohei Ooka, whose book *A Prisoner's Journal (Furyoki)* became a Japanese classic, could later write of his capture (in this case in the Philippines): "I did not regard capture by the enemy as the heinous disgrace our drill instructors had pictured. . . . Soldiers in the field had every right to abandon hopeless resistance. Yet once I had fallen captive, how discomforting, how reprehensible it felt to be idly enjoying life among the enemy while my brothers in arms continued to risk their lives in battle. I felt a sudden urge to throw myself into the ocean and kill myself. . . ."

At 10th Army G-2 interrogation headquarters we mobilized every Japanese speaker in American uniform—officers and noncoms, army, navy, and marines—to extract militarily useful information from our prisoners. Because of the numbers involved, we sometimes interrogated POWs in groups—for the first time in our experience. Various interrogators were assigned to different Japanese units to elicit information on their tactics during the campaign, all the while screening prisoners for further questioning. In addition, we were on constant call to accompany intelligence officers from various division headquarters, in efforts to talk out the last survivors of 32nd Army battalions from their cave hideouts. Generally we were unsuccessful. And time and time again the attempts of individual soldiers to turn themselves in were frustrated by the determined resistance of hard-liners in these caves who wished "Death for the Emperor!" to be the fate of all.

At one point we were led by an engineer captain, just taken prisoner, to a cave where General Amamiya and many of the surviving 24th Division troops had blown themselves up. With 7th Division intelligence officers, I went down to one of the cave entrances and crawled in. After a walk through a long tunnel we came on a huge underground cavern and one of the ghastliest sights I ever saw. Here lay General Amamiya, surrounded by his staff and some two hundred officers and men. They had all killed themselves, most with grenades, although Amamiya had thoughtfully given himself a lethal injection to avoid the rigors of ritual suicide. The cave floor was literally carpeted with corpses.

In the middle of this carnage we found one survivor, a private who had been the general's orderly. Amamiya had told him to stay alive and report how they died—to the Emperor, presumably. The orderly had faithfully remained, prepared to do so. He found an underground spring that gave him a steady water supply and subsisted for almost a week on bits and pieces of rations which had been left behind by the suicides. The captain who had taken us to the cave was unhinged by the experience. He suffered, to put it mildly, a mental breakdown; it took him a long time to recover. But the general's orderly, once released from the cave, seemed to shrug off his ordeal. Late that afternoon I saw him in one of the prison camp yards playing volleyball with his fellow captives.

In the course of this bizarre fieldwork I managed to get to the Mabuni headquarters cave of 32nd Army on the same day the generals had committed suicide. This was probably just as Yahara was leaving. With an intelligence officer from the 7th Division, I attempted to go into the cave to talk out any survivors. There was still some Japanese sniper fire in the area, so 7th Division infantrymen covered us as we entered. No one was alive there, however. We found only the corpses of several Japanese staff officers. They were dressed in full uniform, swords at their sides. One of them, I recall, wore his tunic with decorations and his ceremonial aiguillettes.

Tenth Army, it must be remembered, was ticketed to land in Japan as one of three invading armies: 6th, 8th, and 10th. Until August 15, therefore, we lived in a climate of military urgency. Even when the word came a few days earlier of the A-bombs dropped on Hiroshima and Nagasaki, we were far from convinced that the war was over. Until the actual surrender announcement, our experience with the die-hard resistance on Okinawa seemed to presage an even bloodier struggle for the Japanese homeland.

Colonel Yahara was quite ready to review and explain the Japanese side of the Okinawa operation, as we called it, but he was reluctant to discuss anything bearing on the future. Only once did we press him. We had just attended a long staff conference at 10th Army G-2, in which various landing areas were considered for the invasion of Japan's main island of Honshu. After the merits and faults of a variety of beach areas were argued back and forth, a consensus among American staff officers finally agreed that the best place to strike was Kujikuri-hama—literally Ninety-nine Ri Beach (the old Japanese measure *ri* being roughly equal to two and a half miles) in Chiba Prefecture east of Tokyo. (This is not too far from the present Narita Airport.) When Lamott and I dropped in that evening at Yahara's quarters, we asked him rather casually where *he* would try to land an invasion force in Japan. "Why, Kujikuri-hama, I suppose," he said, "it's the obvious place."

As the bad news kept coming from Japan, Yahara grew more depressed. Given the surrender, there was no longer any rationale for him to report the battle. It was an anticlimax. Increasingly, he brooded over his survival, reflecting that almost every one of his colleagues had committed suicide or gone down fighting. His withdrawn, almost despairing mood was quite obvious.

One afternoon, to break the routine, I suggested that he might like to see the changes on the island since his capture. Dismissing the camp guards, I buckled on my forty-five, started up the jeep, and took the senior staff officer on a drive around the island. He was amazed at the network of roads that had been built over the past two months, not to mention the new barracks and office area around headquarters. We went to the top of one hill and got out of the vehicle, looking at much the same landing beaches that Yahara had viewed from Mount Shuri only a few months before. I pointed out new construction, as well as the new docks and storage areas for the cargo from the transports and freighters in the nearby anchorage. We talked a good bit, and his spirits seemed to pick up.

Not long afterward Yahara got into a conversation with a young American army PFC, one of his guards, and talked a bit in English about his circumstances. "Why are you so down?" asked the soldier. "You've done your duty. It's hard to understand this impulse to suicide among Japanese soldiers, when things go wrong. Countries, governments, battles—they're all like business. When business goes bad, you start over again, but you don't kill yourself."

To Yahara this homespun logic seemed to make a lot of sense. It marked something of a turning point for him. After he was transferred to another camp, he shook off his lethargy, assembled his notes, and began to set down his record of the campaign. In January he was repatriated. As his transport headed north, he took a last look at the island and wrote a final poem:

How sad to watch the peaceful Kiyan Cape
Now carpeted in green,
After it was dyed red
With the blood of warriors.

On reaching Tokyo, he went back to what was left of the old Imperial Army Headquarters, now called the First Demobilization Ministry. He found a lieutenant general he knew and proceeded to report briefly on the battle, as Cho had ordered him to do. The general heard him out, with formal sympathy, then excused himself for lunch. He did not invite Yahara but asked him to wait. Lunch for the general's staff was apparently served in the next room. Through a thin partition the colonel heard the general mention the name Yahara, then the word "prisoner." Harsh laughter followed. Shortly afterward, Yahara left.

At his home in Yonago he was reunited with his family and started eking out a living there. He was called back once by the Demobilization Ministry in July 1946, to help wind up the paperwork of 32nd Army. He worked there for about half a year, just to make a little money for his barely subsisting family. Some years later, when the government began organizing the National Police Reserve that later became the Self-Defense Forces (*Jiei-tai*), he was asked to serve as a cadre instructor. He declined. There was to be no more military life for him. He did give lectures years later to Self-Defense Force officers about the history and tactics of the Pacific war.

His book was quite successful, going through several printings since its first appearance in 1972. Income from the royalties enabled him and his wife to move from Yonago to Kamakura, the venerable seaside town just outside of Tokyo. It was in Tokyo where I met him again.

I had seen the book advertised and read most of it. I was fascinated by its tone. So I asked him to lunch one day. We met at the Keio Plaza Hotel in Tokyo's Shinjuku section. He was relaxed and happy to talk about the old days. He emphasized his desire to set the record straight with his book, particularly since he had been so heavily criticized by other surviving military men for making his escape. He still attended reunions of his class at the Military Academy, but that was about all the contact he had with his old comrades in the Emperor's Army.

He kept himself well informed about politics and international affairs, although he grew increasingly pessimistic about current attitudes of the Japanese public. Japan's high-growth era had begun. Business seemed to absorb the country's attention. International politics was something to read about in the newspapers—a secondary spectator sport. About the power of communist China and Vietnam, most Japanese seemed curiously unaware. In wartime days the same public had been hopelessly uncritical of the militarists, patriotic to a fault. Now, he thought, they were going pacifist in the same uncritical fashion.

He showed considerable interest in my work editing the Japanese-language version of the *Encyclopaedia Britannica,* and he seemed pleased that I had kept up with my Japanese language. Then, as we talked again about Okinawa, he added a personal historical footnote.

"You know, Mr. Gibney," he said, "when you sent away the camp guards and drove me on that sightseeing trip around the island that August day, it was before the surrender and I was still under orders to escape and report to Tokyo. . . . You were totally unwatchful. While you were proudly pointing out the new road network to me, I could have easily grabbed your pistol and knocked you over the head. Conceivably, I could have driven your jeep up the coast and found a boat to escape north. I thought about it, but decided that it would not have been a very nice thing to do. So I stayed put."

I was riveted to my seat. That possibility had never occurred to me at the time. I was so used to prisoners, once captured, accepting their fate. Had Yahara, colonel in the Imperial Army, escaped, the consequences would have been embarrassing for Lieutenant (jg) Gibney USNR, I thought. Even if I survived the experience, a court-martial would have ensued. Portsmouth Naval Prison, I had heard, is not a very nice place. I was thankful.

We did not meet again. After once recovering from a stroke, Yahara continued to live quietly. He died in his sleep at Kamakura, in 1981, at the age of 78.

Prisoner-of-War Interrogation Reports

Introduction to the
Prisoner-of-War Reports
By Frank B. Gibney

These two reports are copies of field interrogations conducted in Okinawa in late July and early August, 1945. Colonel Yahara was interrogated by Lt. (jg) Kenneth Lamott, while I interrogated Mr. Shimada, who as General Cho's friend and private secretary (with some Intelligence connection) was of great importance to us. Lamott and I shared our notes during both interrogations, which covered much the same ground.

At the time these reports were written, we fully expected that the war would continue, culminating in landings in Japan. Tenth Army was to be part of the landing force. The thrust of our line of questioning was to prepare for this eventuality. Ironically enough, Lamott's interrogation was distributed on August 6, the day the A-Bomb was dropped on Hiroshima.

CICA/KCL
6 August 1945

PRISONER OF WAR INTERROGATION REPORT

Tenth Army Interrogation Report #28.

1. PERSONAL DETAILS

Name   : YAHARA, Hiromichi
Rank   : Col
Duty   : Senior Staff Officer, 32d Army
Date of Capture   : 15 July 1945
Place of Capture : YABIKU Civilian Compound
Age   : 42
Residence   : TOTTORI Pref
Occupation   : Army officer

2. ASSESSMENT

a. Details of Capture:

After attending the dinner preceding the suicides of
Generals USHIJIMA and CHO, Col YAHARA, in civilian clothes,
proceeded to carry out orders received from General CHO -
"After participating in the final defense of OKINAWA Island,
Staff Officer YAHARA will proceed and take part in the defense of the homeland". He made his escape from the MABUNI
caves in spectacular fashion, rolling over a cliff when
observed by Blue troops, inadvertently firing his pistol
during the descent. This performance was apparently the
basis for rumours that YAHARA had been killed at MABUNI.
Alive, though bruised by the fall, Col YAHARA joined a group
of civilians in a cave, intending to remain with them and
to work his way north, hoping eventually to reach Japanese
Territory by small boat. When Blue troops approached the
cave YAHARA led the group out and accompanied them to the
YABIKU civilian compound where he successfully assumed the
guise of a school-teacher. Three days on a labor detail
depleted YAHARA's already weakened endurance; he collapsed
and spent the next two weeks resting. The presence of an
idle but complaining stranger aroused the suspicion and resentment of an alert Okinawan who took Col YAHARA aside and
demanded an explanation. YAHARA revealed his identity but
appealed to the man's patriotism and begged his silence.
To his chagrin the Okinawan immediately reported his presence to local CIC agents who returned and took YAHARA, bitter but unresisting, into custody.

b. Evaluation:

Quiet and unassuming, yet possessed of a keen mind and
a fine discernment, Col YAHARA is, from all reports, an eminently capable officer, described by some POWs as the
"brains" of the 32d Army.

-1-

His life falls into the pattern of many career officers of the Japanese service. The son of a small country land-owner, Y.H.R. won an appointment to the Military Academy, graduating in 1923. Although promotions came slowly he won some distinction as a junior officer and attended the War College, graduating, according to his account, fifth in his class (officer POWs attribute this to native modesty, hold-ing that Y.H.R. led his class). His subsequent assignments included duty in the United States, in CHINA, and as a plain clothes agent in SIAM, BURMA, and MALAYA. Col Y.H.R. attri-butes his frequent change of duty to a propensity to dis-agree with superior officers which made him an undesirable among certain old-line officers.

Col Y.H.R. discusses the OKINAWA operation freely though he has indicated that he will not divulge information which he considers vital to the security of the Empire. There is no reason to believe that he has made any attempt at decep-tion. It should be borne in mind that his observation of the campaign was made from the comparative safety of SHURI castle and that in some instances his narrative may differ from that of front-line troops.

The present report deals only with the OKINAWA operation, making no attempt to delve into the Col's pre-Okinawan ex-periences.

3. INTELLIGENCE
    a. Chronology

__1923__
        Grad from Military Academy. To 54th Inf Regt (OKAYAMA).
__1925__
        To 63d Inf Regt
__1926__
        Entered Army War College
__1929__
        Grad from War College. Returned to 63d Regt.
__1930__
        To Personnel Dept of War Ministry
__1933__
        To US as exchange officer. Wilmington, Boston, Wash-
        ington D.C.   Att 8th Inf Regt for six months at Fort
        Moultrie.
__1935__
        Returned to Personnel Dept, War Ministry
__1937__
        Appointed as instructor (strategy and tactics) at Army
        War College.
        Three months in China as staff officer with 2d Army
        (N CHINA Exped Force)
__1938__
        Returned to Army War College as instructor.
__1940__
Sept As Japanese agent to Siam, Burma, Malaya.
Nov
Dec   To General Staff as expert on SE Asia.
__1941__
July To Bangkok as Ass't Military Attache
15 Nov Received secret orders to staff of 15th Army (SAIGON).
        Remained at Bangkok and participated in the negotiations
                              -2-

for the peaceful occupation of SIAM.
Then participated in the BURMA operation with the 15th army.
Apr
      Became ill and returned to Japan.   Again assigned to
      War College as instructor.
1944
16 Mar To OKINAWA as advisor from Imperial Staff.   32d Army
      Hq soon formed and assigned as Senior Staff Officer,
1945
15 July Captured.

b. Pre-L-Day Estimates and Preparations:
    The successful US invasion of the MARIANAS convinced
staff officers both in the 32d Army and the General Staff
that the US would attempt a landing either on TAIWAN, the
RYUKYU RETTO, or HONGKONG within the year. The 32d Army
staff believed that, because of its strategic position,
OKINAWA would certainly be invaded; opinion in TOKYO remained
more indefinite, some favoring TAIWAN. The attack was expected either as (a) an immediate landing based from and using
troops available in the MARIANAS or (b) an attack mounted
from the SOWESPAC area when the tactical situation should
permit the withdrawal of troops from that area. The first
possibility was regarded as a more dangerous threat since
OKINAWA was totally unprepared to repulse enemy landings
at that time. The landings on the PALAUS and on LEYTE
came as a respite, indicating that US plans did not include
an immediate attack in this area. The Landing was then
expected from late March to June 1945, on the assumption
that the situation in the PHILIPPINES would have eased
sufficiently by that time to permit the withdrawal of troops
and the use of LEYTE as a staging area. The OKINAWA landing was expected to take place before the IWO landing because IWO was considered of lesser importance. Some false
confidence was inspired by intelligence reports that not
enough troops were available to effect a landing on OKINAWA
for some time to come. However, in late Feb reports of shipping concentrations in the MARIANAS and LEYTE convinced the
32d Army staff that the attack would come in late March or
early April.
    From an early date the principle guiding the Japanese
plan of defense was that since it was impossible to defeat t
the invading enemy, the most successful plan would be that
which denied him t c use of the island for as long a period
as possible and cause him the greatest casualties. The
following plans were suggested, the first being that which
was adopted.
    1.   To defend, from extensive underground positions,
the SHIMAJIRI sector (i.e. that part of OKINAWA S of the
NAHA-SHURI-YONABARU line) the main line of defenses being N
of NAHA, SHURI, and YONABARU. Landings N of this line will
not be opposed; landings south of the line will be met on
the beaches. Since it will be impossible to defend KADENA
A/F, 15 cm guns will be emplaced so as to bring fire against
the airfield and deny the invaders its use.
    2.   To defend from prepared positions the central portion
of the island, including the KADENA and YONTAN A/Fs.

-3-

3. To dispose one Div around the KADENA area, one Div in the southern end of the island, and one Brig between the two Divs. To meet the enemy wherever he lands and attempt to annihilate him on the beaches.

4. To defend the northern part of the island with Army Hq in NAGO and the main line of defense based on Hill 220 NE of YONTAN A/F. The proponents of this course maintained that the terrain in the northern OKINAWA was most favorable for prolonging the defense although, admittedly, the loss of the more highly developed southern section was undesirable.

Although the withdrawal of the 9th Div seriously weakened the forces available for the defense of OKINAWA, the move was not opposed by 32d Army since the Div was removed with the intention of using it to reinforce the PHILIPPINES. Pleas for reinforcements from JAPAN were made in vain to TOKYO. There was a faint hope of getting reinforcements before L-Day, but, Col Y.H.R. states, none whatsoever therafter.

The plan which was adopted, i.e. to defend the SHURI line, presupposed Blue occupation of KADENA and YONTAN A/Fs. Although there was some pressure from TOKYO and certain individuals within 32d Army to include KADENA A/F within the zone of defense, this was deemed impractial, since, due to considerations of terrain. The defense of KADENA would seriously overextend forces barely sufficient for the effective defense of the southern part of the island.

The building of airfields on IE JIMA was criticized, since it was impossible to defend the island for more than a few days. Accordingly, on 10 March demolition of the airfields was initiated. Subsequently, 4 15 cm guns were emplaced in positions on the MOTOBU peninsula from where they could be brought to bear on IE.

The beaches originally considered most probable for Blue landings were (a) the HAGUSHI beaches, (b) the GUSUKUMA beaches (i.e. the beaches W of MACHINATO A/F) (c) the coast between NAHA and ITOMAN, (d) the MINATOGAWA beaches and (e) the NAKAGUSUKU WAN beaches.

By the end of March it was expected that the main Blue strength, probably 6 - 10 Divs would land upon the HAGUSHI beaches, immediately securing the KADENA and YONTAN A/Fs.

It was believed that the invading forces might, following the initial landings, establish beachhead perimeters, each two Divs in strength, 1½ to 3 kilometers in depth, each Div holding 2 km of beach. The perimeters would be maintained until enough supplies had been landed to permit a large-scale attack, using massed tanks and concentrated arty fire. The invaders would rely upon material strength to wear down the defenders rather than making a frontal assault. It was estimated that about ten days would be required to get the HAGUSHI forces in position to attack the main defense line based on SHURI and that during that time the US hoped to force the Japanese to move their main forces to the SHURI line and then to effect a not too costly landing, probably by one Div on the coast some where S of SHURI, probably MINATOGAWA. Additional landings on IE JIMA were expected but the landings on KERAMA came as a surprise, foiling their plans for conducting suicide boat warfare.

-4-

Artillery was ordered not to fire upon Blue shipping and divs were instructed not to oppose Blue reconnaisance or initial landings in their sectors until sufficient troops had been brought ashore to render it difficult to effect an escape by boat. The purpose was two-fold, (a) to attempt to deceive Blue intelligence as to the disposition of the Japanese forces (b) to ensure that any attack on Blue beachhead positions would engage and "annihilate" a sizable force.

The weakest point of the final defense plan was considered to be the CHINEN Peninsula. Landings on CHINEN would give the invaders good observation to direct NGF and a position from which to launch an attack upon the heart of the defensive line.

Accordingly, only the 62d Div, considered to be their best and most experienced outfit, was moved into the SHURI line, leaving the main force prepared to annihilate any enemy force unwise enough to attempt a landing to the south. The 5th Arty Command was ordered to place all its component element in defense of the MINATOGAWA sector. The Arty Command OP was established near ITOKAZU (TS 8364 R). The initial US diversion on the east coast increased their hopes that a landing would be attempted and contributed to the great reluctance with which troops were drawn from the S to strengthen the SHURI line. Until the end of April enough troops were left in the south to deal a severe blow to any landing. Hope of defending the southern coast was given up following the abortive counterattack of 4 May. A new plan was devised by which the event of a landing, 2-3000 troops would fight a delaying action while the main force, giving up NAHA and YONABARU, would establish a circular perimeter around SHURI, extending as far south as TSUKAZAN.

The absence of a landing puzzled the 32d Army Staff, particularly after the beginning of May when it became impossible to put up more than a token resistance in the south. Prevailing opinion was that the Tenth Army wished to obtain as cheap a victory as possible by wearing down the SHURI line rather than committing elements to a possibly hazardous landing in the South in the interests of bringing the operation to a speedier end.

Plans for fleet support of ground forces in the defense of OKINAWA were contemplated but never emerged from a rather nebulous stage. Co-ordination of such activities was in the hands of the OKINAWA Base Force. 32d Army also maintained direct liaison with the Navy General Staff which actually showed more interest in the campaign than did the Army General Staff. No naval personnel ashore were specifically charged with direction of NGF should fleet units succeed in reaching OKINAWA.

The 32d Army profited from the lesson learned on SAIPAN where Japanese arty had been wiped out in the first days of the operation. The overall command of artillery on OKINAWA was in the hands of the 5th Arty Command.

The factors responsible for the failure of Japanese arty in the past were thought to be (1) the lack of cave positions, preferably such that the piece could be fired from inside the cave, and (2) the premature firing, exposing positions before real damage could be done the enemy.

-5-

Consequently, under the Arty Command's direction, preparations were made for canceeling the guns,emplaced in the elaberate system of caves encountered later by Blue forces. Extensive surveying was conducted by the Arty Survey Co, supplying all arty units with data expediting the problem of transfer and massing of fire.

The Japanese realized that ammo was unsufficient for a protracted campaign. Impassioned pleas to TOKYO brough only the information that the shipping situation was acute. The Japanese prepared, accordingly, to make the most efficient use of available ammo.

The caliber of the Japanese general officers charged with the defense of OKINAWA was uniformly high. The following comments by Col Y.H.R. throw some light on the characters of the defeated commanders.

Lt Gen USHIJIMA, Mitsuru, CG, 32d Army: A quiet, reserved but extremely capable officer, held in the highest esteem by all men of his command. He was regarded by some as a latterday SAIGO Takamori (a military hero of the time of the MEIJI Restoration). He delegated all authority to his subordinates, yet took the full responsibility for any decisions made by them. Although an able tactician he took little part in the actual planning; his position was, in fact, little more than an eminently suitable figurehead.

Lt Gen CHO, Isamu, C of S; 32d Army: A fiery individual possessed of tremendous energy, CHO was the driving force behind the 32d Army. Quick to anger and demanding, CHO was not universally popular but no one questioned his ability. CHO made no bones about his epicurean tastes; his cellar was well stocked with better brands of S.KE and an ample supply of Scotch whiskey. Col Y.H.R. believes that USHIJIMA and CHO made a perfect combination, USHIJIMA acting as the balance wheel on CHO's drive.

Lt Gen FUJIOKA, Takeo, CG, 62d Div: Not a war college graduate, FUJIOKA came up through field commands. Quiet and conservative, he was considered the embodiment of the SAMURAI type. Like USHIJIMA he relied heavily on his C of S.

Lt Gen AMAMIYA, Tatsumi, CG, 24th Div: In temperment AMAMIYA resembled FUJIOKA, although more inclined to exert his personal authority. Hardworking and competant, he was regarded as an excellent leader.

Maj Gen SUZUKI, Shigeji, CG, 44th IMB: The least respected of the generals, SUZUKI expressed some resentment that FUJIOKA, who graduated below him at the Military Academy, should hold higher rank. He did a competent job though handicapped by a lack of experienced staff officers.

C. Enemy Operations

The tactical direction of the defense resolved itself! into a struggle between the conservatives, including Col Y.H.R., who advocated strictly defensive warfare, and a group of radicals who proposed that the Japanese take the offensive whenever there seemed to be the slightest possibility of succeeding.

An ill conceived plan for a counter-attack on 8 April was proposed at a staff meeting on 5 or 6 April. At that time the 62d Div alone was on the line, eager to take offensive action. It was proposed to bring up the 24th Div, 44th IMB, and all major arty units and in one massed blow to drive the invaders to the ISHIKAWA isthmus. The 62d Div was to spearhead the attack, having as its objective Hill 220 NE of YONTAN A/F. The 24th Div was to follow, then veer to the east, driving up the east coast. The 44th IMB was to be held in reserve.

The plan met with the vigorous opposition of Col YAHARA and other cooler heads among the staff officers who reasoned that even if the attack should succeed initially the Japanese would be at the mercy of Blue NGF and bombing since no positions had been prepared in the area. Also, the south would be left defenseless against possible landings. The plan was accordingly dropped, reluctantly by a group of fire-eaters, the majority deciding that only a madman could envision the success of such a venture. Another factor influencing the decision was a belief that the Blue forces might set up a defensive line S of the AWASE Peninsula, and proceed with the securing of the northern part of the island, putting off the reduction of the south indefinitely.

The proponents of aggressive action finally were permitted to attempt a counter-attack of sorts on the night of 12 April. The failure of the venture strengthened YAHARA's position as the spokesman of the conservatives.

The 62d Div was still holding the line alone with the 22d Regt of the 24th Div in reserve in the NISHIBARU area. On the night of 9 or 10 April plans were drawn up at a staff meeting calling for 3 Bns of the 22d Regt and 3 Bns of the 62d Div to infiltrate, scattering throughout the area between the lines and the objective line, 1500 yards north of FUTEMA. The sector lines ran through the center of the island, with the 62d Div on the west and the 22d Regt on the east. Within each sector one Bn was to occupy the northern one-third of the area, another Bn the center one-third, and the last Bn the southern third. The men were to hide in caves and tombs, awaiting a suitable opportunity to attack on 13 April.

The main advantage of the attack was that it would prevent the use of Blue NGF or arty since the area would be occupied simultaneously by Blue and Japanese troops, thus enabling the Japanese to fight upon their own terms, i.e. hand-to-hand combat. On the other hand, the 22d Regt was unfamiliar with the terrain. As it turned out, this factor accounted for the complete failure of the attack.

Col YAHARA opposed the attack and succeeded in reducing the forces participation to four Bns.

The attack was launched as scheduled. As Col YAHARA had predicted, the Bns of the 22d Regt were bewildered by the terrain and by dawn had made only 500 yards. They were forced to retreat, suffering heavy casualties. The 62d Div Bns fared somewhat better, one Bn advancing to TA 8378, remaining there throughout the day of 13 April and returning that night with low casualties.

On about 20 April, after the loss of TANABARU, the Japanese began to move troops north in anticipation of a Blue landing in the YONABARU area. The 62d Div, reinforced on the right (east) flank by the 22d Regt was holding a line from ONAGAHCOHI-Hill 187 to the MACHINATO A/F. Even the blindest staff officer was growing aware that Blue forces would eventually break through any defenses the Japanese could establish. As yet the Japanese had not suffered crippling casualties and in the opinion of many officers the time was ripe to strike a "decisive" blow.

Gen CHO, always a proponent of aggressive action, was instrumental in the decision to stage the counter-attack. CHO was vigorously supported by FUJIOKA, CG of the 62d Div,, who expressed the general desire of his men to fight the decisive action in the 62d Div's zone of defense. Col YAHARA opposed the attack as being premature but was over-ridden.

The plan was ambitious. The 23d and 26th Shipping Engineer Regts were to effect counter-landings on the west and east coast respectively during the night of 3-4 May. On 4 May the 24th Div (89th Regt on the east, 22d Regt in the center, and 32d Regt on the west) were to launch an attack with FUTEMA as the objective. The 44th IMB was to follow the 24th Div, bearing west to the coast, thus cutting off the 1st Mar Div. The 62d Div did not participate in the attack.

It was, it is Col YAHARA's opinion, the decisive action of the campaign. The Japanese were so weakened by its failure that they lost all hope of taking any further offensive action. On 5 May Gen USHIJIMA called Col YAHARA to his office and, with tears in his eyes, declared that he would, in the future, be guided by YAHARA's decisions.

On about 20 May it became apparent to the 32d Army Staff that the line north of SHURI would be soon untenable. The pressure exerted upon the line from both Sugar Loaf and Conical Hill forced a decision as to whether or not to stage the last ditch stand at SHURI. The capture of Sugar Loaf Hill alone could have been solved by the withdrawal of the left flank to positions S of NAHA and, in Col YAHARA's opinion would not have seriously endangered the defense of SHURI. However, the loss of remaining positions on Conical Hill in conjunction with the pressure in the west rendered the defense of SHURI extremely difficult.

On the night of 21 May a conference attended by all Div and Brig CGs was held in the 32d Army Hq caves under SHURI Castle. Three possible courses of action were proposed: (1) to make the final stand at SHURI, (2) to withdraw to the CHINEN Peninsula, and (3) to withdraw to the south. The first plan was favored by the 62d Div which was reluctant to withdraw from what they thought of as their own territory. Other factors favoring the adoption of this plan were the presence of large quantities of stores in SHURI and a general feeling that a withdrawal would not be in the best traditions of the Japanese Army. It was recognized that to stay would result in a quicker defeat and consequently it was discarded in accord with the 32d Army policy of protracting the struggle as long as possible. A retreat to CHINEN was regarded with no great favor by anyone and was deemed unfeasible due to the difficulties of transportation over rough and mountainous terrain. The discussion resolved in a decision to conduct an ordered retreat to the south, influenced to a great extent by the presence of 24th Div positions and stores in that area.

The transport of supplies and wounded began on the night of 22 May. The burden of the operation was in the hands of the 24th Tpt Regt, an unusually proficient organization commanded by a Col N.K.MUR. who later received a commendation for the masterful way in which the operation was carried out. While in CHINA the Regt had been intensively trained in night driving, apparently with some success.

The occupation of YON.B.RU on 22 May came as a surprise to the Japanese who did not expect such a move during the inclement weather prevailing at that time, assuming that Blue infantry would be unwilling to attack without tanks which were thought to be immobilized by the mud. On 23 May elements of the 24th Div were despatched to retake the town. The attack continued with no success on the 24th and 25th. May.

At this time the 62d Div sector consisted only of less than a 2000 yd front north of SHURI held by one Bn. The main force, consisting of about 3000 men was in SHURI, several hundred yards to the rear. Since the pressure directly north of SHURI was relatively light it was decided to place the Bn on the line under the command of the 24th Div and to send the rest of the 62d Div to assist the 24th Div in the attack on YON.B.RU. On 25 May the 62d Div left SHURI and travelling by a circuitous route approached YON.B.RU from the South, three days being required for the maneuver. The arrival of the 62d Div failed to relieve the situation.

The mass retreat from SHURI took place during the night of 29 May. Combat units left one-fifth to one-third of their troops behind to hold the line for another day with orders to retreat the night of the 30th. A temporary line from the mouth of the KOKUBA G.WA on the west coast running N of TSUK.ZN to T.A 8069 and then bearing south through K.R.DER.A to Hill 157 in T.A 8367 was occupied on 1-2 June with the 44th IMB manning the sector from the west coast to KOKUBA, The 24th Div from KOKUBA to CH.N, and the 62d Div from CH.N to the east coast.

The 44th IMB retreated through ITOM.N, then bore east going north of M.K.BE and through MEDEER.A to occupy the western portion of the line based on Y.EJU D.KE, arriving on 3 June. The remnants of the 62d Div (2500 men) fell back through T.M.-GUSUKU MUR. and GUSHICH.N MUR. occupying the sector south of M.K.BE and west of M.BUNI D.KE on 4 June. The 24th Div (7-8000) men withdrew through the center of the island, taking up the east flank on 4 June.

The message from General Buckner, offering USHIJIM. an opportunity to surrender did not arrive at 32d Army Hq. until 17 June, a week after it had been dropped behind the Japanese lines. Col Y.H.R. states that the delay was normal for frontline to Hq communications at that stage of the operation. The message was delivered to Col Y.H.R. who bucked it to Gen CHO, after showing it to his staff officers. The staff officers were unimpressed and treated the matter lightly. Gen USHIJIM.'s reaction is not recorded.

D. Enemy Intelligence

32d Army intelligence was admittedly poor. Although a
staff officer was charged with intelligence he was hampered
by assignment to other duties and by the general lack of interest in intelligence among front-line troops. Div staff
officers looked upon intelligence as minor matter; below
division, there were no personnel concerned with intelligence.
Col Y.H.R. admits that an unfortunate attitude that intelligence
work belonged properly only to officers incompetent for operations work prevailed even in the highest echelon.

Col Y.H.R. states that the greatest single source of intelligence was US news broadcasts indentifying units on the
island and describing the general progress of the operation.
Such broadcasts were monitored in T.I.W.N and transmitted from
there to OKINAWA.

Practically the only other source of intelligence was documents taken from bodies and wrecked tanks. Although a civil
service official supposedly qualified in the English language
was assigned to Army Hq, he proved himself incompetent and
Col Y.H.R. read captured documents personally. A tank destroyed shortly after the 27th Div came into the line yielded an
OpPlan of that Div. The document was taken to 32d Army Hq
where it was examined by Col Y.H.R.. Most of the document
was not of immediate interest, however, the "Estimate of Enemy
Capabilities" aroused great interest and amusement. On 5 May
a Marine enemy situation map, captured during the 4 May counter-
attack caused great consternation because of its accurate appraisal of Japanese dispositions. Some valuable OB information
was taken from addresses on personal letters taken from Blue
dead. The presence of the 1st Mar Div on the southern line
were discovered in this fashion.

The only US POWs of which Col Y.H.R. admits knowledge
are one navy ensign or Lt(jg) shot down off KER.M., and 2 or
3 unidentified flyers captured in March. The first POW was
interrogated on OKINAWA and apparently revealed movements of
his task force (it is not known how accurately; the Japanese
accepted his account at face value) but when questioned as to
future operations advised his interrogators to consult Admiral
Nimitz. This POW was subsequently flown to TOKYO for more intensive interrogation. Col Y.H.R. can furnish no information
on the POWs captured in March, beyond the fact that he thinks
they were flown to TOKYO immediately to be worked over by
competent interrogators. No POWs were reported to 32d Army
Hq during the operation; if any were taken they were dealt with
on the spot. Orders directing units to attempt to take prisoners
were issued with no results. Several Okinawans suspected of
acting as US agents were turned in but, without exception, they
were found to be insane.

Occasionally staff officers listened in on Blue voice transmission but, due to their imperfect English, gained no information of any value.

Indicative of the character of Japanese intelligence are
two reports received at Army Hq. The first, received shortly
after the 1st Mar Div moved into the southern line stated that
Chinese and Negro marines had been observed being driven to

the front by tanks, presumably to prevent their desertion.
A second report, received from an infiltration team, described a gala party, complete with orchestra, chinese lanterns and dancing girls, which had purportedly been seen in progress at FUTEMA.

E. Battle Lessons

The 32d Army staff was somewhat puzzled by certain phases of Blue tactics which were in conflict with accepted Japanese tactical doctrine.

The Blue attack against the Japanese line was often characterized by the exertion of uniform pressure against the entire line. When weak points were discovered in the Japanese line they were generally probed by Blue patrols yet no efforts were made to effect a break-through, if only to gain a temporary advantage. This seemed at variance with what the Japanese considered sound tactics, which would advise an attack in force upon weak points with the objective of causing the enemy heavy casualties, if not of disrupting his defense. The seemingly over-cautious policy came as a disappointment to many Japanese staff officers who had hoped to force a decision once the Blue forces had engaged the SHURI defense line and before the Japanese had been appreciably reduced in strength.

Col Y.H.R. and other staff officers became of the opinion that the 10th Army had been committed to taking the island as cheaply as possible. In retrospect he declares that the policy was probably wise, insofar as it reduced total casualties, although more aggressive action would probably have shortened the campaign appreciably.

Blue methods of tank warfare also came as a surprise to the Japanese. Col Y.H.R. expressed the belief of the Japanese that OKINAWA was ideally suited to large-scale tank warfare, at least in comparison with the home-islands of JAPAN. (In this connection, Col Y.H.R. remarked that the CHIBA Peninsula was probably the only area in JAPAN suited by terrain for armored warfare. The Japanese themselves find difficulty in conducting maneuvers on terrain characterized by paddy fields and irrigation systems.) The Japanese envisioned Blue tank attacks comparable in scale to those of the European war, involving 5 or 6 waves of 100 tanks each. Indications that such attacks were not contemplated came as a great relief to the Japanese. Col Y.H.R. is, however, of the opinion that Blue superiority in tanks was the single factor most important in deciding the battle of OKINAWA.

The Japanese were forced to admit that their countermeasures were ineffective; AT guns were of little use in well-concealed positions and were soon destroyed if moved to positions with better fields of fire, suicide attacks by personnel bearing explosive charges were disappointing, while bringing arty fire against tanks was difficult because of poor communication and the undesirability of firing during the daytime when under air observation. Some comfort was derived from the observation that tanks would sometimes withdraw in the face of a show of strength or when accompanying infantry were fired upon.

-11-

At one point there was a rather wistful discussion of the
possibility of retrieving damaged US tanks and after repairing
them to use them in the field. The scheme soon proved to be
impractical. A light AT weapon such as the bazooka is badly
needed by the Japanese.

The tactical maneuver causing the greatest concern to
the Japanese was the so-called "horseback attack" (UMANORI
KOGEKI), i.e. the double envelopment of cave positions. Although the Japanese positions were constructed so as to be
mutually self-supporting certain unexpected factors entered
the picture. It was discovered that double-envelopment tactics
had been successful not so much because of inherent defects in
the construction of the positions, but simply because troops
in nearby positions were reluctant to endanger their own safety
by opening fire on positions which had been enveloped. Orders
were issued that an officer or NCO would remain on watch at all
times in each positions and that there would be no delay in
opening fire upon Blue troops attacking other positions.

Flame-throwers were countered by constructing caves with
the main passages at right angles to the entrance. To further
minimize the effect of flame-throwers, entrances were covered
with blankets, shelter-halves, or other heavy materials thoroughly wetted. Col Y.H.R. believes that these measures were
fairly successful against brief attacks, although admittedly
unable to withstand prolonged attack.

Blue night attacks were particularly effective, taking
the Japanese completely by surprise. The Japanese had so
accustomed themselves to ceasing organized hostilities at
nightfall, and, except for the ubiquitous KIRIKOMITAI, re-
organizing and relaxing during the night that attacks in these
hours caught them both physically and psychologically off-
guard. Col Y.H.R. believes that such attacks could have been
successfully exploited to a much greater extent than they were.

The 32d Army had experienced considerable bombing and were
reasonably certain that their cave positions gave adequate protection. There was, however, general consternation at the prospect of being under NGF. Col Y.H.R. was informed by an arty
officer that on BB had firepower equivalent to the arty of
7 Inf Divs; this naturally caused him some anxiety which was
relieved only when, after the first naval bombardment of the
island, he inspected the results and found that well constructed
cave positions were vulnerable only to direct hits. The following conclusions were drawn as to the effectiveness against NGF,
bombing, and arty fire.

1. NGF, bombing, and arty directed against an area the
size of OKINAWA will not have much effect against disciplined
troops in well-constructed cave positions.. Important positions
must be such that no amount of bombing or shelling will destroy
them.

2. After positions have been overrun or destroyed by the
enemy, dispersion is vital. All movements must be at night.
3. The final result will be by hand-to-hand combat.

The enemy's first taste of Blue arty was the bombardment
by pieces emplaced on KEISE SHIMA, which caused the enemy no

-12-

little annoyance, particularly since they had not anticipated any such move. Counter-battery brought against these batteries was believed to be partially successful.

The effectiveness of Blue arty was countered, successfully to a great extent, by the elaborate system of under ground fortifications. Heavy bombardments, such as came before attacks caused relatively low casualties.

Blue observation planes were a constand threat to the Japanese. They learned quickly that the presence of an observation plane overhead usually presaged enemy fire. And, although they appeared to present fine targets, observation planes were tantalizingly hard to hit with small arms. Observation planes were, therefore, treated with great respect, all movement being kept to an absolute minimum while these planes were overhead.

DISTRIBUTION:

COMPHIBPAC	(1)	Chief Military Branch	
G-2 TENTH ARMY	(5)	MIS, Room 2D-825, Pentagon (for PACMIR)	
CINCPFPAC	(4)	Washington, D. C.	(1)
CINCPOA Adv	(1)		
FMF PAC	(3)	Capt Appleman	
III Phib Corps	(5)	Historian	
XXIV Corps	(5)	G-2 XXIV Corps	(1)
CTF 31	(4)		
ASCOM (I) APO 331	(3)	Hq AFMIDPAC	
310th CIC Det (ASCOM)	(2)	Historical Section G-2	
File	(5)	APO 952	(1)

-13-

CICA/FBG
24 July 1945

PRISONER OF WAR INTERROGATION REPORT

Tenth Army Interrogation Report #27.   Ref: RYUKYU RETTO Map
                                                1:25,000

1. PERSONAL DETAILS:

POW Name	:	SHIMADA, Akira	Rank:	Civil Service Official
Enemy Serial No	:	None		(Attchd to Army)
Unit	:	32nd Army	Duty:	Sec to Lt Gen CHO, C/S,
Place of Capture:		GUSHICHAN, (TS 8160)		32nd Army.
		SHIMAJIRI GUN, OKINAWA.		
Date of Capture	:	24 June 1945		
Age	:	35		
Education	:	15 years		
Residence	:	NAHA (TS 7471) OKINAWA		
Vocation	:	Film Industry		

2. ASSESSMENT:

a. Details of Capture

POW claims to have been the last person in 32nd Army Hq to leave the Army CP at Hill 89, MABUNI (TS 7857) on 24 June. With no particular purpose in mind, he attempted to make his way northward, but was captured by Seventh Division MPs later the same day at GUSHICHAN. At the time of capture he was carrying on his person the only remaining copies of personal letters written by General CHO before his death to the Minister of War, the head of the Imperial Rule Assistance Association, the Poetry Master of the Imperial Household and other officials. These were taken away from POW and thrown aside by the MPs who searched him; on returning to the spot two days later in the company of intelligence personnel, he found only a few burned-fragments of the documents.

b. Evaluation

POW is an extremely shrewd individual blessed with a glib tongue and a very rational way of thinking. His memory and powers of observation are excellent and the reliability of his information is far above that of the average officer POW. Impelled by motives of expediency as well

- 1 -

220

as idealism, he has offered his services to the United States to assist
the speedy winning of the war in whatever way he can. From his background, general knowledge and native ability, it seems evident that he
could be of great service in this connection; he has already given information which should lead to the apprehension of at least one important
32nd Army Staff officer.

For the past eight years POW was an intimate friend of the late Lt. Gen
CHO Isamu, Chief of Staff, 32nd Army and he served as CHO's personal
secretary throughout the campaign. (His official rank in this capacity
was that of a Higher Civil Service Official of the Sixth Class - equivalent to a Captain in the military.) His association with General CHO
and other members of the 32nd Army Staff has enabled him to contribute
considerable information not previously known about the plans and activities of the 32nd Army during the battle for OKINAWA. In addition his
former affiliation with the TOKUMU KIKAN, the Japanese secret intelligence
organization should be of great interest and POW's knowledge of this
agency, as well as the large body of general information in his possession
should be further exploited by detailed higher echelon interrogation.

3. INTELLIGENCE

Chronology

1932
January   Entered the Army at KUMAMOTO (13th Regt)
1933
April   Commissioned 2nd Lt. Released from service shortly thereafter.
1933 - 39
              In business in TOKYO - publicity department of TOHO Motion
              Picture Co.
1939   Entered TOKUMU KIKAN (Special Service Agency) as a Military
              Civilian (GUNUZOKU) Agent; worked for a year in the Propa-
              ganda Dept in the PEKING TOKUMU KIKAN.
1940
July   Transferred to the TATON (DAIDO) Branch of the PEKING TOKUMU
              KIKAN.
1941
July   Received a discharge from the TOKUMAKIKAN on medical grounds.
              Returned to TOKYO.

- 2 -

1943
May   Moved to OKINAWA. Became manager of the NAHA Theatre.
1944
October   Moved to SHURI (TS 7872) after the Blue airraids.
1945
25 March   Attached to 32nd Army as General CHO's secretary.

32nd Army Operations

The 32nd Army was activated on 1 April 1944 and put under the command of
General WATANABE Masao, with General KITAGAWA Kiyomi as Chief of Staff; the
original Headquarters were at ASATO (TS 7572) northeast of NAHA. In the
summer and early fall of that year the units which were to form the main
strength of the 32nd Army arrived in OKINAWA and plans were made for has-
tening defense preparations on the island.

General WATANABE had been in poor health since arriving on OKINAWA and con-
sequently was unable to play any active part in the direction of his command.
As the Chief of Staff was considered a rather ineffective personality and a
second-rate strategist, the WATANABE-KITAGAWA combination left much to be
desired and it was replaced at the end of August 1944 by Lt Gen USHIJIMA
Mitsuru as Commanding General and Lt Gen CHO Isamu as Chief of Staff. (Lt
Gen WATANABE is no longer on active service; KITAGAWA is Asst C/S, 10th
Area Army.) USHIJIMA arrived immediately before the departure of his pre-
decessor; CHO however remained in TOKYO for final staff conferences at
Imperial Hq and did not reach OKINAWA until late in September. (It should
be noted that prior to assuming his post as Chief of Staff, CHO had visited
OKINAWA in June or July 1944 as a tactical advisor from Imperial Hq and
had held conferences with the 32nd Army Staff at that time.)

After the arrival of USHIJIMA and CHO there were considerable revisions made
in the personnel of 32nd Army Staff section. The staff which emerged was
in general distinguished by its ability and comparative youth and low rank -
there was an unusually large number of majors in positions which might ord-
inarily be occupied by officers of the higher field grades. Even General CHO
and Colonel YAHARA, the Senior Staff Officer were young for their rank and
responsibility.

With the reorganization of the 32nd Army Staff completed, work was hurried
on the defense plans of the island. The withdrawal of the 9th Division to
FORMOSA in December on the orders of Imperial Hq made the situation critical,
as it became evident that JAPAN lacked sufficient shipping to send any reinforcements to OKINAWA to replace this unit. In January, General CHO went to
TOKYO for a final conference at Imperial Hq on the strategy to be used in the
defense of OKINAWA. It was at this conference that CHO was told that 32nd
Army units were not to fire on Blue Shipping in the event of an attempted
landing on OKINAWA; Imperial Hq assured him that the KAMIKAZE suicide planes

and similar units were enough to insure the destruction of the greater part
of Blue naval forces, without forcing shore batteries to give away their
positions by premature firing.

After the departure of WATANABE, Army Hq was moved to SHURI and in January
1945 work was begun enlarging the system of caves beneath SHURI Castle for
eventual use as 32nd Army CP. Construction continued on field fortifications
for the various Army units and in February POW accompanied the Chief of Staff
on an extended inspection of the positions to the north of SHURI, at which
time CHO criticized and changed various entrenchments along the lines.

Commencing in January 1945 an effort was made to mobilize virtually the entire
civilian manpower of OKINAWA for use as Army auxiliaries . Additional Home
Guard levies were made, designed to supplement the earlier conscriptions of
the fall of 1944. Almost the entire student body of the Middle Schools,
the Vocational Schools and the SHURI Normal School was organized into
guerrilla units, the most prominent of which was the celebrated Blood-and-
Iron-for-the-Emperor Duty Unit (TEKKETSU KINNO TAI). The students were
trained in infiltration tactics by a Capt HIROSE, an expert on guerrilla
warfare who had been sent to 32nd Army from Imperial Hq for the express
purpose of coordinating the activities of infiltration groups and similar
irregular forces.

On 10 February 1945, POW was told by General CHO that word had been received
from Imperial Hq that an invasion of OKINAWA was imminent. On 15 February
the last passenger ship for JAPAN left OKINAWA with a cargo composed mainly
of refugees. From that time (with the exception of several small AKs, the
last of which left OKINAWA in early March) there was no surface communications
between OKINAWA and the Japanese home islands. Continuous radio communication was of course maintained until the very end of the campaign with TOKYO,
FORMOSA and the other islands of the RYUKYUS. However, from the time of
Blue landings Imperial Hq made no attempt to interfere in the conduct of the
OKINAWA campaign, nor did the Formosan Army (10th Area Army); 32nd Army
directed its own operation from start to finish.

When in late March it became evident that the Blue landing was about to take
place, the 32nd Army Staff was faced with the problem of a final disposition
of its forces to deal with the invasion in the most effective way possible.
It was already committed to a defense of SHIMAJIRI GUN, and   ,
accordingly had evacuated its main strength from the rest of OKINAWA to the
southern part of the island, leaving behind the so-called KUNIGAMI Detachment to defend the North as long as possible. (Although this course meant
the virtual abandonment of the YONTAN and KADENA airfields to Blue forces,
it was felt that the advantages of fighting with ones forces concentrated
in a restricted area easily defended both by location and the nature of the
terrain more than compensated for the loss.) In addition a landing on the
HAGUSHI beaches or possibly further south on the west coast was expected.
The pressing question was whether or not an additional landing - possibly

the principal one - would be made on the eastern coast off MINATOGAWA (where
a Blue landing feint was later made). There was a long and sharp discussion
on this point among the staff members. Col YAHARA, the Senior Staff Officer
insisted that a diversionary landing would at'some time be made in the MIN-
ATOGAWA region; in order to crush this move it was necessary to keep a size-
able portion of the Army's strength in that area, i.e. south of the SHURI-
YONABARU line. Major YAKUMARU, the Intelligence Officer held that no such
landing would be made and that the only Blue landing would come in force on
the HAGUSHI beaches or thereabouts. Needless to say, YAHARA's prestige and
arguments won the day and POW records that YAKUMARU, bitterly disappointed
at the final decision, went off for the next few days to inundate his sorrows
in prolonged draughts of expensive sake.

As a result of the Staff's decision, the L-Day dispositions of the principal 32nd Army units were as follows:

The 62nd Div with Hq at SHURI Castle had its component units disposed north
of the SHURI area in northern SHIMAJIRI and southern NAKAGAMI GUN; the 12th
IIBn was farthest north with a line front running through OYAMA, FUTEMA,
(TS 8481), ATANIYA (TS 8681) and KUBA (8980); the 63rd Brig had its CP at
NAKAMA (TS 7975), with the 13th IIBn along the KAKAZU line (TS 7668), the
14th IIBn on a line from NISHIBARU to KANIKU and the 11th IIBn on the
TANABARU (TS 8275) - OUKI front; the 64th Brig with Hq at DAKESHI (TS 7874)
held the coast sector from MACHINATO (TS 7978) to AMIKU (TS 7473).

The 24th Division with Hq at YOZA (TS 7661) was deployed south of SHURI in
central and southern SHIMAJIRI GUN. Its sector was bounded on the west by
MATAMBASHI (TS 7669), TOMIGUSUKU (TS 7468), GIBO, TAKAMINE (TS 7360) and
ARAGON; on the east by GUSHICHAN, MINATOGAWA (TS 8361), ARAGUSUKU (TS 8162),
KAMIZATO (TS 8066), TOYAMA (TS 8462), FURUGEN (TS 8190), and KANEGUSUKU
(TS 7387).

The 44th IMB occupied the CHINEN (TS 9165) Peninsula area with its sector
bounded on the west by MINATOGAWA, TAKAMIYAGUSUKU (TS 7268) and ITARASHIKU
(TS 8469): the Brig CP was at TAKAMIYAGUSUKU. The OKINAWA Naval Base Force
was charged with the defense of the OROKU Peninsula.

In addition to the above major echelons with their attached units there was
a considerable body of provisional infantry troops available as a reserve.
In accordance with previously laid plans, the greater part of 32nd Army
service and specialized troops had been converted to an infantry organization at the time of Blue landing. In general they were held in rear areas
until later in the campaign.

The first and for a short time the only unit to engage Blue troops was the
12th IIBn; by 4/5 April short shrift had been made of this detachment and
the remnants drew back along the east coast in an attempt to reach 62nd
Div Hq at SHURI. As the lines pushed southward it soon became for the
Japanese a question of holding to the line from KAKAZU through NISHIBARU
to TANABARU in the 63rd Brig sector. By the latter part of April the

- 5 -

62nd Div had sustained heavy losses and Army decided that it was necessary
to strengthen the Division's front. Accordingly, one battalion of Army infantry (IN: under the direct control of 32nd Army), one regiment of the 24th
Div (IN: 22nd Regt) and an u/i element of the 44th IMB were sent to the lines
in front of FUTEMA on about 20 April as reinforcements ; they were attached
to the 62nd Divs.

At the beginning of May plans were made for a counter-attack on the eastern
side of the front, using all three infantry regiments of the 24th Div. On
the night of 3 May there was a conference of Brigade and Division CGs at
the SHURI Hq and final arrangements for the attack were made. The order to
the units involved was given that night and the attack began on the morning
of the next day. It had for its objective penetration of Blue lines on a
wide front as far as FUTEMA, which was believed to be the Tenth Army CP area.
Despite the ambitious aim of this assault, it met with no success; on the
contrary the Japanese were forced to fall back to a line extending from
YAFUSO (TS 7775) through NAKAMA, MAEDA (TS 8075), KOCHI (TS 8174), and GAJA
(TS 8372). It was (the failure of which was attributed partly to transport
difficulties in bringing the troops up to the line), after this ill-starred
action that General CHO abandoned all hope of a successful outcome of the
operation and declared that only time intervened between defeat and the 32nd
Army.

To bolster the lines, a battalion of Shipping Engineers (IN: probably the
remainder of the 26th Shipping Engr Regt) under Lt Col HARAGA was moved into
the line from AMIKU (TS 7573) along the ASAGAWA and the main strength of the
44th IMB took up positions on the ASATO-AMIKU line; by this time the 24th Div
had taken over the old 62nd Div sector; the 62nd Div, which had been very roughly handled in the past month, occupied the zone between the 24th and the 44th
IMB. In the TSUKAZAN (TS 7868) - NAHA areas to the south, the 32nd Army
Freight Depot, the Ordnance Depot and other service units had been organized
into two provisional infantry battalions with Hq at KAKAZU. These were to
cooperate with the OZATO Guard Unit (IN: An informally named provisional infantry unit with attached Navy units which was posted at the approaches
to the CHINEN Peninsula) in opposing a possible Blue breakthrough or landing behind the lines.

It is interesting to note that throughout this time and until the evacuation of SHURI the 32nd Army was constantly expecting an attack by Blue
paratroops. Patrols were continually posed - particularly in the TSUKAZAN
sector, where it was thought an attack would be most likely - to guard
against this eventuality.

By the latter of May the situation of the SHURI line had become increasingly critical and Blue successes on both flanks of the line threatened
ultimately to isolate the defenders in the city and surrounding areas.
Accordingly a staff meeting of the 32nd Army unit COs was held at the Army
CP to decide on the next move. Opinion was divided on the advisability of
retreating. One group led by Lt Gen FUJIOKA, 62nd Div CG, advocated remain-

ing in SHURI for a last stand; although this view seemed for a time to pre-
vail, it was ultimately decided to withdraw to the MABUNI area and orders
were given to all units to make their retreat at the end of the month.   On
29 May 32nd Army Hq moved from 2100 until dawn, organized into four echelons.
CG, 32nd Army was in the second echelon which moved to TSUKAZAN by way of
SHICHINA and ICHINICHIBASHI (TS 7869). The third echelon, which included the
Chief of Staff, made its way to TSUKAZAN via HANTAGAWA and the south HAEBARU
road. After the departure of the fourth echelon, demolition squads under a
Capt HAYAKAWA were left behind in various points of the Army CP to carry out
demolition work.

Army Hq. staff personnel spent two nights in TSUKAZAN and proceeded to MABUNI
in two 24th Div trucks, followed by the Hq. troops. From 1 June to the end
operations were directed from the Army CP at Hill 89. MABUNI. (As an indic-
ation of 32nd Army Staff's withdrawal, it should be noted that only 20 days
supply of rations were taken from the Army CP.

The remnants of 32nd Army retreated from SHURI, fighting as they went and
attempted to regroup for a last stand in the southern part of SHIMAJIRI GUN.
The 24th Div established its CP at MADEERA (TS 7759) with its units disposed
on a line extending through NAGUSUKU (TS 7258) KUNIYOSHI, OSATO (TS 7561),
YAEZU DAKE (TS 7861), and OKA. The last of the 62nd Div and other 32nd Army
units held a final resistance line on Hill 96.3 north of MABUNI and KOMESU
(TS 7657). 44th IMB concentrated at GUSHICHAN and NAKAZA.

As a result of continual Blue pressure, the remaining Japanese troops by
20 June had been pushed into two pockets - one in the MABUNI, KOMESU and
YAMAGUSUKU area with the Hill 89 CP as its center and the other, composed
maily of 24th Div troops, isolated at MADEERA. On 19 June a final meeting
of the Army Staff was held, at which General CHO ordered certain staff
members to leave the island for the purpose of conveying various official
messages and comments on the operation to Imperial Hq. These officers
were to make their way north - in civilian clothes - from MABUNI to OKU KO
(TS 4048) at the northwestern end of the island; from there they were to
proceed to TOKUNO JIMA by small boat (via YORON and OKINOERABU JIMA). and
thence by airplane to JAPAN. They were to be accompanied by Okinawan students
(attached to Army Hq as orderlies, ect.) who were to act as guides on the
journey. On 19 June Major YAKUMARU, Army Intelligence Officer, Major NAGANO,
Asst Operations Officer, Capt SUNAGA (Intelligence) and Capt ANZAI (Air
Corps) left the CP; on 20 June they were followed by Lt Col KIMURA, Air
Officer, Major MIYAGE, Communications Officer and Capt WASAI (Intelligence).
Later the same day an infiltration party of 40 men commanded by Major
MATSUBARA made a sortie from the cave position, sustaining heavy casualities.

On 21 June at 2200 the last message was sent to Imperial Hq; General CHO
issued the last 32nd Army order on the same day - a general exhortation to
all units to fight to the utmost. Observing that the CP was no longer
tenable, USHIJIMA and CHO made preparations for suicide. After copious
farewell toasts with the remains of the case of Black and White which the
somewhat hedonistic CHO had kept with him to the last, the CG, 32nd Army

and his Chief of Staff met their death together at 0400 on 22 June. POW witnessed the suicides. On 23 June Col YAHARA, the Senior Staff Officer (later taken prisoner) left the CP in an attempt to reach northern OKINAWA and ultimately JAPAN on the orders of General CHO. Shortly after all the remaining personnel in the CP - about 200 - made a last attack on Blue positions under the command of Major ONO, Chief of 32nd Army Code Section. On 24 June POW left the cave, having stayed for an extra day to care for the wounded who remained there.

POW is uncertain of the fate of the 24th and 62nd Div commanders. It Gen WADA, CG 5th Arty Command was killed at the head of his surviving troops in a suicidal assault against Blue force on 21 June. The whereabouts of Maj Gen SUZUKI, CG 44th IMB remain in doubt; POW had heard at the MABUNI Hq that SUZUKI, accompanied by about ten soldiers, had left his command in mid-June in an effort to slip through Blue lines to KUNIGAMI GUN.

32nd Army Relations with Other Echelons

As a result of the isolation of 32nd Army Hq and its main strength after the Blue landing on OKINAWA, subordinate units on other islands of the NANSEI SHOTO formerly under the command of 32nd Army were detached and assigned to other echelons. On about 15 April control of the 28th Div and other forces in the SAKISHIMA GUNTO was transferred to the 10th Area Army (Formosan Army). The 64th IMB and attached units in the AMAMI GUNTO were not taken from the 32nd Army's jurisdiction until late in the campaign, however; POW stated that in June they were put under the command of the Western District Army, which has been converted to a tactical command. There was never any attempt made to secure reinforcements from TOKUNO JIMA or any other islands of the NANSEI Group, as it was recognized by 32nd Army Hq that the units stationed on these islands had barely enough troops to defend their assigned terri- tories. While Army Hq was at MABUNI, two soldiers from AMAMI OSHIMA reached there; they declared that they had been sent from NAZE OSHIMA in company with an officer bearing a message to 32nd Army Hq; the officer had been killed en route and they had no idea of either the contents of the letter or the purpose of their mission.

Aside from the transmission of intelligence reports and the despatch of a few technical advisors to the 32nd Army to assist in the operation, Imperial Hq played a very insignificant part in the conduct of the defese of OKINAWA. There was a Major or Lt Col on the staff who was charged with the duty of acting as liaison between Imperial Hq and the 32nd Army Staff and collecting Battle Lessons of the 32nd Army and similar information about the campaign; he exercised no influence on the conduct of the battle however. (This officer had previously visited OKINAWA from October 1944 to January 1945 for staff conferences.) In February 1945 a Major KYOSO, an artillery expert and an instructor at the Artillery Staff College was sent to 32nd Army Hq on temporary duty to assist in the preparation of defense plans. He gave daily lectures to groups of officers on the defense scheme of the island, stressing the artillery situation. Unfortunately for Major KYOSO, the Blue landing came somewhat prematurely for his expectations and he unable to

return, but was attached to the staff of the 44th IMB. POW believes that
this officer remains at large in KUNIGAMI GUN. In January, 1945 a Major
JIN was sent to 32nd Army Hq from Hq 6th Air Army to act as liaison officer
between the two commands. He was ordered to return to JAPAN at the beginning of June with observations made by 32nd Army on the effects of the
KAMIKAZE suicide plane attacks on Blue targets and suggestions for their
improvement. Although it had been arranged that a float plane from TOKUNO
was to pick him up off MABUNI for the flight to JAPAN, the aircraft was not
forthcoming and JIN was at last forced to set out by small boat for the islands to the north on about 4 June. His efforts were apparently rewarded,
as Imperial Hq later sent word to OKINAWA that the Major had safely reached
JAPAN.

At the outset of the OKINAWA operation Imperial Hq sent a dispatch to the
32nd Army signed by the Asst Chief of the General Staff wishing the Army
the best of luck in the coming battle and deeply regretting the fact that
it was being forced to fight a large-scale action on such slender resources;
POW records that the message was received with bitter amusement. Although
consistent appeals for reinforcements were made by USHIJIMA and CHO, Imperial Hq only reply was exhortations and encouraging words; no actual
promises of any surface-borne reinforcements were made. According to POW,
Imperial Hq at one time planned to return two regiments of the 9th Div to
OKINAWA at the beginning of 1945, but was compiled to abandon this idea
because of inadequate shipping facilities. (IN: This information is completely unsubstantiated by other sources.)

32nd Army Hq was notified by TOKYO that an airborne infiltration would be
carried out on YONTAN A/F on 24 May, with the object of doing as much damage as
possible to Blue aircraft and installations there; any survivors from among
the infiltrators were ordered to attempt to join Japanese units in KUNIGAMI
GUN. In addition it was reported from TOKYO that the 6th Air Army was to
send six battalions of airborne infantry to OKINAWA by glider at the beginning of June.

From the beginning of the OKINAWA campaign to the breakup of 32nd Army Hq
on 20 June, 32nd Army Battle Lessons (SENJI KUNREN) were radioed almost
daily to Imperial Hq by Major YAKUMARU (Intelligence Officer) and Major
NAGANO (Asst Operations Officer). The Battle Lessons, a compilation of
32nd Army Hq and lower echelon reports on the OKINAWA campaign, gave a detailed history of the action, as well as comments on tactics used by both
sides and suggestions for improvements in combat techniques. The longest
one sent was the account of the 3 May counterattack and its failure written
by Col YAHARA. POW can recall only two specific tactical recommendations
made in the Battle Lesson: one that the standard A/T satchel charges be
increased in weight from five kilograms to seven or eight kilograms and the
other that they increase the distance between the so-called "octopus pots"
(KAKUTSUBO) foxholes in preparing defensive positions in front of caves and
similar entrenchments.

- 9 -

32nd Army Intelligence

Before the beginning of the OKINAWA campaign, 32nd Army Hq had little advance information on the nature and size of the Blue forces about to attack the island. POW declared that a report came in March from the HARBIN TOKUMU KIKAN saying that the 1st and 6th Marine Divisions were preparing to attack OKINAWA. The identity of the other divisions involved remained unknown until after the Blue landing. POW was familiar with Tenth Army, the 7th, 96th and 27th Divisions, but had not heard of the presence of the 77th Div, the elements of the 2nd Marine Div or either of the two corps.

Intelligence of Blue troop movements, order of battle information, etc. was largely secured by special teams of espionage personnel called SHOKO SEKKO TAI (Officer Patrol Units) operating behind Blue lines for short periods. These teams were usually composed of an officer and four or five NCOs all dressed in civilian clothes; most or all of the NCOs were Okinawans or Okinawan-speaking and the patrols usually traveled by day with groups of Okinawan civilians - many of them were in MG custody at various times - noting positions and troop activities. When specific information was desired by 32nd Army about an area in Blue-held territory, it would forward the information desired to the subordinate unit most directly concerned. This unit (Generally one of the divisions or the brigade) would then send several of its Officer Patrol Units through the lines to get the information. The patrols were usually gone for a period of four to ten days, and POW asserted that the great majority of them returned safely through the lines. Despite this ease of maneuver, the espionage teams were not too accurate in their appraisals of Blue positions. They located the 96th Div CP at FUTEMA, but erroneously thought it the Tenth Army CP. Later in the operation, they found III Phib Corps CP in NAHA but misidentified it as the 6th Marine Div CP. Other than this, they were unable to find any Blue Division CPs; they reported to Army Hq that, as Blue divisions moved about very frequently, it was extremely difficult to locate their CPs. In addition to this rather unimpressive information, however, POW believes that the patrols did furnish considerable intelligence on troop movements and dispositions.

There was little information obtained from captured documents - POW knew of only one, a gridded map of OKINAWA which had been captured early in the operation. With the exception of two pilots captured in March, there were no American troops taken prisoner during the operation. The two airmen, according to POW, were flown directly to JAPAN after capture.

Oddly enough, the Japanese believed that Blue forces on OKINAWA were using Okinawans as espionage agents behind the Japanese lines. A number of "suspicious characters" were apprehended and questioned at Army Hq by various amateur interrogators, including POW. Nothing was proved against them, however.

32nd Army Personalities

Generally speaking the 32nd Army Staff Section was distinguished among Japanese army staffs for its progressiveness. It had been completely reorganized by CHO after he became Chief of Staff and included a great number of the 'bright young men' of Imperial Hq. As a group it operated smoothly and the intelligence and alertness of its members is in general reflected in the ability with which the defense of OKINAWA was conducted. Col YAHARA, the Senior Staff Officer is a comparatively young man with wide experience and an excellent capacity for tactical direction. A cool and rational thinker, his appraisal of the Okinawan situation was from the first pessimistic and he served as an effective brake on some of the more impulsive designs of other staff members.

Lt Gen USHIJIMA Mitsuru was a quiet-spoken competent officer with a faculty for choosing capable subordinates. He had the quality of inspiring confidence among his troops and was held in great respect by them. Early in the war he had been an infantry group commander in BURMA; prior to his assignment as CG, 32nd Army he was Commandant of the Japanese Military Academy at ZAMA. He was to be promoted to General in August 1945.

CHO, Isamu was a Lt Gen at the age of 51, when most of his classmates at the Military Academy were still colonels. He was a keen, vigorous man with an extremely agressive personality who was feared as much as he was respected. Known in the Army and even in private circles as a strict disciplinarian requiring order and exactness in the smallest details, he did not, however, fall into the error - common to the so-called 'spit and polish' soldier - of letting an obsession with minor details injure his grasp of major issues. He was known as an extraordinarily efficient staff man and manifested this very noticeably in his conduct of the Okinawan campaign.

In the early 1930s CHO was sent to the United States as an exchange officer and spent two years there. On his return to JAPAN he was stationed for a considerable time at Imperial Hq in TOKYO until 1939, when he was ordered to CHINA, serving there as Chief of Staff of the 26th Inf Div and Asst Chief of Staff of the North CHINA Expeditionary Force (North CHINA Area Army). He was promoted to Maj Gen in October, 1941. As the outbreak of the GEA War he became Asst Chief of Staff of the Southern Army and participated in the MALAYA and BURMA campaigns. In July, 1942 he was transferred to the Military Affairs Bureau of the War Dept, where he remained until receiving his appointmen as Chief of Staff, 32nd Army.

Although believing in the creed of the Japanese military man with orthodox fervor, CHO retained a logical outlook and a well-balanced view of the situation. He recognized that it was impossible for JAPAN to win the battle of OKINAWA without large reinforcements. Therefore his hope in the campaign was to fight a delaying action until these reinforcements could arrive. He continued sending appeals for additional troops as late as 10 May and until that time believed that Imperial Hq would at least attempt to send some, for it was his firm conviction that the fall of OKINAWA meant the loss of the war. There was never any question of surrendering in his mind; when the surrender

- 11 -

message from General Buckner was received at 32nd Army Hq, CHO and USHIJIMA both laughed and declared that, as SAMURAI, it would not be consonant with their honor to entertain such a proposal. (It should be noted that this message was received at 32nd Army about 17 June - approximately one week after it was dropped within the Jap lines.)

When it finally became evident that resistance was at an end, CHO prepared for suicide. However, he remarked that he saw no reason for all members of the staff to do likewise and accordingly sent various staff officers to TOKYO on his own initiative. feeling that it would be senseless for them to die in OKINAWA , when they could be more useful in the future both to JAPAN and to themselves if they remained alive. CHO was not at all pleased with the prospect of dying himself; POW believes that, had the Chief of Staff heard of the precedent set by General YAMASHITA's alleged escape from the PHILLPPINES, he would have abandoned the idea of committing suicide and attempted to make his way north with the others.

Before his death CHO handed POW copies of letters which he had written to several high officials in JAPAN, requesting POW to deliver them if he were at all able to escape from OKINAWA. Although the letters were taken from POW and destroyed by the MPs who captured him, he was able to recall the substance of them, which follows:

(1)
     To: Dr CHIBA Taneaki, Imperial Household Poetry Master

     The 32nd Army under its commander has fought a good battle. Our strategy, tactics and technics - all were used to the utmost and we fought valiantly, but it was as nothing before the material strength of the enemy. With this I shall commit suicide, bearing the responsibility for a beaten army. I beg of you the favor to tell Imperial Hq, after my death, of my views and of the sad manner in which I met my end.
     It has become evident to me that defeat of the nation's armies is inevitable, if precious strategy is continued. Please convey my humble apologies. Thank you very much for your previous favors; I shall never forget your great kindness.
     I am forwarding my opinions and the Battle Lessons on the OKINAWA operation to Imperial Hq through Lt Col (IN: name u/i) OKINAWA Operation Staff Officer (OKINAWA SAKUSEN SHUNIN SAMBO).

(2)
     To: General ANAN, Minister of War
         Field Marshall UMEZU, Chief of the General Staff

     The OKINAWA campaign has ended and I can but apologize by my death for its outcome. I pray for your success in war.

(3)
> To: HASHIMOTO Kingoro, Head of the Youth Assistance Assn
> OGAWA Shumei, Head of the Strong JAPAN Assn (KENKOKKAI)
> IWATA, Ainosuke, Head of the Patriotic League (AIKOKUSHA)

(IN: The Imperial Youth AssT Assn is a national organization embracing all Japanese youth 15 years of age and above as members; the other two groups are the strongest of Japanese patriotic organizations.)

Before material supremacy one can do nothing. With my own words I assume responsibility for the defeat. American physical resources are too much for present-day JAPAN; it is essential that JAPAN reflect on this. I hope that my countrymen will struggle to the utmost to overcome this handicap. Many thanks for your previous favors.

Okinawan Civil Officials

The governor of OKINAWA Prefecture, SHIMADA Akira (no relation to POW) was a comparatively young man who had formerly been Chief of Police of SHANGHAI. Although he had taken office only recently, he had the reputation of an efficient, just administrator and was well-liked in OKINAWA; the high regard in which he was held was in contrast to the bad feeling which had been borne by Okinawans towards his predecessor. He had flown back to OKINAWA from FORMOSA just one day before the initial Blue landing and remained with the 32nd Army in SHIMAJIRI GUN until the end.

On 19 June Blue forces equipped with flame throwers attacked the cave at MABUNI (just below the 32nd Army Hq cave) where the govener was living, in company with the Prefectural Chief of Police (ARAI) and the Chief of the Internal Affairs Bureau (NAKASONE). From that time nothing was heard of them and POW believes them dead. It is POW's opinion that the governor would have responded to an appeal to surrender at that time, had it been made.

TOKUMU KIKAN

(IN: As a full interrogation on this organization lies outside the scope of this report, it is emphasized that information herein given is admittedly incomplete; it should be supplemented by exhaustive higher echelon questioning.)

POW entered the TOKUMU KIKAN in 1939 as a military civilian (GUNZOKU) agent and served in the Propaganda Section (SENDEW BU) of this organization in North CHINA. He stated that he had applied for this work and had been accepted as a result of the influence of Lt. Gen CHO, when POW had known in TOKYO. It was because of this powerful intercessor that POW was immediately received into the TOKUMU KIKAN without having to attend the special school maintained for training the members of this organization. However, due to this fact he was not qualified as a field agent and had the classification of a specialist in propaganda work. He served for two years in the TOKUMU KIKAN Office in PEKING and its branch at TATON (DAIDO); in July 1941 he secured a discharge on grounds - admittedly somewhat spurious - of physical disability, and returned to civilian life in JAPAN.

The TOKUMU KIKAN is a worldwide Japanese secret service organization with Hq in TOKYO and branches in almost every nation. Its duties include espionage, counter-espionage, pacification of occupied countries, surveillance of civilian populations and the dissemination of propaganda. Its sphere of operation is generally different from that of the KEMPEI TAI and it concerns itself for the most part with civilian rather than military affairs. Its activities are little publicized, to say the least, so great is the secrecy in which it operates that few TOKUMU KIKAN personnel could identify even all the people working in their own immediate organization.

Although a military organization, the majority of its personnel is composed of military civilians with a status similar to that which POW enjoyed while one of the brotherhood. Many of these military civilians were among the groups of extremist young officers who engineered the assasinations of prominent moderate Japanese statesmen in the notorious 'incidents' of 15 May 1931 and 26 February 1936. Exiled for participation in these affairs, they retained a very real if unofficial connection with the Japanese Army and became active agents for the TOKUMU KIKAN in the various locations they had chosen for their places of exile.

The TOKUMU KIKAN has always been active in foreign countries; before the war it had agents at every Japanese embassy, where they were responsible to the Military Attache. The centers of prewar activity were the United States, USSR and Germany; according to POW there was an especially flourishing HAWAII branch. POW believed that the outbreak of the GEA War put an end to the activities of the TOKUMU KIKAN in the United States, although he thought that numerous agents remain scattered throughout the South American countries.

The largest and most efficient establishment of the TOKUMU KIKAN is in CHINA. According to POW the TOKUMU KIKAN had managed to inject itself into every section and stratum of Chinese life, including the CHUNGKING government, which was rather carefully watched by TOKUMU KIKAN agents. Agents in the field were thoroughly trained in Chinese language, customs and conditions and, in fact, included hundreds of native Chinese among their number. Headquarters personnel are also competent specialists in propaganda , counter-espionage and the coordination of various intelligence activities.

In addition to the CHINA TOKUMU KIKAN, there are large units in JAPAN, MANCHURIA (the HARBIN TOKUMU KIKAN is known as an especially efficient espionage collection center) and the occupied regions of Southeast Asia. The organization in JAPAN is directly under the control of the TOKYO Hq. Activities in MANCHURIA are directed from Hq of the KWANTUNG Army, in MALAYA, INDO CHINA NEI etc from the Southern Army Hq at SINGAPORE, and in CHINA from the CHINA Expeditionary Army Hq and the Northern Area Army Hq. POW insisted that there has never been any TOKUMU KIKAN activity on OKINAWA, due to the docile nature of the civilian population.

- 14 -

POW confirmed the existence of the Navy TOKUMU KIKAN, organized on the same lines and with the same purpose in mind as its Army counterpart. Although smaller than the Army organization, it, too, apparently operates on a world-wide basis. In JAPAN or Japanese-held areas, TOKUMU KIKAN Branches are attached to the various Fleets and the Headquarters of large naval shore establishments. There is a particularly large Navy TOKUMU KIKAN Branch at AMOY.

In general Army and Navy TOKUMU KIKAN operate in different assigned sectors and there is seldom much conflict between the two, except in the case of areas like SHANGHAI where there are large detachments of both - a condition which inevitably gives rise to the usual inter-service bickering, no where more prominent than among rival intelligence organizations.

According to POW there was no cooperation between the TOKUMU KIKAN and similar undercover groups of other nations. In the case of the GESTAPO POW noted that, far from cooperating with that agency, Japanese authorities have caught and executed a number of GESTAPO agents since the outbreak of the GEA War.

The TOKUMU KIKAN Branch at PEKING to which POW was attached in 1939-1941 operated under the orders of the North CHINA Area Army and Imperial Hq with subsections (called BUNSHITSU) at TATON (DAIDO), CHIJANSHIANG (SEKKASHO), JISHANG (JOSHU) and KAIFANG (KAIFU) and numerous smaller posts scattered throughout North CHINA. It was commanded by a Col SHINODA and had a staff of over 400 at the time. It was divided into four sections each commanded by a Major: Operations (SAKUSEN), Pacification (SEMBU), Intelligence (JOHO) and Propaganda (SENDEN). Although the four sections were theoretically on a level, in actual fact Operations and Pacification exercized a controlling power over the other two, which were primarily field agencies. Pacification and Propaganda were the two more obvious sections of the TOKUMU KIKAN and little attempt was made to conceal their identity. Operations and Intelligence, however, were scarcely known and operated in the greatest secrecy.

Operations, with a staff of about 20, concerned itself with the obtaining of tactical intelligence from civilian and other sources and was principally a planning and coordinating unit. Intelligence, with some 3000 personnel, including a few officers, numerous Chinese spies, informants and an assortment of odd Sax Rohmer characters was charged with the actual securing of intelligence information and forwarding it to H.... ...... Headquarters. Pacification, a group of about 10 specialits in propaganda techniques, directed its efforts towards the creation of a Chinese population friendly and holding favorable dispositions in general towards the Japanese forces.

Propaganda, with about 100 personnel including a number of Chinese, worked directly with the civilian population and for the most part was engaged in carrying out the projects conceived by Pacification, as well as promoting good will among the Chinese in a general way.

As a member of Pacification, POW's work was divided into two categories - civilian propaganda and POW propaganda. In the former connection, he wrote various propaganda leaflets for general distribution, supervised the spreading of goodwill among different civilian elements by the presentation of plays, free entertainments, ect and the writing and dissemination of popular slogans along the lines of MEKKYO WAHEI, which can be roughly translated as "Return to peace by killing off the Communists". The other half of his work consisted of the indoctrination of captured Chinese POWs with an eye to their use by the Japanese. On the arrival of a group of recently captured Chinese POWs, POW would bustle out to greet them with food, entertainers, and a fairly effective propaganda line about their part in the new Japanized CHINA. After the prisoners had been rendered favorably disposed as a result of the efforts of POW and his assistants, POW selected about half of them - the best physical and mental specimens of the group - and enrolled them in the Japanese-controlled puppet army, with an officer's commission given to the highest ranking person among them. The remaining POWs were sent to the coal mines to help dig out the foundations of the GEA Co Prosperity Sphere. POW regarded this system as quite efficient and could recall few instances of its breaking down.

In general the propaganda line followed in CHINA was founded on fear of Communism and the desire of building up a Sino-Japanese uniracial movement. Cultural similarities of CHINA and JAPAN were stressed and Japanese propagandists like POW professed to be great admirers of the Chinese and their ways. According to POW, Japanese propaganda in North CHINA was eminently successful, despite the admitted propensity of POW and others like him for pursuing the local fleshpots with more arder than the official policy of Greater East Asian cooperation.

Defense of JAPAN

The coming Blue invasion of the Japanese home islands was a continual topic of conversation among 32nd Army staff officers both before and after the landing on OKINAWA. Although there was considerable disagreement as to where an invasion would take place, the majority opinion was that the landing would be made in HONSHU, probably in either CHIBA, SHIZUOKA or KANEGAWA Prefectures; General CHO believed that CHIBA would be the place selected. POW pointed out at this juncture that in recent years the problems involved in a defense of CHIBA and SHIZUOKA Prefectures against an enemy landing had received special attention at the War College and all Army staff schools. These areas have long been the traditional maneuvering and training grounds for Japanese Army unit and nowhere is the Japanese staff more familiar with the quality and potentialities of the terrain.

At the time of Blue landings on OKINAWA, 32nd Army Hq received a report from Imperial Hq that 50 new divisions were being activated in the Japanese home islands out of all remotely able-bodied men not already in the Army or the Navy. In March prior to this broadcast, a Capt (Arty), 1st Lt (Inf) and other officers from the OKINAWA Regimental District Hq were flown to 6th Depot Div Hq at KUMAMOTO to join a new division which was reportedly forming there.

In November 1944 POW visited JAPAN for a month and observed many signs of preparation for an invasion. He observed coast defenses in MIYAZAKI and OITA Prefectures — elaborate systems of pill-boxes, caves and other entrenchments dug in the hills just inland of the beaches — which were already being manned. However, at that time there had not yet been any order for civilians to evacuate coastal areas. He had heard that a powerful network of fortifications was being constructed in southern KYUSHU and along the Pacific coasts of SHIKOKU and HONSHU, the latter areas under the direct supervision of the Eastern District Army.

POW observed a large paratroop unit training at TAKACHIHO in MIYAZAKI Prefecture KYUSHU. He estimated from the number of barracks that three regiments were stationed there. While he was in the vicinity (December 1944), they held jump practice almost every day.

DISTRIBUTION

COMPHIBPAC	(1)	Chief Military Branch	
G-2 Tenth Army	(5)	MIS, Room 2D-825, Pentagon (for PACMIR)	
CINCAFPAC	(4)	Washington, D. C.	(1)
CINCPOA Adv	(1)		
FMF PAC	(3)	Capt Appleman	
III Phib Corps	(5)	Historian	
XXIV Corps	(5)	G-2 XXIV Corps	(1)
CTF 31	(4)		
ASCOM (I) APO 331	(3)	Hq AFMIDPAC	
310th CIC Det (ASCOM)	(2)	Historical Section G-2	
File	(5)	APO 952	(1)

Index

1st Marine Division (U.S.), 33–34
III Amphibious Corps (U.S.), 36
Fifth Fleet (U.S.), 32
6th Marine Division (U.S.), xxiii
    battle for Sugar Loaf Hill and,
        60–61
    on Oroku Peninsula, 125, 185
6th Special Regiment (Japanese)
    Amekudai battle and, 59, 61–62
    Mixed Brigade and, 42
7th Division (U.S.)
    Kiyan battle and, 108, 132
    Yonabaru battle and, 95, 121
9th Division (Japanese)
    Okinawa deployment of, 12, 14
    redeployment of, 31–32, 46, 71
10th Area Army (Japanese), 16, 60,
    92, 196
10th Army (U.S.)
    infiltrating tactics used against, 36,
        37
    Kadena landing of, xi–xiv, xx,
        xxiii–xxiv
    preparations for Japan invasion by,
        201–2, 206
15th Independent Mixed Regiment
    (Japanese)
    Amekudai battle and, 58, 61–62
    Okinawa deployment of, 12, 14
21st Independent Mixed Regiment
    (Japanese), 3, 10
22nd Regiment (Japanese), 53, 84
23rd Shipping Engineer Regiment
    (Japanese), 75, 76
XXIV Corps (U.S.)
    artillery intelligence of, xxiii, xxiv
    hand-to-hand fighting by, 33–36
24th Division (Japanese)
    certificates of merit awarded to, 108
    command post of, 84, 87, 96

counteroffensive of, 36, 37, 42, 43
field hospital of, 117
Kiyan battle and, 129, 131–33, 146
Kiyan deployment of, 113
Kiyan troop strength of, 111–12
last-stand positions and, 69, 72
offensive retreat strategy and,
    80–82, 87, 94
Okinawa deployment of, 31
Shuri line and, 60, 63, 67, 79
Tsukazan stand of, 107
Yonabaru battle and, 77
31st Army (Japanese), 4, 9
32nd Army (Japanese)
    airfield construction by, 7–8
    creation of, 3–4
    fortifications of, 35, 37, 184
    infiltrating tactics of, 36
    jikyusen strategy and, 32
    last-stand positions and, 103
    Okinawa headquarters of, 5–6,
        53–55, 61, 83–85, 87, 93
    Okinawan civilians and, xxiv
    Operation Victory plans for, 20–26,
        31
    staff changes for, 16, 18, 19
    surrender proposals and, 136, 137
    U.S. army landing at Kadena and,
        xi–xiv, xx
    Watanabe, General, and, 6, 18
44th Independent Mixed Brigade
    (Japanese)
    defense position of, 14, 15
    Kiyan battle and, 121–24, 129–31,
        133, 140, 142, 151, 170
    Kiyan deployment of, 113
    Kiyan troop strength of, 111–12
    offensive attack by, 37, 42, 43
    offensive retreat strategy and,
        81–82, 87, 94

237

44th Independent Mixed Brigade
  (Japanese) *continued*
  Okinawa deployment of, 3, 12
  Shuri line and, 79
  Sugar Loaf Hill and, 57, 60
  torpedo attack on, 31
62nd Division (Japanese)
  Amekudai battle and, 57, 59, 60
  counteroffensive of, 36, 37, 42, 43,
    44
  Kiyan battle and, 124, 131–32, 151
  Kiyan deployment of, 113
  Kiyan troop strength of, 111–12
  offensive retreat strategy and,
    80–82, 89, 90, 94–96
  Okinawa deployment of, 31
  reputation of, 64
  Shuri fortifications and, 71–72, 79,
    129
  Tsukazan stand of, 107, 108
  Yamagusuku command post of, 119
89th Regiment (Japanese), 75–77, 99
96th Division (U.S.), 35

Air Force (Japanese)
  attack on U.S. Fifth Fleet by, 32, 45
  importance placed on, 4–5, 11, 16,
    37, 49, 50, 91, 195–96
  losses in, 30
  Ryukyu Islands defense and, 3–5,
    7–9
  U.S. army landing at Kadena and,
    xiii–xiv, xviii, 32
Air power (U.S.)
  carrier sweeps by, 29
  Japanese mainland raids by, 30
  Japanese positions and, 57
  Marianas line attacks by, 30
  Task Force 58 and, 31, 33
Akinaga, Lieutenant, 149, 150
Amamiya, Lieutenant General
  Tatsumi, 75, 200–201
Amekudai
  Japanese defense of, 57–62, 75

reserve force losses at, 76
Amphibious landings (Japanese), 36
Anami, General Korechika, 41, 146
Antitank tactics (Japanese), 12–13, 35,
  50
Arai, Police Chief, 44, 106, 133
Arakaki, Major, 151
  escape from Mabuni of, 159, 161,
    163–64, 167, 170–71, 183
  in U.S. custody, 175–77, 179, 184
Arikawa, Major General, 90, 96
Arikawa Brigade, 57, 63–65
Arnold, Major General, 95
Artillery (Japanese)
  ammunition shortages and, 59, 95,
    196
  Kiyan battle and, 121–24, 129, 142,
    143, 151
  Kiyan deployment of, 114
  Kiyan troop strength and, 111–12
  Shuri retreat and, 101
  strategic importance of, 24–25, 32,
    34, 43, 81, 82
  U.S. destruction of, 76
Atomic bombing of Japan, 192, 201,
  206
Atomiya, General, 12–13
Attu, battle of, xii

Baldwin, Hanson, 156
Banzai charges, xii, xvi, 162
Blood and Iron for the Emperor
  service units, 105, 116, 141
Boeitai, xxiv
British navy, xiv
Buckner, Lieutenant General Simon
  death of, 146
  Japanese counteroffensive at
    Yonabaru and, 95
  on Japanese retreat strategy, 108
  surrender proposal of, 136
  U.S. army landing attack and, xii
Bushido, xix, xxii

Casualties
  civilian, 156, 179, 186–87, 200
  Japanese, 109, 156
  U.S., 156
Caves. *See* Fortifications
Chiba, Warrant Officer, 144, 151
  escape from Mabuni by, 159–62,
    183
China Incident, xvii, 47
Chinen Peninsula
  civilian withdrawal to, 105
  Japanese retreat options and, 69
  U.S. occupation of, 108
Cho, Major General Isamu
  Arikawa, General, and, 64, 65
  bravado of, 31, 51
  civilians and, 106, 117
  command changes authorized by, 80
  death of General Buckner and, 146
  fitness reports and, 84
  General Staff Office and, 15
  Imperial commendation and, 144
  intelligence reports and, 119
  Jin's Tokyo mission and, 115
  Kiyan battle and, 123, 133, 134,
    137–38, 140–41, 143, 147
  last-stand positions and, 70–72
  at Mabuni headquarters cave,
    117–18
  military career of, xvii–xviii, 16–18
  Naval Base Force and, 127
  Shimada, Akira, and, 168–69, 199,
    206
  Shuri retreat and, 87–88, 91, 96,
    101–3, 107
  strategy and tactics of, 11–12, 13,
    32, 36, 37, 42, 49, 55, 68, 92, 153,
    196–97
  suicide of, xvi, 141–42, 143, 145,
    150–56, 196, 199, 201
  U.S. army landing attack and, xi
Chocolate Drop Hill, 67
Churchill, Winston, 47
CIC (Combat Intelligence Center),
  189–90

Civilians, Okinawan
  casualties among, 156, 179, 186–87,
    200
  conscription of, xxiv, 59, 76, 112,
    123
  construction projects involving, 8,
    93
  culture of, 5, 181
  Japanese military propaganda and,
    xvii, 106
  Japanese treatment of, xxiv
  in Mabuni headquarters cave,
    116–17
  as refugees, 100, 101, 105–6, 142,
    168, 170–77, 179–83, 185–87, 189
  U.S. bombing raids and, 31
  as U.S. military laborers, 183–84,
    186
  U.S. propaganda and, 136
Clausewitz, Carl, xix
Combat fatigue, 122
Comfort girls, 50, 83, 90–91, 117

Daitojima, 10–11, 16
DDT, 180
Defense Headquarters (Japanese),
  military perspective of, 10–11
Deserters, 122, 168
Disguises, 141, 145, 161, 183–84
Domei News Service, 45

Ely, Colonel Louis B., 193

Fifth Fleet (U.S.), 32
Fortifications (Japanese)
  at Amekudai, 59
  conditions in, 50–51, 83, 102, 118
  food supplies stored in, 185
  on Kiyan Peninsula, 91, 112–13
  at Mabuni, 102, 115–19, 135
  on Mount Shuri, xii–xiv, 37, 55, 69,
    71, 129, 135, 197
  reverse slope construction of, 35

Fortifications (Japanese) *continued*
    strategic importance of, 24, 32, 53,
        60, 69, 184
    U.S. capture of, 58
Fujioka, Lieutenant General Takeo
    command style of, 72–73
    Kiyan battle and, 131, 132
    Takushi withdrawal and, 65
Fusozaki Village, refugees housed in,
    179–82, 186–87

General Staff Office (Japanese)
    military perspective of, 10–11
    Okinawa troop deployment and, 15
    See also Imperial Headquarters
Guerrilla warfare, 140, 147, 180
Gunjin, xvi

Haneda, Captain, 126
Hara, Colonel (13th Battalion), 124,
    129
Hara, Lieutenant General (9th
    Division), 12, 14
Hara-kiri. See Suicide
Hasegawa, Kazuo, xxii
Hashimoto, Lieutenant Colonel
    Kingoro, 17
Hattori, Colonel Takushiro, 4, 46
Hayashi, Major Tadahiko, 12, 19
Hazeyama, Major, 19
Heshikiya, Miss, 117, 151, 155
Higuchi, Colonel, 75–77, 94, 113
Hiraga, Lieutenant Colonel
    Amekudai battle and, 59, 61
    Shipping Engineer Unit, 185
    Yaezu hill fortification and, 113,
        123, 124
Hiraoka, Colonel, 122
Hirayama, Major, 93
Hirohito, Emperor, 46, 144, 192
History of the Sixth Marine Division,
    60
Hodge, General John, 35
Hongo, 63

Horiuchi, Lieutenant, 119
Horse-mounting attacks, 63, 64, 109

Ichinichi Bashi, 89
Iizuka, 129
Ikeda, Lieutenant, 147, 150
Imperial Headquarters
    32nd Army and, 8–9
    air power and, 4–5, 16, 24, 36, 49,
        50
    Amekudai battle and, 62
    army communications with, 46–47
    commendation telegrams from,
        143–44
    Kachen Peninsula siege and, 139
    Kadena landing and, 196
    Kiyan battle and, 131, 138, 139, 155
    offensive strategy of, 92, 196
    Operation Victory plans and, 19, 24
    philosophy of, xix
    postwar operations of, 203
    preparations for defense of Japan
        by, 183
    Ryukyu Islands defense and, 9–10,
        12–15
    Shuri line and, 68
Inagaki, Takeshi, xix
Infiltration tactics (Japanese), 36, 59
Inoue, Colonel, 3
Inoue Battalion, 58, 61
Ito, Captain (32nd Infantry
    Regiment), 192
Ito, Colonel (4th Special Regiment),
    80
Ito, Vice Admiral Seiichi, 33
Ito Battalion, 67
Iwo Jima, U.S. attack of, 30

JICPOA (Joint Intelligence Center for
    Pacific Ocean Areas), xx, 30
Jikyusen, xv, 32
Jin, Major Naomichi
    on tactics of Hiromichi Yahara,
        xviii

Tokyo mission of, 49–50, 54, 85, 115, 119, 131, 139

Kachin Peninsula, seige of, 139
Kadena, U.S. army landing at, xi–xiv, xxiii–xxiv, 196
Kakazu, Dr., 106, 150
Kakazu Ridge, XXIV Corps and, 35
Kamikaze
  attack on U.S. Fifth Fleet by, 32–33, 49–50
  strategic use of, 30
  success of, 156
Kanayama, Colonel, 75, 77
Kataoka, Captain, 109
Kato (operations secretary), 152
Katsuno, Lieutenant Colonel, 102, 116, 145, 150
Katsuta (naval battalion), 113
Katsuyama, Corporal
  escape from Mabuni by, 159, 160, 162–64, 183
  Kiyan seige and, 116
  Mabuni headquarters cave and, 118, 149, 151
  personality of, 84–85
  Shuri retreat and, 88–90, 99
Kaya, Lieutenant Colonel, 53–54, 96
Kerama Islands, 36
Kidani, Colonel
  last-stand locations and, 71, 72
  Kiyan battle and, 124
  Shuri retreat and, 84, 87
Kimura, Lieutenant Colonel, 12, 19
  final mission of, 140, 142
  Kiyan provisions and, 116
  Mabuni headquarters cave and, 119
  Shuri retreat and, 87, 96
Kinjo, 116
Kitagawa, Major General, 6, 7, 16
Kitajima, Lieutenant Colonel, 71, 80, 132
Kitamura, Captain, 58

Kiyan Peninsula
  accommodations for wounded soldiers at, 109
  battle for, 121–24, 129–38
  communications at, 112, 119, 122, 131, 133, 134, 151
  description of, 102–3
  fortifications at, 91, 112–13
  provisions at, 108, 116
  troop strengths at, 111–12
  U.S. tank assault on, 121, 123, 133, 142, 145, 149
  withdrawal to, 68, 70, 72, 76, 80, 81, 94–95, 101, 107–8, 111
Kobayashi, Lieutenant General, 11
Kochinda, Japanese retreat through, 100
Kojima, Major, 88, 89, 116, 147
Koshino (operations secretary), 152
Kugimiya (staff officer), 19
Kushibuchi, Lieutenant General, 12
Kusunoki, Masashige, 53
Kusunose (staff officer), 95, 132
Kuwahara, Lieutenant Colonel, 96
Kyoso, Major
  Amekudai battle and, 58, 61
  Kiyan battle and, 130–31, 139, 140
  last-stand positions and, 71, 72
  Lieutenant Moriwaki and, 50
Kyoso (staff officer), 123

Lamott, Lieutenant (jg) Kenneth C., xx–xxi, xxiii
  interrogation of Hiromichi Yahara by, 191–92, 199, 202, 206
Leyte, U.S. attack on, 30
Liang, Zhuge, xix
Lice, 118, 170, 180

Mabuni
  headquarters cave at, 102, 115–19, 132, 135, 201
  Japanese retreat to, 101–3
  U.S. tank assault on, 142, 145, 149

MacArthur, Douglas, 29
Maekawa, Captain, 126
Manchuria, Japanese occupation of, xvii
Marianas line
  Japanese defense of, 4, 9–10, 24, 30, 31
  U.S. troop movements and, 7, 11, 15, 19, 22
Masai, Major, 145, 147
Matsubara, Major, 119, 140, 152
Matsui, Lieutenant, 145, 149
Matsunaga, Captain, 118, 119, 147, 150
Mazaki (staff officer), 140, 151
Medical treatment (for Japanese soldiers), 109, 117
Merrill, General Frank D., 193
Midway, Battle of, 30
Miike, Lieutenant, 127
Mita, Colonel Seiko, 12, 14, 58, 60
Mixed Brigade. See 44th Independent Mixed Brigade (Japanese)
Miyake, Major Tadao, 13, 19
  civilian reports to, 117
  counterattacks and, 43
  final mission of, 140–42, 183
  Jin's Tokyo mission and, 115
  Kiyan provisions and, 116, 119
  Shuri retreat and, 84, 85, 87, 96
Miyazaki, Major General, 3
Morale (Japanese)
  failed counterattacks and, 44
  fortification conditions and, 50–51
  during Kiyan battle, 133, 135–37, 151
  offensive retreat strategy and, 83–84
Moriwaki, Lieutenant, 50, 94, 131, 139
Mount Shuri. See Shuri
Murakami, Lieutenant Colonel, 67

Nagameshi, Major, 124
Nagano (staff officer)
  attrition strategy and, 92
  final mission of, 140–42, 183

  fitness report on, 84
  Kiyan battle and, 133–34
  last-stand positions and, 68, 70, 73
  at Mabuni headquarters cave, 117, 118
  offensive retreat strategy and, 80
  Shuri retreat and, 87–89, 91, 93, 95, 102
Nagaya, Engineer, 164
Naha
  description of, 5, 6
  U.S. bombing of, 31
  U.S. occupation of, 59, 61, 185–86
Nakajima, Lieutenant General, 63, 96, 131
Nakamoto, Miss, 117, 150
Nakamura, Lieutenant, 53, 72, 108
Nakamura, Private, 151
Nakao, Lieutenant, 71, 72, 126
Nakatsuka, Private, 89, 116, 151, 155
Nanjing Massacre, xviii
Napalm, 135
Naval Base Forces (Japanese)
  infiltration units of, 59
  offensive retreat strategy and, 81, 82, 95
  at Oroku Peninsula, 114, 122–23, 125–27, 185, 200
Nawashiro, Major, 77, 84
Nazi Germany, collapse of, 46, 47
Night assaults (Japanese)
  naval infiltration units and, 59
  preparations for, 61
  tradition of, 36
  at Yonabaru, 77
Nii, Lieutenant Commander, 59, 60
Nijin, Colonel, 193
Nimitz, Admiral Chester, xx
  Okinawa strategy of, 70
  Pacific strategy of, 29, 31
Nishimura, Major, 58
Nishino, Major
  escape from Mabuni by, 159, 161
  final mission of, 140, 147, 151, 153

Mabuni headquarters cave and, 118, 119

Naval Base Force capitulation and, 126–27

Nishiura, Colonel, 12

Nurses (Japanese), 50–51, 200

Obata, Lieutenant General, 9

Ogata, Major, 84

Ohki, Lieutenant Colonel, 123, 142

Okuyama, Captain, 62

Ono, Major, 143, 152, 154–55, 162

Ooka, Shohei, 200

Operation Victory plans, 19–26

Ota, Rear Admiral Minoru, 59, 76, 125–26

Ozaki, Captain
Amekudai battle and, 58, 63–64
Gushichan stand of, 113, 122
Yonabaru battle and, 77

Pacific Fleet, U.S., xiv

Peace, Japanese consideration of, 45–46, 138 (see also Surrender)

Peleliu, U.S. attack on, 30

Philippine Sea, Battle of, 30

Potsdam Declaration, 192

Prisoner's Journal, A, (Ooka), 200

Prisoners of war (POWs)
Japanese military tradition and, xvi, xxii, 195, 200
Japanese propaganda on U.S. treatment of, xvii, xxii, xxiii, 200
Japanese treatment of, xxii
Ou Island compound for, 176
U.S. interrogation of, xxi–xxiii, 31, 190–93, 199–200, 201–2, 206–36

Propaganda (Japanese), on U.S. treatment of prisoners of war, xvii, xxii, xxiii, 200

Propaganda (U.S.), Kiyan siege and, 136

Rainy season, 79, 83, 89, 94

Refugees. See Civilians

Richards, Corporal, 191

Roosevelt, Franklin Delano, 45, 47

Ryukyu Islands
Japanese air defense of, 3–5, 7–9
U.S. attack plans for, 30

Saigo, Takamori, 18, 154

Sakaguchi, Captain, 13
escape from Mabuni of, 159
Kiyan provisions and, 117
Mabuni headquarters cave and, 115
Shuri retreat and, 88, 99
suicide of Japanese generals and, 152–53, 155–56

Sakiyama, Miss, 150

Samurai tradition
bravery myths and, xix
offensive thrusts and, 36
ritual suicide and, xvi, xxii

Sato (paymaster)
Isamu Cho and, 90, 91, 145–46, 149, 151
suicide of Japanese generals and, 155, 156

Sato, Sergeant
escape from Mabuni of, 165, 167, 171
in U.S. custody, 175–77, 179, 184

Sayamoto, Captain, 107, 119

Shibata, Colonel, 9, 13, 14

Shimada, Akira
escape from Mabuni of, 168–71
U.S. interrogation of, 199, 206, 220–36

Shimada, Governor, 106

Shimajiri Area Garrison, 80

Shimomura, General, 9

Shimura Battalion, 53, 54, 192

Shinba, Rear Admiral, 10, 14

Shitahaku, Japanese retreat through, 100, 101

Shuri
    fortifications at, xii–xiv, 37, 55, 69,
        71, 129, 135, 197
    possible loss of, 70
    retreat from, 87–97, 99–103, 108,
        125
    U.S. bombardment of, 54
Sims, Sergeant, 191
Sonan, Ryoji (and civilian refugees),
        179–81, 184, 186–87, 189
Special attack aircraft
    attack on U.S. Fifth Fleet by, 32–33
    battle at Amekudai and, 62
    U.S. army landing at Kadena and,
        xi-xiii
Stilwell, General Joseph A., 191
Submarines (U.S.)
    attacks on Japanese shipping by, 29,
        30
    sinking of *Toyama Maru* by, 12,
        13–14
Sugar Loaf Hill, U.S. battle for,
        60–61
Sugimori (staff officer), 71, 84, 96, 146
Sugimoto, Major, 63
Sugiyama, General, 46
Suicide
    of Japanese officers, xvi, 137,
        141–42, 143, 145, 150–56, 160,
        191, 195, 196, 199–202
    of Japanese regular soldiers, 109,
        199–201
Suicide bombers. *See Kamikaze*;
    Special attack aircraft
Sunano, Lieutenant Colonel
    counteroffensive defeat and, 43
    Kiyan battle and, 121–23, 135,
        142–43
    Kiyan deployments and, 114
    last-stand positions and, 71, 72
    Shuri retreat and, 94, 95, 101
    Yonabaru battle and, 76
Surrender
    Japanese prohibitions against,
        136–38

    of Japanese regular soldiers on
        Okinawa, 199
    Potsdam Declaration and, 192
Suzuki, Major General Shigeru, 3, 14
    Amekudai battle and, 58, 60
    Kiyan battle and, 124, 129, 140
    Shuri retreat and, 88, 108
    Yaezu hill fortification and, 113
Suzuki, Prime Minister, 45–47

Tagawa Battalion, 53
Taiwan
    Japanese defense of, 19–20
    U.S. attack plans for, 30, 31
Takahashi (staff secretary), 89, 152
Tanaka, Lieutenant Colonel, 3
Tanamachi, Captain, 126
Task Force 58 (U.S.), 31, 33
Tatsuno, Lieutenant Colonel, 159
Tojo line. *See* Marianas line
Tokkotai, 32–33, 49
Toyama Maru, sinking of, 12, 13–14
Tsubakida, Lieutenant, 152
Tsuchida, Lieutenant Colonel, 80
Tsukazan, Japanese command post at,
        93, 96–97, 99

Udo, Colonel, 14
Ueno, Colonel, 64, 65, 71
Umezu, Colonel, 90, 133
Umezu, General Yoshijiro, 41, 146
Untamamui hill, U.S. bombardment
        of, 75–76
Ushijima, Lieutenant General Mitsuru
    Arikawa, General, and, 64, 65
    civilian evacuations and, 105, 106
    command style of, 6, 18–19, 71
    death of General Buckner and, 146
    fortifications of, 35
    Imperial commendation and, 144
    influence of Isamu Cho on, 36, 37,
        42
    Jin's Tokyo mission and, 115

Kiyan battle and, 124, 131, 133, 134, 140–41
Kiyan provisions and, 116
Kyoso, Major, and, 131
last-stand positions and, 72
Mabuni headquarters cave and, 117, 119
merit certificates and, 84
Naval Base Force and, 125–26
Operation Victory plans and, 19, 196
Shuri retreat and, 87–88, 91, 94, 99, 101, 102, 108
Sugar Loaf Hill and, 61
suicide of, xvi, 141–42, 143, 145, 150, 152–56, 199, 201
tactics of, 49
U.S. army landing attack and, xi–xii
U.S. surrender proposal and, 136

Wada, Lieutenant General Kojo, 32, 34, 143
Wada, Major, 90
Wasai, Captain, 119, 147
Watanabe, Lieutenant General, 6, 13, 18

Yabumoto, Lieutenant, 152
Yaezu hill
  Japanese defense of, 123–24, 129, 131, 132
  Japanese fortification of, 113

Yakumaru, Major, 19
  counterattacks and, 43
  final mission of, 140–42
  Kiyan battle and, 119
  Kiyan provisions and, 116
  last-stand positions and, 72
  offensive retreat strategy and, 80, 95
  Shuri retreat and, 84, 90, 94, 107
Yamaguchi Battalion, 64, 75, 76
Yamamoto, Lieutenant Colonel, 53–54
Yamane, Captain, 122
Yamashita, General, xix
Yamato, sinking of, 33
Yamazaki, Major, 160, 161
Yasaka (staff officer), 19
Yasuda, Lieutenant, 152
Yogi, Miss, 117, 150
Yokota, Lieutenant Colonel, 14
Yomitan, assault on, 196
Yonabaru
  Japanese counteroffensive at, 95, 184–85
  U.S. occupation of, 75–77, 79
Yonabaru, Major, 116, 151, 159–61
Yoshida, Colonel, 132–33
Yoshida, Mitsuru (ensign), 33
Yoshinaka, Lieutenant General, 10, 11
Yoshino (staff officer), 140, 151
Yoshio, Adjutant, 87

Zhanggufang Incident, 17